Capitalism and Nothingness

ALSO AVAILABLE FROM BLOOMSBURY

Working Aesthetics, Danielle Child
The Rise and Fall of Neoliberalism, ed. Kean Birch and Vlad Mykhnenko

Capitalism and Nothingness

Critical Theory in Unwanted Times

Peter Fleming

BLOOMSBURY ACADEMIC
LONDON • NEW YORK • OXFORD • NEW DELHI • SYDNEY

BLOOMSBURY ACADEMIC
Bloomsbury Publishing Plc, 50 Bedford Square, London, WC1B 3DP, UK
Bloomsbury Publishing Inc, 1359 Broadway, 12th Floor, New York, NY 10018, USA
Bloomsbury Publishing Ireland, 29 Earlsfort Terrace, Dublin 2, D02 AY28, Ireland

BLOOMSBURY, BLOOMSBURY ACADEMIC and the Diana logo
are trademarks of Bloomsbury Publishing Plc

First published in Great Britain 2025
Reprinted 2025

Copyright © Peter Fleming, 2025

Peter Fleming has asserted his right under the Copyright,
Designs and Patents Act, 1988, to be identified as Author of this work.

For legal purposes the Acknowledgements on p. 204 constitute
an extension of this copyright page.

Cover image by Amelia Seddon

All rights reserved. No part of this publication may be: i) reproduced or transmitted in any form, electronic or mechanical, including photocopying, recording or by means of any information storage or retrieval system without prior permission in writing from the publishers; or ii) used or reproduced in any way for the training, development or operation of artificial intelligence (AI) technologies, including generative AI technologies. The rights holders expressly reserve this publication from the text and data mining exception as per Article 4(3) of the Digital Single Market Directive (EU) 2019/790.

Bloomsbury Publishing Plc does not have any control over, or responsibility for, any third-party websites referred to or in this book. All internet addresses given in this book were correct at the time of going to press. The author and publisher regret any inconvenience caused if addresses have changed or sites have ceased to exist, but can accept no responsibility for any such changes.

A catalogue record for this book is available from the British Library.

A catalog record for this book is available from the Library of Congress.

ISBN: HB: 978-1-3504-4188-0
PB: 978-1-3504-4187-3
ePDF: 978-1-3504-4189-7
eBook: 978-1-3504-4190-3

Typeset by Integra Software Services Pvt. Ltd.
Printed and bound in Great Britain

For product safety related questions contact productsafety@bloomsbury.com

To find out more about our authors and books visit www.bloomsbury.com
and sign up for our newsletters.

In the open-air prison which the world is becoming, it is no longer so important to know what depends on what, such is the extent to which everything is one. All phenomena rigidify, become insignias of the absolute rule of that which is. There are no more ideologies in the authentic sense of false consciousness, only advertisements for the world through its duplication and the provocative lie which does not seek belief but commands silence.

T.W. Adorno, *Prisms*

Contents

Foreword by Stefano Harney: Principium individuationis viii

Introduction: Ghosts from the future 1

1 Point blank capitalism 9

2 No-dimensional man 31

3 Beyond the leisure principle 53

4 Gothika economica 71

5 Meat machines 91

6 Necromathmatics 109

7 Requiem for touch 131

8 Fragments of failure 153

Conclusion: Ideology and the void 169

Notes 176
Selected bibliography 196
Acknowledgements 204
Index 205

Foreword

Principium individuationis

Stefano Harney

In this extraordinary book Peter Fleming stares into the eyes of capitalism, and nothing stares back. One of the best places to catch capitalism's eye is the corporate workplace, a focus for much of this book. But make no mistake. It is neither the corporation nor management that is Peter Fleming's target. He has his sights set on capitalism's ultimate fantasy, a world without labour, a world without workers and indeed a world without humans, or at least the project of humanity. Of course such a project has never been realized, not just because of capitalism's hostility to it even as the unrealized project is often put to work. But now it appears that the false premise of that project itself is being abandoned with equally devastating consequences.

For example, speaking about the term 'racial capitalism' – foundational to his masterwork *Black Marxism* – Cedric Robinson would often say that he borrowed the term from South African comrades. And indeed in his time living in South Africa, Robinson witnessed an extremely racialized capitalism. But Robinson was also being somewhat understated by saying he borrowed the term.

Because while honouring what he saw, he also transformed the term from a political and sociological one to an ontological one. In Robinson's brilliant reworking of the term it ceases to be about two systems of oppression and exploitation merging. It becomes instead an analysis of the essential nature of capitalism. And that essential 'identity' of capitalism is *brutality*, and more particularly the brutality of separation and individuation. Along the way to this formulation Robinson rejected the idea that brutality is external to the capitalist production process, noting it was insufficient to talk about primitive accumulation as a phenomenon unfolding before the capitalist production process matures or away from it and in support of it. Nor was brutality merely an enforcement mechanism to keep capitalist relations in place and the class struggle at bay. Robinson supplies a far more revolutionary definition of racial capitalism: brutality is the chief factor of production inside the capitalist production process because separation and individuation are the ontological conditions of racial capitalism.

This brutal separation and individuation occurred at all levels, people from land, people from animals, people from people, body from mind, reason from spirit. The major theorist of the European imposition of separability, as well as causality and linearity, Denise Ferreira Da Silva talks about these ideologies as part of pursuit of 'total value'. Therefore from the beginning this separation of all things was experienced in vastly different ways, but chiefly as either a separation causing death or a separation and individuation visiting death. It was far more thorough than being separated from the means of production or being separated from the land you farm or forage, or the tools and workshop you operate. Indeed, as has been frequently observed the separation of people from the earth and everything that dwelled in it made the 'world', a place full of objects to be observed and manipulated. There had been other instances in history of separating the world into subject and object, but none before so engined and reinforced by the same operation in the material production of society and its pursuit of total value. This brutal separation distinguishes man from all around him in thought and in production, and it would soon produce speciation, the brutal separation of 'man' from people who cannot or will not separate and individuate themselves properly.

But the separation of the material and intellectual means of production under racial capitalism necessarily occurred on both sides of this historical experience of death and death dealing. The imperial project of the individual is often called the rise of the bourgeois individual because it is amidst this class that the project begins. And indeed the European bourgeoisie are the first to wilfully separate themselves from their own means of production through the privatization of their labour, their bodies and their minds, greatly aided by the laboratories of colonialism. Or to put it differently, they were the first to insist that they were their own means of production. This insistence on being self-sovereign brutally disappeared their entanglement and dependency on other people and on the earth and was powered by a narrative death squad, the narrative of Western philosophy, politics and economics.

Nor was it to end there. What Angela Metropoulos called the democratization of sovereignty soon spread this terror far and wide, with chosen others also offered this dangerous fantasy of individuality while most would have to continue to be speciated to support this nefarious narrative. These others are subject to 'exclusive inclusion', as Peter Fleming puts in these pages, a suspension of the very possibility of individualism, while still being judged against it.

This exclusive, cataclysmic fantasy of individuation and the resulting monstrous individual it tries to sustain continue to haunt both organic and non-organic life. It is the rise and potential fall of this imperial project of individuation that Peter Fleming documents and analyses so brilliantly in what follows. In the death throes of empire it throws up grotesque levels of individual display against a background of mass failure to maintain the facade of the original claims of the bourgeois individual, and evermore speciated populations relegated to working for the failing fantasies of others' individuation. Today on one side of racial capitalism are those who're dealt death. They experience the geocidal and genocidal separation on a planetary scale. Meanwhile on the other side of racial capitalism, the death dealing side, the fantasy turns back on the fantasists devouring their own interiority, separability and agency. Peter Fleming illustrates this deterioration on both sides of the experience of racial capitalism. His chapter on the Australian mining company that blew up the sacred Aboriginal lands demonstrates both sides of the brutality of separation in racial capitalism brilliantly, in an episode he calls 'collective aphantasia' or elsewhere in the book 'the organized ignorance of corporate leadership'.

And as Fred Moten and I have regularly done, it is important to make a distinction here between brutality and violence. Violence can be the ongoing tendency for things, like us, to return to entanglement, to kink up, to re-materialize, to gather. In this way violence is not the opposite of care or love. Violence is not so much the forcing of things together but rather the force that allows for this return. Brutality, on the other hand, is the forced individuation and separation of living and non-living things, imposing the fantasy of the individual on oneself and all things, straightening yourself out as the apodictic prerequisite to straightening out others. These are not moments of singularity. This force is the imposition of a dematerialization in the face of the violence of the collective return to indistinction. With the rise of the two towers of capitalism and bourgeois individualism, the brutality of dematerialization has intensified. Or as Peter Fleming phrases it in the realm of paid employment: 'working today means abasing oneself to an idealized abstraction that refuses to recognize your categorical and shared materiality'.

For Cedric Robinson, the concept of the ontological totality is both a violent concept and a conception of violence. Those who insist on living all incomplete, as he puts it in *The Terms of Order*, will be in a constant war of collective self-defence of their shared materiality, even against those who would reduce shared materiality to materialism. The readiness of the all incomplete to die for this ontological totality is tied to the ability to conjure it, out of what seems to others like nothing, after what looked like complete separation. Moreover for those subjected to this war, amongst the dangers faced are those proposing to self-manage their individuation and emerge from their self-imposed immaturity to claim that they can indeed use their understanding independently of the influence of others. This can only lead to betrayal and to acts of brutal correction directed at the undercommons in an always insufficient and therefore endless and intensifying demonstration of what Saidiya Hartman called 'a burdened individuality'. This is individuality which must always be burdened and always for some more than others.

According to Cedric Robinson in *The Terms of Order* this burdened individuality is the basis of the Western conception of politics, whether conceived as the citizen, that is 'the one', or conceived as a class, that is, 'the many'. Here then it is not the systems of racial and capitalist oppression and exploitation that work together. It is the automatic subject of capitalism and history of dominant Western political thought that conspire to produce this brutality. In this sense the separation of means of production under racial capitalism occurred on both sides of this historical experience. Robinson demonstrates that this reliance on the one and the many as individuated fantasies underpins all major Western political thought, including Marxism and Anarchism. Despite contradictory signals, both Marxist and

Anarchist thought remain wedded to politics through the projection of the free or the new man in a new order. Or conversely the reliance on 'the political' as a system of thought depends on that individual free or new man. It is against this system of thought that Robinson deploys the concept of people being all incomplete. Not so much in headless societies, because such societies have leadership, organization, even direction but they don't have anyone who conceives of themselves, including whoever is temporarily leading, as separate from others in the society or from the earth they inhabit, or sufficient without their shared-ness and influence.

And this brings us back to the 'nihilolithic' hauntology Peter Fleming pursues. His analysis goes beyond Frederic Jameson's formulation that it is easier to imagine the end of the world than the end of capitalism. He is instead haunted by the idea that the end of the fantasy of the individual chronicled in these pages means the end of politics, and therefore even of class politics as an eminently political instance of thought of the one and the many. But Peter Fleming's hauntology is also an invitation to reject our separability and to recover our incompleteness, along the way dispensing with the future, even one in the past, as yet another example of that separability. We could not ask for a better guide.

Introduction

Ghosts from the future

In early 2016 I was invited to give a talk in Lyon, France. Living in London at the time, I agreed. Any opportunity to escape that dirty town for a few days was always welcome. We set a date and travel arrangements were made. A week before the trip, however, a colleague reminded me of the class I'd promised to teach in London on that same day. Ah, damn it. I contacted my Lyon hosts to apologize and request a raincheck. No need, they said, you can 'beam in' instead and have plenty of time to make your class afterwards. *Beam in?* What do you mean? 'Beam' was a high-tech telepresence robot. After the speaker logged on (which took around fifteen minutes), their face appeared on a screen fixed to the robot's head. The bot – roughly the size of an actual person – was mounted on wheels that allowed the virtual speaker to roam the room. I was warned to be careful, though. The machine was prone to tumbling on uneven surfaces and could seriously injure anyone misfortunate enough to be in its path.

Back then I was amazed by this remarkable new communications technology. Beam was a huge advance compared to Skype. I did a little research on its development and still have the notes. One of its main functions was remote workplace monitoring. Managers could teleport into distant locations in robot form and check up on workers. A training video shows Beam appearing unannounced amidst a group of mildly perplexed employees. To be honest, when reading my notes today, I'm embarrassed by their tone of wonderment. Beam ... a gamechanger? In the wake of virtual meeting platforms like Zoom and Teams – not to mention bossware surveillance that can collect vast amounts of data about the workforce – what could be more clunkier than being beamed into a physical robot that cost thousands of dollars and was a safety hazard in most office settings? But my estimation in 2016 was very different. Beam was emblematic of a brave new world of work, a mega-leap forward in dark technology that was fascinating and frightening in equal measure.

The anecdote offers several insights concerning contemporary capitalism, which I will extend in this book. That this transition – from Beam to AI-controlled datascapes, spyware and the ubiquity of Zoom – took less than a decade is simply breathtaking. In terms of technological advancement, our underwhelming appraisal of Beam today was simply unavailable in 2016. And the same blind spot probably applies to our appreciation of capitalism today. Indeed, there's a good chance that a reader of this book twenty years from now will laugh at the 'naïve' systems of exploitation described therein. Huh, he thought that platform capitalism was bad ... look at what was just around the corner! As Hegel famously remarked, the owl of Minerva only takes flight when the shades of night are drawing, long after the decisive moment has passed.[1] Critical theory is always arriving too late. Or more accurately, being born too soon. In any case, its knowledge is left stranded, little more than an intellectual indulgence in the shadow of overwhelming exigencies.

I think this inadequacy is partly due to the synthetic retroactivity some critics use when giving shape to emergent structures of dominance. 'Now-time' is the end point of a preceding telos. And that telos has forever been fulfilled like some hidden god. There is no 'in-between-time'. For example, compared to Beam, the corporate technophere today looks far more menacing because it seems to have reached an apotheosis. However, when that retroactivity echoes back to us from the past, we lose something important: our capacity to apperceive the future as a break in the continuum of history. We are always approaching the end and thus never able to begin. Debates about the future of work – a topic I discuss at length in the book – exemplify this conceptual afterwardness. The question is asked: What will employment look like five decades from now? Present wishes, anxieties and demands are then projected based on historical presuppositions and antecedents. There is no dialectical externalization of the totality, making historical thought impossible. Only when 2075 rolls around do we – or those who come after us, at least – see how off the mark our predictions were, even the wildest ones. This projective cecity thwarts critical reason. It consequently fails in one of its central objectives: to help society understand its perennial outdatedness, no matter how mesmerizing our technological wonders may appear today. Only through this methodological anachronism can we cut through the ideology of presence that has transformed 'now-time' into an eternity and the future an unintelligible mystery.

In the field of socio-economic action, this expansive futural openness is not interpreted as an index of freedom because it has been violently decontextualized. A void appears in the political imagination. A future that doesn't know itself is terrifying. It becomes a blank screen upon which monsters appear, and a niggling suspicion that what awaits will be infinitely worse. The following chapters will investigate this phrenic expurgation in several domains. We'll observe it in the workplace, in the diffusion of sophisticated digital technologies, the predatory state apparatus and the unrelenting corporate suspension of democracy. If a post-pandemic spirit of capitalism does exist, then it is a sick one, an inward turning vacuity that cannot step beyond the exaggerated present.

Let me present a more concrete example. The Covid-19 pandemic debunked the mythology of work once and for all. In rich countries at least, many jobs were suspended during the crisis, prompting massive government stimulus and subsidy schemes. It turned out that the institution of paid employment wasn't rooted in biological necessity at all. It was a social ritual reflecting a specific set of power relations. Economic scarcity too was a manufactured condition that could be adjourned at a moment's notice. Notwithstanding this new cultural awareness, it was business as usual when the crisis subsided. Everyone must return to the struggle for existence like before and act as if working is akin to hunting and gathering in prehistoric times. The self wilts. Suffering is bad, but pointless suffering contorts the soul.

Returning to the question of technology, the wave of digitalization that rendered Beam antediluvian in a mere decade has assumed almost sacred qualities in recent times. A 'religion of technology' has flourished around the advent of AI, neural nets and algorithmic computation, something to be both revered and feared, but mostly *believed*. This is objective mysticism, and scary monsters stir in the umbra. The idea can be connected to Mark Fisher's groundbreaking writings on hauntology.[2] Typical sociopolitical hauntings originate from past traumas (e.g. the murder of democratic socialism) that return as a ghostly demand for retribution. Just as important for Fisher, however, are those past realities that *never were*: beautiful utopian plans and projects that were euthanized before they began. He mentions early 1970s militancy, including Black power, libertarian communism, feminist syndicalism and the radical ecology movement. This betrayal haunts us 'not because of some unrecoverable and unrepeatable confluence of factors, but because the potentials it materialized and began to democratize has to be continuously repressed'.[3]

Technicity is important in this regard due to the forsaken potential it conveys. That we got Facebook and SpaceX instead of e-Communism is a tragedy. Yet the latter persists in spectral form. Fisher's focal temporal unit is understandably the past. But can we be haunted by the *future* as well? I believe so given how technological fatalism has sought to eradicate any negation of its own impossibilities. But it's a tricky supposition to elucidate. Let's try. If the contemporary capitalist subject is politically delimited by a retroactive history of the present (timeless 'now-time'), then perhaps he or she is also haunted by a retroactive *future* of the present. The feeling is familiar. Something horrific is ahead, but what exactly? This kind of haunting was perfectly depicted in Nigel Kneale's lost 1964 television play *The Road*.[4] Set on a remote British estate in 1768, farm workers report seeing an apparition in the forest. A young woman describes a supernatural cobbled road, the sound of growling chariots and crying children. Local squire Sir Timothy Hassall believes the spot is haunted by the Celtic warrior Queen Boudica. A grisly massacre occurred there centuries beforehand. Hassall's friend Gideon Cobb isn't convinced. He is an arch Enlightenment sceptic in the vein of Hume. Ghosts? More like wind in the trees and peasant superstition. As they travel to investigate, the sun fades in the Western sky. Cobb is besotted by technological progress and waxes lyrical about the imminent machine age. It will be amazing. Authentic human history will finally begin. He raises the question of slavery (his 'servant' Jethro is from the Caribbean). Bonded labour will naturally die out because

> machines will supplant it. The great steam pumps we see now are going to have a million descendants. In 250 years, machines will do all the world's fetching and carrying, they will carry men through the air and over the seas. They will free man from his folly and savagery.

Then the ghosts appear. A blinding flash of light turns the night white. A vision is unveiled. Groaning cars gridlocked on a large highway. Honking horns. Panic. Children whimpering ... and a nuclear mushroom cloud growing on the horizon. Cobb suddenly realizes that an event deep in the future is taking place, one so alien that it could be from another world. A desperate mother holding her daughter runs to Cobb. 'Help her, please help her!' In tears, Cobb replies, 'I can't, I can't, we will be dead before she is born.' A grid of black missiles descends. Mother and child are instantaneously vaporized. 'Impossible machines, *impossible* ...', Cobb sobs.

The play succeeds because of its timing. A significant temporal rupture is necessary for the haunting to be more than just a dystopian projection of the present. If *The Road* was set in 1920 – as quantum mechanics was gathering steam – it wouldn't be the same. The machines foreseen would be possible and commensurable. Moreover, the futural spectre always attracts someone awkwardly primed, in this case Cobb and his proud techno-positivism. Only he can decode the meaning of the apparition by repudiating the scientific universalism he so faithfully embodies. The ghosts are speaking to him for this reason. The 'impossible machines' Cobb observes shatters the symbolic order and retrospectively (from a distant future past) establishes a new relationship with *technē*. In an ironic twist, the BBC wiped the original tapes of the television broadcast, and Kneale's script of *The Road* is all that remains.

But if the haunted future described in Kneale's story is successful, insofar as the ghosts allow Cobb to confront his world as an open and indeterminate negation (i.e. freedom), then there are also *unsuccessful* hauntings. They are the worst. Why so? Because its victims are trapped by a trauma born of its own circular return. These spectral instantiations gather energy not from any positive content but from an internal emptiness that seeks an unattainable redemption. To redeem is to return. Hence, like the gravitational pull around a blackhole, a pervasive nothingness marks the current historical moment. While this emptiness keeps the wheels of commerce turning, the old adage still stands, *ex nihilo nihil fit*, nothing comes from nothing. In other words, the ghosts we must face today are not only arriving from the past. They come from times unpast too. Their sound and fury, including the phantom pains they levy, are the subject of this book.

1
Point blank capitalism

1

Twenty thousand years ago – during the Late Glacial Period – several figures from a local tribe enter a dark rock shelter deep in the Western Australian outback. Here they eat food foraged during the day, light fires to warm themselves against the desert night and tell creation stories – the Dreaming – in which ghostly ancestral figures emerge from the surrounding natural environment. The land is central to Dreamtime. Not only are the people and country one but the geological formations – like the cave they occupy – recall previous generations that stretch back thousands of years. The stones, wildflowers and birds are loved ones manifest and demand the utmost respect. Mythical creatures lurk in the scorched countryside too, leaving an indelible trace on the land. For example, the Gaagudju people of the Northern Territory believe that the rock escarpments in their country were created by Crocodile-man (or *Ginga*). After being accidentally burnt during a ceremony, *Ginga* jumped into the river and carved magical waves into the cliff face, which can still be seen today. Some tribes see the land as their mother. She is included in important decisions and given right of place in the Dreamtime when she returns to her children.[1]

The Juukan Gorge shelters in the Pilbara region of Western Australia are a sacred site of the Puutu Kunti Kurrama and Pinikura (PKKP) people. Archaeological excavations have found evidence of continuous human occupation for 46,000 years. Grindstone tools and one special find – a long plait of human hair woven from several different individuals – have been unearthed in two ancient rock shelters (known as Juukan 1 and Juukan 2). Unfortunately for the local community, in the earth beneath the shelters was something so evil that no Dreamtime creature could defend them from its iniquity: *iron ore*.

The mining giant Rio Tinto has been quarrying this part of the country for years. Headquartered in London and Melbourne, rich iron ore deposits in Western Australia have generated super-profits. The Chinese market alone is worth billions. The Juukan Gorge is situated close to the Brockman 4 mine, which opened in 2010. Due to the significant seams of ore found there, Rio Tinto aggressively expanded its operations. The corporation and Juukan rock shelters were soon on a collision course. Having gained governmental consent to proceed with a new extension and ignoring protests from the PKKP and archaeologists, the caves were dynamited on 24 May 2020 and destroyed forever. Within a matter of days, 8 million tonnes of iron ore had been torn from the earth.

What kind of corporate mentality could commit such a flagrant act of cultural vandalism? Some argued that greed was the culprit. Blended with the pressure to increase production and keep share prices high, a culture of avarice blinded senior managers. Increased output meant more revenue since annual bonuses were linked to quotas. Other commentators pointed to Rio Tinto's organizational structure. Its iron ore division was semi-autonomous, and bad decisions could be made without oversight from central administration.

These explanations alone are unsatisfactory. After trawling through the screeds of testimony provided by Rio Tinto executives during a two-year parliamentary enquiry following the disaster, one is struck by the remarkable vacuity in the testimonies provided.² Of course, there are the obligatory displays of contrition *post factum*. But the move to increase production – despite the dire ethical implications – wasn't compelled by the mountains of cash they would make. Nor were these managers especially stupid, another explanation broached by outraged newspaper columnists. In fact, they appeared to be fairly intelligent people. But when it came to describing the decision-making processes close to the actual blast, these executives had almost nothing to say. They constantly divagated to mitigating circumstances, legal precedent and vapid clichés. Whereas at 'ground zero' a complete void of human reflection is evident. Perhaps, then, the question 'what were they thinking?' misses the point. Flawed cognition was not to blame. Instead, these individuals were not thinking at all. Like the machinery, spreadsheets, Ghant charts and digital logistic systems enveloping them, these frontline agents of extractive capitalism were incapable of thinking beyond the narrow KPI-world view governing their actions. To grasp how this evacuation of moral apperception could occur, we require a theory of *organized non-thinking*.

2

The writings of Hannah Arendt may be useful in this respect. Her reports on the 1961 trial of Adolf Eichmann – the infamous Nazi 'desk killer' – are a textbook study of *bannus malum*.³ It goes without saying that Rio Tinto's wrongdoing doesn't compare to the crimes of Eichmann, who sent millions of victims to their deaths. But we can still glean some ideas from Arendt's study to help understand how managerial mindlessness functions. As Arendt famously pointed out, while Eichmann's deeds were monstrous, the actor himself was dull and unremarkable. He was certainly no diabolical genius or fanatical ideologue, unlike other senior Nazi officials (a conclusion that landed Arendt in hot water with the Jewish community). When observing Eichmann's defence testimony, Arendt noticed that he seamlessly adapted to the rhythms of the courtroom. This was telling because 'he had not the slightest difficulty in accepting an entirely different set of rules. He knew that what he had once considered his duty was now called a crime, and he accepted this new code of judgement as if it were nothing but another language rule'.[4]

This unusual propensity for social acclimation was matched by the nugatory nature of Eichmann's personality. He spoke only in stock phrases, evincing a shallowness that was bereft of any reflexivity about his crimes and imminent fate. This made Eichmann problematic for Arendt. A wanton villain is easy to spot and condemn accordingly. Not Eichmann, however. He was an evildoer who simply displayed no evidence for the capacity to think. Was this Arendt's way of calling Eichmann an idiot? Not at all, a topic she elucidates upon in a lecture called 'Thinking and Moral Considerations', published ten years after his execution. The 'inability to think is not stupidity; it can be found in highly intelligent people, and wickedness is hardly its cause, if only because thoughtlessness as well as stupidity are much more frequent phenomena than wickedness'.[5] How does this incapacitation of thought result in terrible lapses of conscience?

Arendt defines thinking in a specific manner. For her – building on Kant's distinction between reason and intellect – thought is different to knowledge: 'our desire to know, whether arising out of practical necessities, theoretical perplexities, or sheer curiosity can be fulfilled by reaching its intended goal'.[6] The outcome is then accumulated and stored. However, thinking – or what Kant calls our desire to ponder beyond the limitations of what we know – has no calculable telos. And it doesn't leave anything tangible behind or exhibit worldbuilding properties as with knowledge. Thought is for itself and thus resultless.

By the same token, thinking does influence the thinker. Arendt's argument has three parts. First, unlike knowledge – which considers extant data to obtain a result – thinking deals with objects and people that are absent. Hence its objectlessness, at least in pragmatic terms. Conjuring that absence requires imagination to lift us out of our phenomenological immediacy. When lost in thought we are not present. But the converse is true also, when lost in thought, the present – as we formally knew it – is not present either. Now it's something unusual. In short, the thinker splits themselves between what is (e.g. a well-oiled authoritarian bureaucracy) and what is not (e.g. a world different and juxtaposed to preexisting conditions). Such abstraction is missing in Eichmann because he merely duplicates social reality as he finds it, be this the courtroom or a Nazi meeting in Wannsee. There is no gap or dissonance. Eichmann cannot exceed his situation, which is the predicate of moral freedom in Kantian philosophy. Furthermore, the inner space that thinking clears often demands we struggle against knowledge – especially knowledge that has been certified by power. This makes thinking uncomfortable, almost unnatural. For the thinker, the world around them feels out of order.[7]

By inducing this variance between self and reality, thinking interrupts the routine of full presence. This is the second part of Arendt's argument. Thought forces the individual to stop and pause, 'and it may have a paralysing effect when you come out of it, no longer sure of what had seemed to you beyond doubt while you were unthinkingly engaged in whatever you were doing.'[8] How does this translate into moral reason? There is no guarantee it will.

Indeed, if evil is banal then so is being good. The third part of Arendt's argument is interesting in this respect. When thinking separates itself from what we are, it initiates an inner cross-examination (her famous two-in-one). It aims to test the tenability of remaining who one is. The thinker asks: Can I live with you now that I understand who you are? If the answer is 'no', then anguish awaits, a theme long explored in literature (e.g. Shakespeare's haunting exchange in *Richard III* when the monarch asks, 'Is there a murderer here? No. Yes, I am.').

Arendt's conceptualization of non-thought can help us explain Rio Tinto's mindless decision to blast the Juukan Caves. Of course, greed, annual bonuses, deep seated racism and the pressure to meet 'stretch targets' all played a role. This is a cut-throat industry well known for its rapaciousness. But given the enormity of the transgression – one that even a child would recognize – those factors alone cannot deactivate the ability to think. KPIs are powerful, but can they reach into the human brain and stun it? We need a better account of how reflexivity is compromised in the corporate world today. A limitation of Arendt for this purpose is her adherence to ontology. Hers is a metaphysical project and that won't do in the realm of economic practice given its swerving and undulating contingencies. We instead must locate non-thought within the historical development of capitalism itself. It metastasizes within a specific constellation of economic power relationships. When historicized in this manner – particularly with reference to management ethics, the main concern of this chapter – corporate unthinking can be interpreted as the latest institutional pathology forged in the fire of global commerce. My primary argument is this: the contemporary corporation is a thought-terminator. And this termination process is symptomatic of significant shifts in how labour and life are objectified and exploited today. Let me unpack this proposition in more detail.

3

Managerialism does not simply involve the instrumental task of managing others. It also expresses a *Weltanschauung*, or world view, one that ideologically frames other human beings in a specific manner. When assessing any given social field, managerialism foregrounds the importance of efficiency, obedience, monetization and solutionism above all else. Objectifying people in this way invariably constitutes its own subject position. The managerial personality is often presumed to be a cold-hearted rationalist. Frederick Winslow Taylor's mania for mathematical expediency comes to mind. But it has a less mentioned facetious side too, peopled by all manner of wounded characters who are often anything but rational.[9] This is largely due to power. Whether in the public sector or private sector, corporations or universities, charities or governmental agencies, power fosters mystical qualities that transcend its functionality. Masters feel more than just a master. Fantasies of giftedness, superiority and resentment so often sprout from the fertile soils of social domination. Similarly, servants are more than just a servant. Their subjugation exceeds the role in uncanny ways. Inferiority is primarily a psychological category after all. Authority spellbinds both bearer and victim, even in the most elementary asymmetrical relationships. Monstrosities arise on both sides amidst the surfeit of meaning that inequality produces. Here we must resist the wisdom of philosophers at all costs. There is absolutely nothing natural about social power. At any rate, depending on the medium through which it's exercised, power converts the deformities of an institutional matrix into personal values.

I will take the deindustrialization and decline of Fordism in Western countries – the early 1970s and abandonment of the gold standard – as my beginning point. From then onwards, three successive managerial character-types (including their accompanying malignancies and dysfunctions) have haunted the halls of big business. In what follows, I want to present a speculative genealogy of these business pathologies to explain the appearance of the latest and most disturbing figure in the world of corporate managerialism: the irredeemable *non-thinker*.

Before I do so, though, a brief note on method is necessary. Histories mapping the ideologies that accompany successive stages of capitalism typically suffer from teleological rationalism. Each phase builds upon its preceding intellectual bloc and turns out to be more 'calculative' (in the instrumental sense of the term), a historical approach perfected by Max Weber, of course. A recent example of this is Nicholas Lemann's well-researched *Transaction Man*.[10] It charts the evolution of US corporate ethics over the last century and identifies three distinct personas. The first is *institutional man*, corresponding with the birth of modern management (i.e. the separation of ownership and control, and roughly paralleling William Foot Whyte's 'organizational man'). Following that – along with the rise of neoliberal capitalism – we have *transaction man*. He embodies the logic of the stock market and futures trading. Emerging today finally is *network man*, personifying the triumph of Big Tech and its fetishization of pseudo-connectivity. Lemann's story is not a happy one. He laments the decline of the American dream and the restoration of a ruthless superelite. The narrative depicts the escalating rationalization of economic life, a super-honing of social calculation that is increasingly coordinated through dark finance and logarithmic theorems.

I want to do something different. Each 'man' (the masculine overtones of these corporate personalities are hardly mentioned by Lemann but will be important for my argument) could be read as a regressive plateauing of moral reason, an intellectual depletion that feeds on itself before cascading into something worse. The decline will be traced in two ways. First, I'll identify a formal ideal-type, the distinct 'spirit of capitalism' germane to that stage of economic development. Second – and especially relevant for our purposes – is the pathological underside of each corporate personality, the nefarious 'snakes in suits' who appear from nowhere and wreak havoc. Each deformity is superimposed onto its predecessor like a palimpsest, I suggest, which finds its terminus in today's managerial emptiness. This corporate character doesn't think twice. He doesn't even think once. Moved by an institutional momentum that is impervious to sustained reflection, the decision to blow up a sacred indigenous site literally means *nothing* to him. Welcome to Point Blank Capitalism.

4

The crisis of Fordism in the 1970s was no sudden break but more a catabolic slow-motion implosion. This was particularly so concerning its effects on the proletariat in developed countries. While still integral to capitalism, the working class, especially as a political entity, gradually became irrelevant vis-à-vis global value chains, international arbitrage and the incessant proliferation of the shipping container. In the United States it would take nearly forty years before the 'deaths of despair' caused by this irrelevance was finally acknowledged. Back in the 1970s, this major reorganization of the capitalist mode of production placed the manager in pole position. Prior to this, managers were midrange supervisors. By contrast, post-industrialization thrived on the symbolic value of managerialism – not the technique but the discourse. And here we meet our first corporate personality. *Amoral man*. He temporarily brackets ethical deliberation in the pursuit of economic gain. Vestiges of Fordist authority remain important for his agenda, especially scientific expertise. As is well known, the management profession originated in the field of engineering.[11] From Frederick Taylor onwards, it involved wrestling knowledge away from workers towards the apex (Taylor was a virulent union buster). Scientifically trained managers could then better optimize production, it was argued, by quantifying every detail of the labour process.

This exploitation-by-numbers was frequently couched in the language of paternalism. Taylor's condescending exchange with 'Schmidt' – a pig iron labourer whose real name was Henry Noll – epitomizes this. Taylor called Schmidt a hard-working but dim-witted fool. Like a strict but fair father, the scientific manager can best care for his workers by educating them about 'the one best way' and the mutual advantages of piece-rate work. Numbers trumped politics in Taylor's universe. But not morality, however. Taylor believed scientific management contained a strong ethical code because the natural superiority of the manager resulted in worker betterment and a 'win-win' financial outcome. Reading *The Principles of Scientific Management* as an economic fable, in the vein of Mandeville, is essential for understanding its underlying intent.

During the 1970s, Taylor's moralism was evoked less as the class war from above moved out into the open. Labour intensification failed to halt the falling rate of profit. This left only metrics and technocratic opprobrium to do the dirty work. The kind of managerialism built during this period was masculine to the point of caricature, as can be noted in large companies like Kodak and General Electric. Measurement, production statistics, targets and optimization are amoral man's weapons of choice. His pathological side became apparent as capital radically revolutionized the means of production from within. We might term it *quantitative psychosis*. Executives come to believe that numerical representation *is* reality. Numbers don't lie. However, the implication is that people generally do, or at least make judgements that often confound quantitative veracity. Hence why internal cost accounting becomes so salient in this period, dramatically altering corporate cultures accordingly, even prior to digitalization. Ethical contemplation may still occur but is momentarily compartmentalized or quarantined for the greater good of the firm. Moral reason is only permitted on Sundays and at funerals. Never at the office.

A good example of quantitative psychosis in full bloom can be found at Ford Motor Company when led by Lee Iacocca. In the early 1970s more fuel efficient Japanese automobiles flooded the US domestic market. To compete, Iacocca ordered engineers to design their own compact model, the Ford Pinto. The 1971 oil crisis gave the project urgency because Ford was haemorrhaging cash. Development and production deadlines for the Pinto were drastically reduced. One cost-saving feature was placing the gas tank closer to the rear bumper. But would the car pass the National Highway Traffic Safety Administration's 20 mph rule? (i.e. withstand a rear-end collision by another vehicle travelling at this speed). None of the prototypes passed the test. All exploded on impact. Indeed, collisions at faster speeds crumpled the doors inwards, making it impossible for occupants to escape the blazing inferno.

Following an extensive advertising campaign – the radio jingle even chimed, 'Pinto will leave you with a warm feeling' – the model began to sell like hotcakes and became a financial lifeline to the corporation. But as more burnt-out wrecks were sent back to the factory for inspection, executives needed to make a decision … and fast. Should they proceed with the faulty design or remodel the fuel tank (which would cost about $US11 per vehicle in a planned production run of 12.5 million units or $137.5 million). To help decide, managers did what they were trained to do at business school: a cost-benefit analysis. They compared the (monetary) benefit of making the life-saving modifications with the cost of doing so. But how much is a human life worth if killed by being burnt alive? Considering funeral expenses, lost-productivity, lawsuits and medical expenses, Ford priced it at US$200,725 per individual in 1971 dollars. They expected at least 180 fatalities. Now they could do the analysis. The benefit of redesigning the car and saving those lives was US$49.5 million. The cost was US$137.5 million. So, the Pinto was given the all clear. Some estimate that around 500 people were subsequently killed in preventable car fires, but the company admitted to only 23.

A former recall officer wrote about the case years later. He remarked that pausing to think and question the decision to keep this death trap on the road was simply not in the company's cultural script.[12] Speed mixed with numerical data overruled all other concerns, a tone set directly from the C-suite. Nevertheless, he considered himself a very ethical person … but only on his own time. Separating personal judgement from the job was a baseline occupational competence in these large conglomerates. Hence the first step towards non-thinking in the contemporary business world.

5

Evolving from this reification of metrics, the next phase of managerial ethics coincided with the deindustrialization of Western economies from the 1980s onwards (aka neoliberalism). Shareholder value and financialization moved centre stage. This was followed by a mergers/acquisitions boom and an unprecedented concentration of capital. A new corporate personality appears in this milieu. Managerialism falls in love with the *investor*. Rational expertise remains important but is supplemented by the mythos of entrepreneurial risk taking. With the benefit of hindsight, it was perhaps inevitable that this trend's final destination was Enron. Such gormless duplicity mixed with mathematicized masculinity could never end well. But for a time at least, these executives were considered the smartest men in the room, a conceit encouraged by MBA programmes in the world's leading business schools.

Given its long-standing veneration of big-shot entrepreneurs, US managers effortlessly transitioned into this era of Wall Street supremacy. In other parts of the world, however, like the UK, Australia and continental Europe, the shift was more discordant. Stewardship and budgetary conservatism remained core values in European capitalism. For example, the CEO of Barings Bank was often spotted taking public transport to work. Then the transition occurred. The management function was no longer considered a colourless administrative responsibility as in yesteryear but an exciting game of beating the market, high-stakes speculation, crushing competitors and enhancing shareholder value no matter what. In the end, the non-US business elite *overcompensated* and identified with the corporate warrior image too much. This overidentification pushed capitalism to the edge. Executives were now charismatic 'leaders' with lush lifestyles. London emerged as a central hub of financial capitalism (along with money laundering and tax evasion) and cultivated corporate cultures of unfazed egoism. By 1995, Barings Bank (founded in 1762) had been reduced to rubble. The perpetrator – rogue trader and compulsive liar Nick Leeson – even seemed proud of the mayhem he had caused.[13]

In most – if not all – Western economies, neoliberalism was a hard sell. The general population didn't buy it at all. It took political force and occasional police violence to railroad through the agenda. In the realm of ideology, governments (assisted by economists) convinced a weary public by cunningly conflating primary narcissism (i.e. self-preservation) with a different instinct, what Rousseau called *amore prope*, or pathological vanity, as opposed to *amore de soi*. Our biological desire to survive was reborn as combative selfishness. It was an impressive confidence trick. Shareholder capitalism soon began to generate windfall profits. This was unadulterated greed. And like that line of half-cut cocaine being snorted in an overpriced restaurant bathroom, there was little 'natural' about it. By the late 1990s a new kind of institutional personality took form. We might call him *antimoral man*. He (and sometimes she) believed that empathy is weak. Altruism is a sham invented by poor people who envy wealth and success. A certain hatred of society was encouraged in this regard. It was fuelled by a misanthropic fantasy of 'the other' (the welfare beneficiary, the public servant, the activist, unions, a more intelligent co-worker etc.) that elevated the ego by casting everybody else as losers. Bret Easton Ellis' novel *American Psycho* wonderfully captures the mindset. Greed is certainly good. But it's not the content of greed that makes it virtuous, on the contrary. Greed offends virtue, which makes it that rare kind of goodness. A certain *jouissance* is acquired from moral transgression, even if only played out in the private cinema of their own minds.

The dysfunctional undercurrent of this managerial ethos is *corporate psychopathy*. Forensic psychologists suggest that the distribution of psychopaths in the population is about 1 per cent, in prisons 20 per cent and in the upper echelons of large business firms around 21 per cent.[14] Although called 'successful psychopaths', they can be just as destructive as their maximum-security counterparts. Besides having no conscience or remorse, corporate psychos practice an extreme form of self-love and enjoy being reckless. General Electric (GE) CEO Jack 'What the Fuck Do I Pay You For?' Welch embodied this type of man. Back in the 1950s GE was a stalwart of welfare capitalism. In 1952, for example, the firm reinvested 30 per cent of revenues back into wages and employee benefits. Only 3 per cent went to investors.[15] That all changed when Welch took the helm. After his predecessor – Reg Jones – handed over the corporation in 1981 at a special ceremony, he announced, 'I give you the Queen Mary, she is unsinkable'. Welch snarled back: 'I don't want the Queen Mary, I plan to blow up the

Queen Mary. I want speed boats.'[16] Share price was his only focus. One way to gain a quick bump was through mass layoffs. Despite soaring profit-margins, Welch gutted the company's workforce. To push things along he pioneered the rank-and-yank incentive system. Staff were annually stack ranked via shonky performance ratings and the bottom 10 per cent automatically terminated. This policy earned him the nickname 'Neutron Jack' because a neutron bomb is designed to annihilate people without damaging the buildings.

In his biography – *Jack: Straight From the Gut* – the CEO boasts that he didn't parcelize his conscience the way previous business leaders did.[17] Instead, like a kind of corporate Übermensch, Welch undertook a transvaluation of all values. Approached from a specific viewpoint, hurting people could also be considered helping them. Hatred is kindness. Terror a form of care. This management philosophy he termed the 'war on loyalty'. By the early 1990s Welch believed that GE's small finance division – GE Capital – was the company's future. No more reliance on plant, labour or concrete goods and services. And screw light bulbs, the company's founding product pioneered by Thomas Edison. Soon high-speed asset trading was being used to offset tax liabilities and game the marketplace. GE Capital grew into a money monster with 30,000 employees worldwide and a balance sheet completely disconnected from reality. But reality eventually bit back. It turned out that actual products did matter. When GE Capital tanked so did its parent company. After reducing GE to a skeletal remnant of its former self, Welch departed in 2001 with a $400-million golden handshake.

6

In the decade preceding 2008 – the year that global capitalism nearly collapsed – these snakes in suits were almost everywhere in big business. The US$74-billion demolition of Enron was completed in

2001 by CEO Jeffrey Skilling. Until then Skilling was considered an entrepreneurial whiz-kid. But in reality, he was a weedy nerd with a male inferiority complex. Hence the regular forays into extreme sports and a five-o'clock shadow that would look more masculine on Preston Playz. Most sinister of all was Enron CFO Andy Fastow. He had zero scruples and was genuinely intelligent. He created accounting instruments so counterintuitive that it took federal investigators years to decipher them. Following his release from incarceration in 2011, Fastow reinvented himself as an after-dinner speaker on the corporate circuit. His topic of choice? Business ethics. The global financial meltdown smoked out some truly frightening characters. Fred 'The Shred' Goodwin – colloquially described as a Seductive Operational Bully (or S.O.B.) – exenterated the Royal Bank of Scotland in 2008.[18] He was widely blamed for crippling the UK financial services industry, not to mention countless lives. Following a £2.1-million tax-free payout, Goodwin still enjoys a £342,500 annual pension. Barclays CEO Bob Diamond and Richard Fuld of Lehman Brothers (who publicly joked about ripping the hearts out of short traders and eating it in front of them) both departed their ruined institutions super-rich men. Ultimately, these and many other S.O.B.'s perfected a kind of 'thinking anti-thinking'. They openly preached moral idealism – perhaps even authentically so – with the purpose of privately obliterating those ideals in the boardroom. This gave them pleasure, a sort of *ethico-sadism*. Thinking as Arendt defines it diminished even further.

The global financial crisis combined with the climate emergency, spiralling inequality and a growing discontent with neoliberal capitalism prompted the partial abandonment of corporate psychopathy. An outward demeanour of empathy and social awareness was now required to placate governmental regulators, shocked shareholders and exploited customers. The concept of

Corporate Social Responsibility (CSR) goes back to the 1950s (and earlier if we include paternalistic factory towns like George Cadbury's Bourneville). After the credit crunch, 'socially correct' capitalism acquired renewed urgency among the ruling elite. This involved a wide range of iterations (replete with buzzwords), including ESG (Environment, Social and Governance), CSV (Creating Shared Value), Stakeholder Theory, Green Capitalism, Conscious Capitalism, Ethical Investing and so on. Even the most controversial industries embraced the idea. For example, US private military company Constellis – formerly known as Blackwater, which committed the Nisour Square massacre in Baghdad – 'considers its responsibility to preserve the natural environment to be of utmost importance'.[19] Similarly, smiling African children and plush green forests festoon the social impact reports of tobacco and oil companies at annual general meetings.

Many critics dismiss CSR as harmless greenwashing. It mostly is. However, that doesn't mean it is entirely innocuous. A worrying trend in this space are declarations by some captains of industry that corporations should go much further than CSR and strive to replace 'failed governments', supplying public goods and services themselves. Why not? They're more efficient than bloated public bureaucracies hamstrung by endless red tape and fickle electorates. BlackRock CEO and billionaire Larry Fink is representative of this ideological shift.[20] In his annual letter to business executives, Fink admonishes governments for being useless. They have not dealt with climate change, runaway inequality and racism. And this is where corporations like BlackRock can make a difference and do the job themselves. Unsurprisingly, this is no act of benevolence. As Fink explains in his 2022 letter: 'we focus on sustainability not because we're environmentalists, but because we are capitalists and fiduciaries to our clients'.[21] Never mind that Fink supported Donald Trump's corporate tax cuts, which undoubtedly exacerbated the erosion of public services he so laments. Nor that

BlackRock *qua* public service provider decidedly wouldn't have a democratic mandate, making it an unaccountable private government with unlimited powers, reminiscent of the Dutch East India Company, which is consistently voted *the* worse corporation to have ever existed (unfortunately for us, records are made to be broken).

Puffed up with self-righteous indignation, executives like Larry Fink, Howard Shultz and many others view themselves as public saviours. They sermonize a win-win doctrine: mega-profits on the one hand and heroic deeds of social welfare on the other. Capitalism doesn't function like this, of course. Oil companies cannot be vehicles of sustainability due to the insurmountable contradictions between their business model and climate justice. Similarly, it is impossible to advocate both financial capitalism and genuine wealth equality ala Larry Fink's proclamations. The two logics are mutually exclusive. Some firms attempt to bypass this tension by championing social causes unrelated to their core revenue stream, including wokewashing (Amazon supporting BlackLivesMatter while exploiting their warehouse workers) and pinkwashing (big polluting airlines championing same-sex marriage). In any case, these diversionary tactics never resolve the underlying antinomy.

The main problem that these managers face is an unavoidable sense of hypocrisy. They don't believe in the trite appeals to social justice and climate change activism and nor does anyone else. Let's call this corporate ethos *faux-moral man*. If only he was a psychopath, then the mismatch between values and practice wouldn't be so troublesome. For those who aren't, however, the hypocrisy can be difficult to live with. Some laugh it off with irony. Self-mockery is another technique. But in most cases, I suggest, this inward barb of shame is assuaged through a manoeuvre that's become a hallmark gesture of modern managerialism. It has two parts. First, corporate morality is *simulated* because it cannot have depth given the contradictions already discussed. And second, the memetic component of this performance is then *outsourced* to either another party (a PR firm) or artefact (glossy brochures and greenwashed websites).

This externalization relieves the manager of ethical agency and activates a sort of pragmatic automaticity. It is different to noetic splitting or compartmentalization we mentioned earlier because thinking is not simply spatially/temporally bracketed until a more convenient time, but indefinitely postponed. The chain of events is now familiar. First comes the corporate scandal. A few heads may roll. Executives claim that the firm's code of conduct was always explicit, but some regretfully ignored it and an internal audit is underway. A penalty is dutifully paid. A press release is posted to the company's website expressing contrition and offering support to victims. And finally, it's back to business as usual.

7

We now have three ethical degenerations in the economic sphere: amoral man, anti-moral man and faux-moral man. Accompanying each character-type is an array of pathologies that have accumulated and folded into each other. Superimposed, their weight has compressed the cognitive/affective foundations – almost to a nullity – that make thought possible. Studying the transcripts of the Rio Tinto parliamentary enquiry, we can detect clear symptoms of this dissolution of reflexivity. Quantitative psychosis is overlaid by traces of psychopathic egoism and then ethical questions are outsourced – to Rio Tinto's Cultural Heritage Management System, for example – facilitating the smooth organization of non-thought. The outcome is eerie. A strategic shutting down of moral reckoning. Beyond the spreadsheets and KPIs, the world does not exist for these executives. Other public enquires reveal something similar, like the one investigating the 2018 bankruptcy of UK firm Carillion.[22] Its CEO Richard Howson wrecked the company through a combination of incompetence and hubris. The enquiry repeatedly questioned him about the inept business decisions precipitating the collapse. His responses revealed a significant lack of mental presence precisely when it mattered: I didn't know about that. My knowledge is limited on that question. I was unaware of this problem, etc. These perfunctory statements indicate a sort of corporate *neo-blindness*, an affected unseeing in the realm of advanced commerce. This blindness derives not from distance but its absence, being *too close* to the myopia of money. The ultimate endgame is economic automaticity. If my argument is correct, then Point Blank Capitalism is characterized not only by its finger-on-the-trigger violence but also by this inability of decision-makers to abstract themselves from the immediacy of administrative praxis, even when the ruins are in plain sight. Under these circumstances, plausible deniability becomes almost an art form among the C-suite.

None of this is to absolve individual agency, of course. Nor deny that some of these people are simply nasty bastards, motivated by avarice, ambition, competition, macho bravado and other traits that make corporations such dangerous institutions. In other words, we shouldn't overintellectualize what may be a simple set of base drives. Even so, our analysis needs to go beyond critical psychology and examine how corporate settings themselves impart specific modes of being and thinking. Or in this case, non-thinking. Here I'm trying to adumbrate a *collective aphantasia* in contemporary capitalism. Sufferers from aphantasia have no 'mind's eye' and are unable to imagine objects or people beyond their concrete situation. Clinical neurologists find a strong correlation between imagination and emotion. Because aphantasics are incapable of this creative thinking they feel little shame or regret. Similarly, to be active participants in the business world today and reap its spoils – especially as the Anthropocene, wealth/income inequality and other bleak trends ramp up – perhaps it is easier to just switch off. A grey automaticity then takes over and does the thinking for them. How else could we explain, for example, disgraced FTX founder Sam Bankman-Fried's habit of playing 'Storybook Brawl' (a videogame) during multimillion-dollar business meetings?[23]

Such routinized non-thinking eventually led to the demise of the Juukan Gorge shelters in 2020. After the parliamentary enquiry was announced, public submissions were invited. Artist and Garrwa man Jack Green submitted nineteen paintings. The works focused on the geological heritage of his peoples, including the long-standing practice of vandalism by the mining industry. One painting called *Diggin a Hole in Our Heart* – submission 154 – depicts rippling rock patterns moving across the canvas, undulating curves that seem to move … as if they were alive. Song lines carry the Garrwa people back to the Dreamtime and ancient ancestors. Then the gaze fixes on an earth mover digging a deep hole in the landscape and a menacing Haulpak truck waiting nearby to receive its load. Inside the growing manmade abyss, the air is yellow and lifeless. The hole echoes the scream of death – the innumerable past generations lost forever – like a black hole sun. As Green explains, 'once you hurt that land, you hurt all of us … we feel cut open'.[24] Whereas Rio Tinto executives felt nothing at all, completely anesthetized.

2

No-dimensional man

1

After being prescribed OxyContin to treat post-surgery pain, Eric Zink – a recovering cocaine addict – recently described the special high that snorting the substance gave him. When swallowed, the tablet dissolves in the stomach and the pain gradually recedes over several hours. Snorting the crushed pill, however, has a very different effect:

> it all of a sudden hits you out of nowhere. It knocked me out almost. It put me to the ground. I didn't want to move. I literally didn't want to do anything. My whole body when blah. A warm blanket came over me. There was no excitement. You are numb. Life is numb. No pain, but numb. It takes you from 100 to zero.[1]

Zink never did it again, sticking to his preferred drug of choice, cocaine. It was a better narcotic for those who wished to feel alive. Whereas OxyContin brings you as close to a 'waking death' as possible. Indeed, when prescribed by medical practitioners, apart from the diminishing pain levels, users are warned of a profound emptiness that may overcome them. 'I was more or less a zombie', another addict said regarding the drug's power to suck the vitality out of everyday existence.[2]

As the ongoing opioid epidemic in the United States indicates, the line between this facsimile death and the real thing is very fine. Often nothing at all. In the late 1990s, OxyContin became the prescription painkiller of choice. A massive wave of overdose fatalities inevitably followed. Between 1991 and 2020 approximately 841,000 Americans died from opioid overdoses.[3] A key cause was the ubiquitous use of OxyContin. Manufactured by the pharmaceutical giant Purdue Pharma (owned and controlled by the Sackler family), the firm aggressively marketed the drug to medical practitioners from the 1990s onwards. OxyContin was advertised as safer, less addictive and more effective than other available painkillers, all of which were a blatant lie. Narcotic analgesics were previously prescribed only by specialists and consultants. Purdue focused instead on General Practitioners, arguing that it can safely be prescribed not only for malignant pain (e.g. cancer) but chronic pain too (e.g. a strained back). This expanded the market significantly.[4] Doctors were invited to luxury resorts – all expenses paid – to discuss OxyContin's amazing attributes. Physicians who had a reputation for overprescribing received extra attention and thousands of 'pill mills' soon sprung up across the country. The privatized US healthcare system helped boost sales because OxyContin was a cheaper alternative for the working poor (compared to physiotherapy, for example), especially the millions without health insurance.

What was originally a medicine for physical pain was now being used to treat endemic *social pain*, which had exploded in America due to record levels of inequality, economic hopelessness and disenfranchisement. Snorting the crushed pill – sometimes laced with fentanyl, etizolam or even worse, xylazine (also known as 'Tranq', a flesh-eating zombie drug) – was a favourite method among addicts. The medical profession quickly suspected the drug was in fact highly addictive and dangerous, not to mention deadly for thousands of its users, but Purdue pursued its defiant sales campaign regardless.[5] The profits were just too good, generating an estimated $35billion. Lobbying, bribing and dissemblance became hard baked into the corporate culture. Doctors continued to overprescribe, and a lucrative black market emerged. In 2003 Richard Sackler stepped down as president but continued as a board member, managing sales behind the scenes but with no formal executive responsibilities. This arrangement would later frustrate criminal prosecutors. In the meantime, the sheer number of deaths and near-fatal overdoses connected to OxyContin couldn't be ignored. By 2019 Purdue was fighting 1000 lawsuits for misbranding the drug. When the Kentucky government sued in 2015 – alleging that OxyContin had destroyed entire communities in Appalachia – Richard Sackler gave an eight-hour disposition. The family fought a long three-year legal battle to keep it secret, but a transcript and video recording eventually appeared in 2019.[6] It presents our first example of *no-dimensional man*. Unsurprisingly, Sackler defends Purdue's marketing approach. Criminal drug addicts are to blame. They abuse an otherwise safe product. However, the four lawyers were taken aback by his almost zombie-like responses when it came to basic questions about Purdue's business model. Sackler said 'I don't know' more than 100 times during the hearing. Look at this segment, for example:

Q. Well, let's talk about the number of Purdue entities there are. How many Purdue entities are there?

A. I don't know.

Q. I've seen upwards of 69 different 16 corporations, perhaps, that the Sackler family owns. Is that correct?

> **A.** If you've counted them. I can't differ with you. I don't know the answer.
>
> **Q.** There are a number of Purdue entities. The Purdue Frederick Company, Inc., does it still exist?
>
> **A.** I don't know.
>
> **Q.** Tell me what companies that you currently have a role with that involve Purdue.
>
> **A.** Purdue Pharma.
>
> **Q.** Do you sit on the board of any other?
>
> **A.** Not to my knowledge.[7]

It is tempting to dismiss Sackler's stonewalling as straightforward deception. And to an extent, it probably was. However, I reassessed that conclusion after viewing the eight-hour testimony video recording. Sackler conveys almost no emotion – be it positive, negative or neutral. No ethical compunction or awareness is visible. Brainwashed by money for sure, but also internally absent as a human being. From the opening remarks to the closing statement – I watched the entire eight hours over the course of a single day – the robotic and expressionless demeanour was unsettling. As I wearily closed my laptop and reflected on the disposition, it struck me that there was a weird congruity between the tranquilized OxyContin addict and Sackler's systematic non-presence in the courtroom. From both the user's point of view, broken by unrelenting economic oppression, and the seller's, bewitched by the unfeeling and predatory pursuit of profit, this sinister drug functions as a chilling metaphor for what contemporary capitalism can do to a person. The purpose of this new ideological matrix is to expunge all internal valence from the sphere of economic praxis. The insensate vacuum that ensues sets the scene for a new persona to step forth: no-dimensional man.

2

Readers will recognize the wordplay used here. Herbert Marcuse's famous analysis of *one-dimensional man* is our point of departure for explaining a series of sociopolitical deformations specific to contemporary economic doxa.[8] Post-war America was tightly controlled by the corporation and capitalist state. Although soon to be shattered by the counterculture and the cumulative horrors of the Vietnam War, Marcuse argued that economic domination was so comprehensive that the individual had been compressed into a one-dimensional mode of existence. By this Marcuse meant the absence of negation or two-dimensionality. Obedience, advertising and a tacit police state flattened out subjectivity, reducing the individual to a mechanistic reflex of work and consumption. *One-Dimensional Man* maintained that these two logics – labour and shopping – had merged into a totalizing drive, an ineluctable mechanism of cultural conformity.

That negative praxis had been entirely purged from this homothetic culture was unsurprising to Marcuse. TVs, fridges, cinema, commuting, happy families and schools pointed only in one direction, forging a social consciousness that mirrored the universal equivalence of exchange value. Add to this the insidious militarization of American capitalism (not only in relation to civic policing but in more subtle domains including daily speech and communication), the economy was duly transfigured into an inexorable performance principle. It couldn't be denied. For the very thought of dissent had been erased from the political vocabulary of mass-produced existence.

One-dimensionality stemmed from the post-war restructuring of liberal capitalism in the United States. Reinforced by the certitude of standardized full employment and sophisticated new methods of social administration, the worker-cum-consumer was pre-programmed from birth (perhaps even beforehand) to obey the precepts of instrumental rationality. Preschool simulated the workplace. Then at high school, the regimentation was immediate, unrelenting and army-like. After that, one-dimensional man enters a faceless workforce, the assembly line or grey office block, which continues the silent war on two-dimensional thinking. Cookie cutter suburbia, the family unit, leisure and even sex did much the same. And let's not even mention funerals in 1950s America. They were deadly.

But this wasn't just a story about dull compliance. Equally as problematic, according to Marcuse, is how the individual grew dependant on this one-dimensionality. Without it, life had no meaning or coherence. More perplexing still is the *enjoyment* one-dimensional existence engendered; men and women (and often children too) embraced their own subordination, openly preferring psychological incarceration over liberation. This facet of capitalist psychopathology was completely anathema to authentic negation and betrayed the core principles of enlightenment, especially man's emergence from self-imposed nonage. One-dimensional man not only evinced a solemn seriousness but also gained pleasure and satisfaction from that unfreedom. Nor does he or she lose their individuality. Instead, it deteriorates into *collective individualism* or a kind of anti-social sociability. This type of individual is scripted to smile, joke and emote on cue. Indeed, self-absorption is central to inculcation on this scale. Consequently, one-dimensional man is unable to experience what Walter Benjamin called the 'deeper solitude' that permits one to be an individual proper, since that is only possible in communities unvitiated by class antagonisms.

In this manner, one-dimensionality extirpated the emotional range and scope of mass society. Take the simple act of laughing, for instance. Perhaps borrowing from his erstwhile colleague and rival T. W. Adorno, Marcuse implies that genuine jollity is no longer feasible.[9] For one cannot disentangle it from the affectation engineered by bad sitcoms and bullies having fun at the office. Often vile and tedious, such mirth was the underside of the lifeless rationality that otherwise predominated. Indeed, history itself could be read as something of a cruel joke. And people lived this joke unconsciously, exemplified by their proclivity for happy violence in the entertainment they consumed. In any case, as small pockets of humanity began to comprehend what had happened to them – galvanized by images of Martin Luther King lying dead on a hotel balcony and babies riddled with bullet holes in Mỹ Lai – a gesture of restorative protest was inevitable, Marcuse maintained.

3

But therein lies our problem: even one-dimensional man retained an elemental indivisibility, albeit minuscule and atrophied. The manufactured ritual of American sociality, consisting of a monstrous cliché wonderfully depicted in Ira Levin's novel *The Stepford Wives*, nevertheless contained a dim glow of incommensurability and deviation. We know this, Marcuse would later suggest, because the rebellious currents defining the late 1960s and early 1970s could never have gained traction otherwise. Some kind of unengineered residue was necessary to jumpstart those mounting refusals.

This latent humanism in Marcuse's book is fascinating, and not only due to the nostalgia it evokes in readers today. One-dimensionality operated as a formidable force of domination, no doubt. But it turned out to be an incomplete actualization of power, perhaps even an unsuccessful one. In other words, despite the hypostatization of absolute technique in the realm of social administration, an external counterpoint – at first minor and inchoate – was able to eventually break through. This radical seed subverted the status quo in escalating waves of opposition, including the radical Kibbutzim movement, the London Free School, the Black Panthers and Yippies. Bureaucratic boredom was challenged by revolutionary play or *homo ludens*. Technological submission mutated into anti-actionality. The mundane grind of consumerism was replaced by the joys of civil disobedience and peaceful sit-ins. And how could the Protestant work ethic ever compete with LSD? In short, repressive desublimation was reconfigured into a moment of libidinal rupture.

Notwithstanding these challenges to the staid norm, escaping the grip of mass media would be no easy feat, especially if revolt itself became its new content. Television, for example, the ultimate technology of pacification, colonizes consciousness subliminally to incapacitate two-dimensional thought. Both its ease and distracting qualities make television highly addictive. Nothing short of cold turkey could break its hypnotic spell. In a famous (and in my opinion hilarious) passage at the end of *One-Dimensional Man*, Marcuse argues this point (again, with a nod to Adorno) as follows:

> The mere absence of all advertising and of all indoctrinating media of information and entertainment would plunge the individual into a traumatic void where he [*sic*] would have the chance to wonder and think, to know himself (or rather the negative of himself) and his society.[10]

In other words, turn that fricking TV off! Marcuse's solution is amusing because it is reminiscent of an angry parent lambasting their child about the ills of excessive 'screen time'. And just think how realistic the possibility of cancelling digital communication would be now. Although the days of interpreting social media as a movement flagbearer for progressive change are long over (indeed, it is astounding that Facebook was ever seen in this light), it is easier to imagine a coming nuclear apocalypse annihilating all of mankind than envisage a world without Instagram.

My point is that Marcuse's one-dimensional man was a failed venture in social programming. He or she could still rekindle a kernel of negation within themselves. Two-dimensionality was only momentarily deferred by the administered order – not deactivated but temporarily eclipsed before the sun reappeared. This critical residue persisted notwithstanding the remodelling of personhood into an identikit of the ideal worker and consumer. That antithetical energy formed the basis of the 'Grand Refusal' and promised to rectify all wrongs and herald a truly emancipated society. Although deeply pessimistic on the surface ('nothing indicates this will be a good end', he writes in the closing pages of the book), a revolutionary humanism lies at the heart of Marcuse's argument.[11] *One-Dimensional Man* was really about why two-dimensionality will triumph despite everything, making it an implicitly optimistic treatise.

4

Marcuse's unstated hopefulness is difficult to sustain today. Our new age of unhappiness – roughly spanning the period from 9/11 through to the depredations wrought by the Covid-19 pandemic and its aftershocks – is characterized by a ghostly non-presence cutting to the core of advanced capitalism. One-dimensionality has decomposed into no-dimensionality in both cultural and economic life. By no-dimensionality, I mean the dissipation of any dialectical relationality between structure and consciousness pertaining to the commodity-form and its human bearer. Unlike one- or two-dimensional man, this persona signals a nullification of inward receptivity. An undoing of knowledge is central to that absence. This is reflected in, for example, the inscrutable workings of financial markets, the code of secrecy observed by corporate elites and a preference for Oxy-addled nothingness over the cold stone reality of economic servitude among the working poor.

This collapse of consciousness has three temporal elements. First, the *present* global system (i.e. shadow banking, shell companies and tax havens, obscure legal arrangements underpinning wealth transfers etc.) largely functions behind our backs, an éminence grise with frightening reach. Most of us have no clue about what's going on in this sphere. Second, regarding the *past*, entire sub-histories of liberatory praxis, including the many missed opportunities, have been erased from awareness after neoliberalism established itself as a kind of timeless eternal present (or what Enzo Traverso calls, 'an insuperable horizon ... a diluted and expanded present absorbing and dissolving in itself both past and future ... a suspended time').[12] And third, concerning the *future*, comprehending what terrifying disasters await the human race is beyond our imagination, especially those precipitated by advanced technologies in the sphere of war, ethnonationalism and the Anthropocene. For sure, our era is no longer marked by the reign of cognitive capitalism but by its negation: anti-cognitive capitalism and the profound undoing of social knowledge.

This non-knowledge is consolidated by a new political economy of counter-experience or experience set against itself. Subjectivity is both totally subsumed by the web of global markets and yet largely superfluous to the accumulation process. For example, we may ignore international debt instruments and it us, but try functioning for one day without somehow drawing on its artefacts. In this sense, we are all capitalist subjects, not by choice but by our inability to act otherwise (unless we move off-grid). Moreover, when Marcuse was writing, everyone had a productive role in the economy and needed cajoling by the industrial complex – the outcome of which was the repressive reformulation of pleasure into technique. Twenty-first-century capitalism is different. Millions play no productive role in the economy and are basically unneeded. It is this symbolic redundancy that informs how the ruling class views the rest of us, even those who do have jobs. The multitude are no longer presupposed as a significant concern in the plans of big business, politics, education and banking. Our thoughts, desires and views are superfluous, almost extraneous to their motives. Richard Sackler's contempt for OxyContin addicts is evidence of this. Users didn't matter and were never part of the business plan (even as they made him a perversely wealthy man). Or to present a more pedestrian example, just try getting a Ryanair or Frontier Airlines service representative on the phone. These firms rely on your cash but will not – under any circumstances – interact with you on any other level. To them you are nothing. If they could do business *without you*, they undoubtedly would, which is a major contradiction in post-millennial commerce. Something similar characterizes government and representative democracy. The colourful displays of counterfeit communication – live leader's debates, for instance – merely underscore an irreparable separation from the voting public. Thence lies a gulf of mutual incomprehension. The mass 'viewer' matters only as a screen for those who rule, a one-way glass that reflects the featureless image of power back onto itself in dormant shades of black. In philosophical terms, the master no longer covets recognition from the servant. Indeed, this heteronomy has become so absolute that it is no longer intelligible. Everything is now branded by its unthinkable overreach. Even the act of contemplation – that final bastion of escape – is like trying to unthink clock time or the state. Dialectical reason flounders.

5

Marcuse believed that one-dimensionality represented rock bottom when it came to class consciousness in advanced capitalism. While he could never have foreseen the unbelievable depths of nothingness that a line of crushed OxyContin could induce, it's easy to understand his supposition. However, the one-dimensional way of life that Marcuse described – albeit as a geometrical flat plane – did entail psychoanalytical extension. Mindless conformity was the outcome of unconscious fear and an attachment to one's own repression. In this sense, and while only negligible, one-dimensional man still had depth via repressed guilt. When the administrative superego – as performance principle – sadistically valorized the outer limits of technical rationality, it *surfaced* – not buried – the libidinal desire for authentic escape and collective recompense.

For this reason, psychoanalysis is ill suited for developing a political philosophy of no-dimensionality. What about existentialism? Sartre famously argued that nothingness can be differentiated from classical self-negation (Hegel) because being-is-not cannot transcend its own absence.[13] Nothingness carries a strange positivity in this respect. His famous café example conveys the point well. Upon arriving at their rendezvous, the unexpected absence of Sartre's friend overwhelms the emotional geography of the room, foregrounding everything else *omnis determination est negatio*. Without digressing into Sartre's ontology too much, I believe we can safely say that existentialism isn't the best way forward either. His philosophy of nothingness invariably exonerates individual consciousness, even if nailed to the cross of infinite freedom. This agentic openness has little to do with the self-divesture we're interested in here. If a rail of OxyContin means anything, then it's not about endless choices but the opposite, a new kind of emptiness that gathers on the horizon like a failed sunset. We must look elsewhere for the intellectual tools to study no-dimensional man.

Let's go out on a limb. Might algebraic geometry and its formulation of dimensions help us? Potentially. The topos of a point is dimensionless, having no length, height or breadth. Mathematicians call this a terminal object. By the same token, points are the primitive building blocks of dimensionality, haunting nullities with internal depth but unable to yield geometric extension in themselves.[14] As an aside, although the ideas of Deleuze and Guattari are now outdated and have proved unsatisfactory guidance for class struggle, I agree with their philosophical privileging of spatiality (planes, segments, poles etc.) over temporality when conceptualizing social control. If time is a genuine dimension, which some seriously doubt, then it's essentially unknowable as J. M. E. McTaggart conceded.[15] To this day, no one truly knows what time is. Nonetheless, the algebraic conceptualization of points (as terminal topological singularities lacking depth) presents an interesting analogical framework for our study.

Marcuse's one-dimensional man embodies a *monolithic* world of conformity (derived from the Latin *monolithus* or a single immoveable stone). Its flat and homothetic surface coincides with the repressive hypothesis. Dissent is sublimated and displaced onto nationalism, sexism, consumerism, work, war and so forth. A theory of points or zeros (*nihil*) instead pictures a *nihilolithic* social formation. By this I mean a subjective (i.e. psychological), social (i.e. organizational) and economic (i.e. meta-structural) functional non-presenting. *Functional* is perhaps the wrong word. Irrespective of whether it is accidental, incidental or useful to the economic order, this productive vacancy generates a loose constellation of sorts. Yet its integrated stability isn't functional in any positive sense but represents a kind of 'catastrophic equilibrium', a reproductive logic that resembles a nasty drug habit as it yields misleading plateaus amidst an otherwise steady decline.

6

To recap, nihilolithic power structures constitute no-dimensional man through the evacuation of knowledge and sense-making at the *psychological*, *organizational* and *meta-structural* levels. The peculiar mental absence that this new spirit of capitalism entails makes no-dimensional man a truly regressive and depressing socio-economic development, even by critical theory standards. Although these countersubjective forces do not unfold evenly across the capitalist division of labour, there is nevertheless a unifying rationality at play. Nihilolithic dimensionality is not simply an ideological tool for the rich. This social apparatus or dispositif absorbs multiple-class factions within its mesh of relations (while distributing very unequal life chances, of course). It connects both the depleted consciousness of the venture capitalist and the Uber driver who hot rolls a gram of Christina before disappearing into the Geosurge algorithm for another endless shift.

Beginning with the psychological level, the business elite exemplify no-dimensional man. Richard Sackler is no outlier in this respect. To be sure, the formalistic cancellation of personality is almost a prerequisite for succeeding in the corporate world today. In the 1980s, the celebration of 'charismatic leadership' was blended with endemic sociopathy and elevated 'character' as a defining value in CEO culture, even the ugly and abrasive ones. Take the cavaliere displays of toxic masculinity that Richard Fuld or 'Chainsaw Al' Dunlap exhibited, for example. The global financial crisis changed this. The archetypical business tycoon first withdrew into grey blandness and then practically disappeared from the theatre of commerce. This was particularly noticeable in the banking industry as the man without qualities attempted to neutralize the Wolf-of-Wall-Street stereotype. That image didn't fit the new era of megaprofits that followed the credit crunch. Indeed, given the quantitative easing windfall and the stockpiling of trillions in cash reserves (which today has reached record highs), a less conspicuous personality was clearly called for.

Multinational companies thus dissolved the 'performative principle' and replaced it with the *vacuity syndrome*. It has worked its way up and down the corporate hierarchy. This is different to mere presenteeism, where workers sit at their desk and pretend to be productive while basically doing nothing. At least that charade concealed an ego semi-present to itself, even if only daydreaming about being elsewhere. In his insider account of business presenteeism, *The Living Dead* (published in 2005 before the rise of no-dimensional man), David Bolchover criticized the empty hours of fake work he observed in a London office.[16] Far more interesting than Bolchover's moral platitudes about indolence, however, are the pastimes he noted flourishing behind the scenes. They included having sex in the office, drinking wine, taking drugs, watching porn, planning revenge against a cheating partner, nursing debilitating hangovers, grieving dead pets and, if they could escape unnoticed for a few hours, visiting a nearby theme park. Calling these individuals 'the living dead' is spurious. They are paragons of life.

No, the 'vacuity syndrome' is different. In the corporate world, at least, it is characterized by a practised and depthless paucity, an existential nullification that runs all the way down. It is telling that business magazines like *Forbes* and the *Harvard Business Review* mention a new trend in white-collar culture they term the 'Great Disengagement', observing how it has swept through the economy like a sleeping sickness. These workers – both at the top and bottom of the ladder – are on autopilot. The causes of this absentification are ultimately connected to transformations in global capitalism, but we can identify more local factors also. For example, inwardly turning off and disappearing might serve as a form of psychic protection, numbing ourselves to the indescribable terrors of the modern office (or even worse, the remote home office, where chronic boredom, damaging levels of stress and ritualized humiliation are mixed with screaming children). Years of overwork combined with pandemic fatigue turn these workers into suited shadows, for just how many Zoom meetings can an individual take?

7

At the organizational level, nihilolithic flows of power are articulated in new institutional norms driving the accumulation process. The corporate sector is instructive once again. Leadership books – often found in airport bookstores or basement bargain bins – are replete with ridiculous prescriptions about good stewardship, typically pandering to the ego-fantasies of the reader. One that recently caught my eye was titled *The Leadership Secrets of Santa Claus*.[17] It argues that the formidable task of producing and delivering toys to the world's children on Christmas Eve is an astounding achievement of industrial entrepreneurship. We can learn much from Santa-as-Manager in this respect. Chapters cover logistics, outsourcing, employee motivation, disciplinary procedures and so forth. Unfortunately, it doesn't seem to have dawned upon the author that 'Santa Claus' is a slang term of derision in corporate America. It refers to an *absent leader*. Employees hate these executives. They appear only once a year – usually at the annual Christmas party via Microsoft Teams – and even then, their concrete existence is often doubted.

Gone is the earlier trend (circa the 1980s and 1990s) of ultra-visibility among upper management, involving vulgar displays of self-aggrandisement like abseiling into general meetings with Fleetwood Mac's 'Don't Stop' blaring from loudspeakers. Secrecy, opacity, inscrutability and institutional minimalism are the preferred modus operandi of the business elite today. Richard Slacker's pathological privacy is a good case in point. Santa Claus managers deploy this cloak of invisibility for several reasons. Life is simply easier without the attention. Maintaining a low profile precludes awkward questions from staff and cultivates an air of superiority (eccentric characters like Elon Musk are exceptions that prove the rule). Moreover, incompetence can be better disguised when transparency is kept to a minimum. This is often assisted by auditing firms (e.g. KPMG, EY etc.) that can introduce Byzantine levels of ambiguity into financial reports, often reducing them to little more than elaborate fairy tales. Some firms don't even bother with this pretence. When cryptocurrency exchange FTX collapsed in 2022, investigators discovered a 'paperless bureaucracy' that militantly resisted all record keeping. Billions of dollars simply vanished into thin air.

This strategic absence has helped sharpen a crucial skill for corporate executives today: *organized ignorance*. It is a neat way of evading culpability when a firm becomes embroiled in scandal or subject to a criminal investigation. A significant debate (sparked in the US by *Global-Tech Appliances, Inc. v. SEB S.A*) is underway in business law on this topic. A distinction is made between unplanned self-deception – where managers take their eye off the ball during the normal course of business – and planned self-deception. The latter takes us into murky legal territory because it suggests that actors can somehow preclude incriminating knowledge without first being privy to that knowledge. This isn't a lie of omission; it is organized non-knowledge and relies on counterfactual analysis to be inferred as such. Organized ignorance implies that these individuals knew what they didn't know what they didn't know. A twist of reasoning that Donald Rumsfeld would have applauded. Hence why illative criminal liability and the 'equal culpability thesis' (where deliberate ignorance and positive knowledge are equivalent) is difficult to substantiate. Prosecutors end up asking absurd questions to obtain the truth, as we observed in the Sackler disposition.

Absent leaders can mix the art of organized ignorance with neoliberal profiteering in ever-sophisticated ways. It represents the highest achievement of institutional stupidity. What we earlier referred to as neo-blindness applies in this regard, confounding a basic legal axiom in commercial law: namely, that presuppositional knowledge never precedes perfect information. In terms of corporate governance, perhaps a new branch of epistemology is required to ascertain whether non-knowledge is in fact a different category of knowledge or the manifestation of some previously unidentified terrain of truth. Regardless, let's call this *false truth* telling.

8

The meta-structural level of nihilolithic power relations consists of the global economic network and it sets the backdrop to the levels previously discussed. A leading contradiction of capital accumulation today concerns the real subsumption of living labour into the economic field on the one hand and its total desertion on the other. Complete integration plus absolute disavowal. Financialization epitomizes this process. The credit system and international money markets have inexorably penetrated every aspect of daily life. Its influence is practically inescapable and is now the 'nervous system' of the social body. On another register, however, that same social body

– namely you and I as workers, retirees, students, consumers etc. – is *irrelevant* to the formal functionality of financial capitalism. It both needs us and yet enforces an unswerving stance of social detachment.

It is only when the system crashes – as with the 2007 subprime mortgage meltdown – that we gain insight into its arcane circuitry. US mortgage-backed securities and collateralized debt obligations (driven by obscure equations like the Black-Scholes algorithm) infected the international economy in such a thorough manner that almost nobody (including the primary perpetrators) could holistically grasp all of its permutations.[18] Many experts – including econometric and actuarial forensicists – still do not entirely understand what transpired, let alone the average person on the street. But it was precisely that person on the street who paid the price when the house of cards collapsed. What did a factory worker in Coventry – laid off and then evicted in the recession that followed – have to do with the Florida housing market? Absolutely *nothing*, of course, but also *everything*. This absent presence by which financial markets absorb the banalities of daily life makes it pernicious for this very reason.

The Panama Papers and similar leaks revealed how megacorps – enabled by wealth fund managers, mailbox companies, complicated tax avoidance arrangements, bribed politicians – truly exist on another planet. It has been estimated that up to US$32 trillion of financial assets are today held in offshore tax havens, stashed away by corporations and wealthy families.[19] Because this capital is cloaked in impenetrable levels of opacity, it's difficult to calculate their worth with precise accuracy. And then there's the shadow banking system: securitization chains, leverage and risk transfer instruments that fall beyond the traditional banking sector and are impossible to regulate. Many analysts argue that shadow banking precipitated the subprime collapse given its lack of regulatory oversight. Nevertheless, while millions of working people still see their income stagnating, the shadow banking sector has gone from strength to strength. Since 2008, capitalization has risen to around US$239 trillion.[20]

It is tempting to critique financial capitalism for its abandonment of the real economy. But that is only partially true. Its no-dimensionality invariably feeds on the all too human dimensionality of living labour circulating in the world system.[21] In other words, it fundamentally structures our lives but enjoys absolute impunity. This oscillating absent-presence is essential to how contemporary international financial markets operate and underlines its nihilolithic tendencies. If only this system did completely disconnect from the social body, the damage it inflicts would be less harmful to those who otherwise bear the brunt of its rent-seeking behaviour.

9

One final topic requires attention. All the examples of no-dimensionality discussed above involve men. Indeed, Marcuse's original critique of one-dimensional man largely elides the question of gender (notwithstanding 1955's *Eros and Civilization*, which is arguably his masterpiece). Marcuse was no stranger to feminist politics, of course, and actively promoted the women's liberation movement. In 1970, *Playboy* magazine offered the ageing philosopher a large sum of money for an extended interview.[22] Marcuse detested the objectification of women and thought the magazine a perfect example of repressive desublimation. After carefully consideration, however, Marcuse agreed to the interview on one condition: that *he* be the nude centrefold for that issue. *Playboy* declined.

Nina Power's *One-Dimensional Woman* presents a corrective to Marcuse's ungendered one-dimensional man.[23] Her opening question – where have all the interesting women gone? – is reformulated later in the book as, whatever happened to our dreams of living differently? The slippage is central for understanding her argument. The co-optation of feminist rhetoric by the neoliberal establishment has reduced it to a question of identity. The power hierarchy is not the problem. We simply need more women and ethnic minorities in those top positions, be it in public institutions, business firms or in universities. The approach – corporate feminism – undermines women's liberation because it diverts attention away from the root causes of gender inequality. This displacement radically redefined feminism from the 1980s onwards. Struggles for economic inequality were divorced from struggles for representational equity. Economic equality was then reframed as diversity. But a diverse elite is still an elite.[24]

The corporate feminist signifies one-dimensional woman par excellence. She believes that women simply want another woman and not the radical transformation of a deeply patriarchal system. It's a numbers game. For example, compare billionaire Sheryl Sandberg's 2013 paean to female leadership – *Leaning In* – with Valarie Solanas' 1967 *SCUM* ('Society for Cutting up Men') *Manifesto*.[25] Sandberg's feminism concludes that 'a truly equal world would be one where women ran half our countries and companies'.[26] Whereas Solanas states:

> Life in this society being, at best, an utter bore and no aspect of society being at all relevant to women, there remains to civic-minded, responsible, thrill-seeking females only to overthrow the government, eliminate the money system, institute complete automation and destroy the male sex.[27]

One can only imagine how Solanas would have reacted to *Lean In*. Reach for her snub-nosed pistol is my guess. At any rate, following Nina Power's lead, is it possible to identify a *no-dimensional woman*? Perhaps. While nihilolithic power networks overwhelmingly recognize and reward men, the rise of *non*-feminism (in contrast to corporate feminism or anti-feminism) among a new generation of women might warrant the descriptor. Valaire Solanas too noted this problematic when referring to 'Daddy Girls'. Men are not the true enemy, she concludes in the *SCUM Manifesto*, because they're weak, puerile and pathetic (e.g. Richard Sackler). No, it's those women who fail to recognize the urgent need to overturn his corrupt society that's the real problem.

The most interesting aspect of the *SCUM Manifesto* lies in Solanas' view of men as less than zero nullities. After taking dominion of the world in such a totalitarian fashion, he chose to reduce it to an uninhabitable wasteland. And now he wants to take everyone (and everything) down with him. Modern man, that nihilistic and empty creature whose idiocy grows evermore craven despite the wreckage piling skyward. Could it be that life *without* him is the planet's only salvation? And in sketching the beautiful contours of this man-free world, might not Solanas be portending the dialectical sublation of *no*-dimensional man and the nature of liberation that lies ahead?

3

Beyond the leisure principle

1

Picture the scene. You knew that office morale had been low for some time, but never dreamt senior management would go to quite such lengths to try and get everyone enthusiastic about their jobs again. You and co-workers board a bus and travel to the Hyowon Healing Centre, where smiling staff are waiting. Attending the 'wellness workshop' is mandatory for all employees, no excuses. As your team enters the large meeting room, an array of aligned coffins come into view. A 'Wellness Counsellor' gives you a supportive pat on the shoulder and then asks you to climb into a coffin – after all, it has your name on it. Inside the casket is your photograph taken years ago when you still had hope: 'now hug the photo' is the final instruction you hear before the coffin lid is closed. Infinite night swallows you.

No, this is not some bizarre scene from a Philip K. Dick novel but an actual motivation exercise used in South Korea.[1] Here capitalism has always tarried with the dark side of modern employment. Undercurrents of negation define the country's economic ethos, as indicated by high-stress corporate cultures and an epidemic of work-related suicides. For this reason, companies have long tried to reconcile the broken individual to their fate as eternal desk-pushers. Perhaps more urgently compared to other economies, corporate Korea asks the question that capitalism has pondered since its inception: How can we push the human body to its limits – sixteen-hour days at the office is considered normal – and still reap the benefits of an optimistic, balanced and sane human being? Or put differently, how can firms enjoy the total subsumption of labour time and yet have the victim embrace their job with passion, and most importantly, repress the temptation to jump from the window of their grey high-rise office tower (or at least jump somewhere else … preferably after business hours)?

Korean-style capitalism has deployed various methods to overcome this generative contradiction. There are 'rage rooms', for example, where overworked middle managers vent their stress by smashing plates and kitchen appliances with a baseball bat. There are company-sponsored binge-drinking sessions or 'hwe-sik', where large quantities of liquor are consumed, often involuntarily and to the point of blackout. And if that doesn't revivify you, karaoke team-building evenings are another strategy. But none seem to have been successful. They merely distract from the symbolic misery that workers instinctively understand is their long-term future. And because the conditions of possibility shaping that future are so entrenched, firms are upping the ante and sending employees to 'death workshops' to shock them back into life. A senior executive explains why he enrolled his team:

> Our company has always encouraged employees to change their old ways of thinking, but it was hard to bring about any real difference … I thought going inside a coffin would be such a shocking experience it would completely reset their minds for a completely fresh start in their attitudes.[2]

The idea works like this: forcing employees to lie in a coffin is supposed to remind them that life isn't all that bad because ultimately death is worse. Anything is better than the horror of nothingness, because once you're gone you can never come back. The sentiment keys into Korean society's paradoxical fear and obsession with mortality. To get them in the mood, employees write fake wills and final letters to loved ones. Then they are led to the casket for a taste of the real thing. After half an hour in his coffin, one confused employee remarked: 'I've realised I've made lots of mistakes. I hope to be more passionate in all the work I do and spend more time with my family.'[3] Both he and his manager know that the likelihood of this hope being realized – especially more quality family time – is minimal.

2

This death workshop violates a basic principle of psychoanalysis. Freud insisted that 'we cannot imagine our own death; whenever we try to do so we find that we survive ourselves as spectators.'[4] Only phantoms can stand outside their own death and watch it as an external event. Perhaps the coffin game, then, is more about becoming a ghost among the living, occupying the position of dead labour in order to apprehend its ontological impossibility. But does it make workers happier? Probably not. Conceivably *worse* because it prompts a stark realization. The death performance, lying in a coffin worrying about a sadistic boss, is not that far removed from what they experience already, languishing in a cubicle wasting away the best years of their lives. What was intended to give these employees optimism – a life worth living and enjoying – regresses into the opposite: a feeling of being trapped on an endless beige treadmill with no way out. Rather than transform their world into a joyous wonder, an hour at Hyowon

Healing Centre disrupts the capacity to endure this post-industrial nightmare and instead highlights just how bad everything is.

An interesting ideological shift in paid employment is evident in this example. Fordism was characterized by the hundred-year struggle to shorten the length of the working day. As Marx noted when discussing the English Factory Acts, the legally limited working day instigated new definitions of formal freedom and the rising organic composition of capital (or relative surplus-value).[5] A durable dialectic then reshaped social reality via the classic spatio-temporal couplet. Personal and ostensibly 'free time' on the one hand. Paid and unfree time on the other. The conjunction proved extremely productive. The human body must reproduce itself beyond the point of production for it to be exploited in any sustainable way. And that ostensible freedom not only legitimizes the externalization of expensive costs (as a private economic responsibility) but also mystifies the unfreedom inherent in the labour contract, giving it an aura of agency.[6]

This temporal bifurcation of labour time and its 'other' was never so straightforward, however. And it's these inbuilt aberrations – once latent and implicit – that are now moving frontstage, converting the culture of work into a curious illness. In one of his most interesting reflections on the topic, T. W. Adorno argued that the traditional work/non-work dichotomy is no simple synthesis of freedom (leisure) and necessity (labour).[7] Because capitalism fetishizes formal freedom, private time is inevitably tied to unfreedom but *never* as an open antagonism. Instead, unfreedom cohabits – as a half-hidden supplement – the act of individual self-determination. This underground connexion explains why even in societies extolling full employment, 'free time is the unmediated continuation of labour as its shadow'.[8] This trace negates the spontaneity that it is meant to advance. The cult of impulsiveness thus gains ascendency precisely when it has become untenable. In this sense, an unconscious and wormlike directive grows inside nominal free time that inscribes leisure with an invisible injunction: it whispers, be yourself ... or else! Without this secret transcript, one could not obey the mythos of work without finding it a general violation of existence.

Adorno acknowledges that this arrangement was unstable from the outset. Consequently, it only took a handful of misguided neoclassical economists to trigger its internal disintegration, mainly by redefining what labour and liberty really meant. As part of a wider class offensive, neoliberal intellectuals rejoiced in pulling back the covers and revealing how your freedom was always just a conceit. Life and labour are synthetic abstractions of the same substance. And both are nothing more than a function of the price mechanism. There is no such thing as 'free time', F. A. Hayek argued, only 'economic time', be that inside or outside the workplace. With the fable of classical freedom dispelled, work and life unify as unlimited living labour. He or she must live and breathe the economy without the comforting illusion that life could be anything otherwise. That universalism *is* freedom according to Hayek, Friedman and their fellow anarcho-capitalists.

A classic Marxian cleansing of the senses should have followed. In other words, when the chimera of classical freedom dissolves and everyone sees the world as it truly is (i.e. naked and shameless exploitation), class consciousness ought to congeal. But it didn't pan out that way. Ideology still weighs on the brains of the living by transmuting freedom into its inverse, enlisting agency to do this rather than proscribing it. The 'new age' workplace often adopts this principle, especially in high-tech corporations smitten by the 'Californian Ideology'.[9] Hip bosses celebrate gay rights and inclusivity, but only insofar as it fortifies an unstated authoritarian prerogative. When he asks you to work in the weekend, the funky boss-cum-tyrant presents the request as a choice. By having the option to say no, the victim feels forced to say yes precisely because of that choice. That's because choosing otherwise – saying no – will have important ramifications, or so you think. In any case, even if you did decline the request, it would be impossible to enjoy that Saturday afternoon with friends and family. A shade of disquietude would fall upon everything. Probably better to have never had a choice in the first place.

When agency is reconstituted in this manner, the relationship between life and work is no longer dialectical. Both instead merge into one apodictic plane, forming an absolute architecture. Society begins to feel like an *open* labour camp ... let's call it a post-modern labour camp, replete with wearables, Teslas and crumbling municipal infrastructure. Now the private home becomes an extension of the office and holidays more like a death sentence, as an overworked corporate lawyer once confessed to me. Vacations inspired dread in him. Any downtime whatsoever threatened to undo the ideological suture that sealed the founding wound of his existence. This is where the Hyowon Healing Centre gets it wrong. It perpetuates the misunderstanding that work addiction occurs when employment assumes a life-or-death status (i.e. I'm nothing without my job). But for the pathic post-industrial worker, employment is rather a life-*in*-death question. My job is nothing if I don't redeem that nothingness in everything else I do. Pointlessness must have a point, even if indirectly obtained from a position of substantial remoteness. Indeed, one can imagine the death workshop backfiring and employees refusing to leave their inner sanctum of nothingness. Finally, I really am no one.

An inevitable urge to flee arises when life outside of paid employment comes to resemble mandatory labour too. But flee from what exactly? A failing marriage? Unjustifiably high rents and predatory landlords? No, something more unshakeable and ubiquitous than that. Given how interwoven life and labour now are, we long to escape *the self*, which is impossible if one plans to live and tell the tale. But there is an element of obfuscation even in this formulation. The conflation of self and 'mere life' is indicative of how work has been radically privatized. The deformed whole is stamped onto the particular. The datum of economic universalism is reproduced via unique individual biographies, all distinct within themselves but basically the same. Despite its appearance of detached independence, then, *principium individuationis* has totalitarian antecedents. A product of too much society rather than a dearth. Most importantly, built into this overdetermined isolation is an allergic reaction to seeing it as such. It naturally follows that the main escape routes available tend towards non-being.

This false interiority – where existence is confused with the manufactured arc of life – invariably locates the source of our problems within the self. What you must resist is within you. This explains a wide range of societal mutations today, from the recent and rather childish fascination with stoic philosophy in the self-help industry (pacifying the self), the devastating fentanyl crisis in the United States (tranquilizing the self), the popularity of react YouTube videos (outsourcing the self) and, most seriously, the suicide epidemic sweeping so many countries around the world (destroying the self). The message is clear. Work is bad. Unemployment is worse. But what remains beyond that bipolarism is truly disturbing, and it prefigures everything about you as an embodiment of the whole gone wrong. Even contemplation – that calm and ethereal time to reflect on the beautiful disasters that will soon befall us – has been stolen. It is now experienced as ennui and boredom. Making matters worse, neo-boredom is not empty time but negative temporal fullness, a surfeit of the incorrect type of time that is endless and without colour or finality. The uncaged sky turns out to be barred by other means.

3

Death has become such a personal and private affair in the modern world. Heidegger even based his ontology of existenz on its insular intimacy. Dying is one of the few things that human beings must genuinely do alone. No one can do my dying for me. So how could something this personal end up being promoted as a motivational exercise in corporate Korea? To find out why, we must think of this managerial technique as an indicator of a wider trend to *deformalize* the labour process in modern capitalism. On the surface this may look like the relaxation of formal rules and thus a welcome development. But it was invented in the United States by right-wing intellectuals. So, it's bad, closely linked to the radical individualization of paid work and the return of arbitrary rule in organizations.

The dominant industrial relations paradigm consolidated during the Fordist period was one of austere formalism. Its essential components had been presaged by Karl Marx (regarding factory discipline) and Max Weber (concerning bureaucratic rationality). The early factory Marx described was alienating because the time workers were compelled to sell was spent on repetitive and stultifying tasks. For them, work was a means to an end (wages) only. Employers regulated the time they owned by deploying machines and managers to robotize the human body, all overseen by an omnipresent clock and unpredictable violence. To say this was dehumanizing would be an understatement. Workers had no rights. Indeed, owners treated machinery better than the workers tethered to them. Astonishingly, up until the 1970s, industrial sociologists (studying plants like Western Electric) found that even speaking on the line was still prohibited. No humanity permitted. Concerning administrative rationality (i.e. office work), Weber famously argued that bureaucracies – invented in ancient China – are efficient because of their military-like depersonalization of social relations. All other forms of coordination pale in comparison. Bureaucracies are designed to strictly separate the official position from the idiosyncratic traits of the office holder. The rational requirements of the bureau meant that all those qualities that make us human beyond the workplace had to be temporarily abnegated. As Weber puts it, the more bureaucracy is dehumanized, the more completely it succeeds in eliminating from official business love, hatred and all purely personal, irrational and emotional elements which escape calculation. This is the specific nature of bureaucracy and it is appraised as its special virtue.[10]

No love permitted. But these abstract templates of factory discipline and administrative depersonalization could never be fully implemented in reality. They served more as aspirational guidelines (Weber's *Gedankenbilder*). Humanity continued to heave behind the scenes: clandestine jokes and games, sabotage on the shop floor, corrupt and nepotistic officials, etc. Nevertheless, this formal fantasy of a human*less* enterprise set the broad tone of economic activity during this period of industrial development.

A change of heart occurred in the early 1980s, epitomized by American capitalism and its lurch to the right. Big business discovered that dehumanized workers didn't really care if the company sank or swam. These workers also found ways to shirk their duties at any opportunity, be it pilfering stock or submitting false overtime claims. Most importantly, and as the post–Second World War period amply demonstrated, they formed trade unions. Despite the intercession of the war, the worst industrial disaster in US history – the Hawks Nest Tunnel incident, which killed a 1000 workers in the 1930s – was still fresh in the minds of union organizers. It was a testimony to the terrible treatment that can befall an unorganized workforce. This contextualizes a major reformulation of managerialism as Ronald Reagan and Margret Thatcher unpicked the capital-labour compact. The ground plan went as follows: to destroy organized labour, we require violence in the political field, without question. But in terms of ideology, particularly in the domain of employee relations, corporations need to capture and replace the sense of solidarity and *esprit de corps* currently being supplied by trade unions. We must commandeer that organic energy away from the socialists and put it to work for capitalism instead. Unions would then naturally wither away.

That was the unofficial strategy. Officially, however, capitalists spoke of the need to care for their workforce in order to address falling productivity concerns. Taking their cue from Japanese industrial relations, corporations like Kodak and General Electric focused on cultivating an intense dedication to the company. Strong *corporate cultures* became all the rage and various indoctrinating devices were used: company uniforms, songs, workshops, retreats, myths, ubiquitous logos, leader worship (often with the 'great man' espousing his philosophy in prerecorded speeches on large telescreens situated in the lobby and cafeteria). All of this was designed to instil the workforce with an undivided loyalty to their employer.[11] Some quietly whispered, 'we're being brainwashed!', but most fell in line, either because it worked or because they feared retribution. And as predicted by business gurus at the time, the 'new employee' toiled until they dropped, no questions asked. Some identified with the firm so much that they continued working into the wee hours of the morning and on their days off. It wasn't only office labour that got the culture management makeover. Factories, retail chain stores and, in one peculiar case, abattoirs did so too.[12] The steady decline of union density followed. This was bolstered by yellow dog contracts insisting that employees forego their right to associate and new legislation scrapping worker protections. The company is your family now. French philosopher Gilles Deleuze got it right in the early 1990s when he remarked, 'we are taught that corporations have a soul, which is the most terrifying news in the world'.[13]

4

In an ironic twist, these high-commitment corporations did eventually depersonalize the workforce in their own way. For instance, company cultures are fundamentally collectivist projects and reward conformity above all else. The private individual was eschewed because nothing outside the firm – including family and least of all trade unions – was permitted to dilute the corporate message. The hegemony of bureaucratic rationality was simply swapped for a regime of values. No wonder why sociologists compared these organizations to wacky cults.[14] Compounding the problems created by mindless conformity – including employees who couldn't use their own initiative when contingencies arose – was another shortcoming noticed by executives. Yes, they had successfully ended the scourge of unionism. But now they had to *care* for their employees, promise them lifelong job security and underwrite pensions. In other words, it was expensive. This commitment also flew in the face of arguments then being made by neoclassical economists: the employment relationship ought to be regulated via market individualism and not closed institutions. This would reduce the economic burden for employers (by shifting the costs of employment onto private individuals) and yield more flexibility to hire and fire as needed.

Heeding this advice, management ideology changed tact once again and we're still dealing with the implications today. The new rationale was cunning: to push through cost-saving reforms, let's appeal to individuality instead, what makes each worker different, unique and standout from the crowd. Once separated from the herd … we pounce. Business gurus of the period lavished praise on individual choice and authenticity. The employment relationship isn't a long-term marriage (as with corporate cultures) but a one-night stand, a temporary arrangement, no strings attached. Now you're free to be yourself and beholden to no one. Most importantly, everyone is different, so let your inner jewel shine. If you want to come to work wearing a florescent-green bandana, great. Have an urge to do the Downward Dog pose in your cubicle? Go crazy! Want to work Saturday mornings instead of Monday afternoons. Groovy. That's between you and your boss. Don't want to join the union, pal? We've got your back!

It didn't take long for this Machiavellian refitting of freedom to bear fruit for big business. Many economies around the world witnessed a massive decollectivization of the workforce from the mid-1990s onwards – not only with respect to unions but career pathways inside firms too as part-time employment, temping and casualization spread. This was assisted by neoclassical economics as it entered the workplace. Human capital theory (concerning the skills you possess and invest in as an individual) was prominent in this regard.[15] Chicago School economists loved the idea because the theory assumed that everyone was already *his own* means of production. We're all capitalists now. It dissolved the left-wing conspiracy that some grave injustice – the expropriation of the means of production – lay at the heart of capitalism. Furthermore, human capital theory never refers to the 'workforce' as a social category. The working class does not exist, only a multitude of independent contractors, free-agents and self-employed business owners do. Management guru Charles Handy claimed (in all seriousness it seems) that 'Karl Marx would be amused. He longed for the day when the workers would own the means of production. Now they do'.[16]

5

Bureaucracy is a prominent *point de caption* in this proto-capitalist mindset. It's particularly salient in the deformalization movement, which shares the same enmity towards bureaucracy that's long been expressed by libertarian economists and business leaders. Bureaucracy is discredited as red tape. It kills innovation and transforms workers into lifeless droids. Here we can note some interesting conceptual affinities between the sociology of Max Weber and arguments latter advanced by anarcho-capitalists.[17] In their hands, Weber's neo-Kantian critique of administrative reason is warped into an anti-state project that seeks to shrink the public sphere at any cost, or at least those parts that cannot be enrolled to advance corporate control. Early renditions of this agenda can be found in Ludwig von Mises' *Bureaucracy* and Anthony de Jasay's truly strange book *The State*.[18] Their antipathy towards workers – who they believed loved bureaucracy because of its socialist connotations – is palpable. Contemporary authors in this tradition, however, employ a more sophisticated rhetorical strategy. They pitch themselves as staunch *allies* of workers. Bureaucracy hurts them as much as capitalist enterprise. The erosive effects of red tape transcend class divisions and ought to unite labour and capital as they confront a common enemy.

Take the bestseller *More Human*, for example, written by Steve Hilton, erstwhile adviser to the calamitous British prime minister David Cameron. I met Hilton in 2015 when promoting our respective books for BBC radio.[19] It was an unpleasant experience. He maintained that bureaucracies are deadly in the modern workplace because they stifle human difference, creativity and morale. These vitiating structures 'eliminate basic humanity and the personal connection, kindness and empathy natural to nearly all of us'.[20] Employers should replace bureaucratic pyramids with decentralized humanism instead and redesign jobs to be more personal and artisanal. Of course, that all this 'red tape' might also ensure health and safety compliance in hazardous jobs or gender equality is never mentioned by Hilton.[21]

A telling contradiction unsettles such calls to debureaucratize capitalism. The kind of informality Hilton wishes to see in organizations isn't existentially indeterminant, something that most philosophers believe is precisely the most human thing about us. No, Hilton's version is ultra-fixed: 'the very notion of enterprise, the calling of the entrepreneur, is profoundly human ... in our system of capitalism, businesses – real businesses – are human'.[22] Clearly, a strong normative ideal is operating here that's unforgiving to anyone who doesn't resemble a mini-entrepreneur. A similar dissonance is evident in recent corporate attempts to harness the 'real' and 'authentic' side of our personalities at work. The management techniques used are hypocritically unreal and scripted, not to mention mandatory. Get into that coffin and pretend to be a corpse ... or leave! When taken to extremes, the results can be painfully embarrassing. Think here of David Brent in *The Office*. He treated his workforce as a captive audience for awful new songs: 'err I suppose I've created an atmosphere where I'm a friend first and a boss second. Probably an entertainer third.' The impromptu performances of 'Thank Fuck its Friday' and 'Don't Cry its Christmas' were meant to be a bit of spontaneous fun. Employees experienced it as the opposite. This kind of managerialism employs an excruciating *formal deformalization*.

With the final frontier of control – the subject's inner and most intimate feelings – now colonized by the logic of paid employment, the sky's the limit for devising novel repertoires of exploitation, as Hyowon Healing Centre's death workshop illustrates. But sometimes employers go too far and violate basic human rights. A good example is the US firm United Health Programs of America.[23] Senior managers wanted to demolish corporate officialdom and inject some humanity back into their lacklustre staff. Unfortunately, what they came up with was plain creepy. One day employees were informed that they were all now followers of a new Christian movement called 'Onionhead'. Consequently, they had to say, 'I love you' to each other, voice their spiritual feelings and pray to God in the office. The reason why

United Health Programs attracted national attention was not due to happiness inspired by the Onionhead faith. Many workers were upset. They didn't love their co-workers. Far from it. Nor were they particularly close to God. But refusing to practice the Onionhead faith could land them with a pink slip. An extensive governmental investigation found that

> Employees were told to wear Onionhead buttons, pull Onionhead cards to place near their workstations and keep only dim lighting in the workplace. None of these practices was work-related. When employees opposed taking part in these religious activities or did not participate fully, they were terminated.[24]

Therein lies the dark side of so-called 'soulful corporations'. Bureaucracy may very well squeeze the life out of your job. But when humanity is unleashed to compensate, it's not only the nice and fluffy stuff we get. Like children and feral animals, humans can be ghastly. And that's what many of those rules and regulations were designed to suppress.

6

Being forced to say, 'I love you' to a despised co-worker or climb into a coffin to satisfy an overzealous line manager only scratches the surface of just how bad these unregulated workplaces can get. The attempt to personalize the employer-employee relationship opens a new horizon of subjection: if you're not willing to go along with it, then your days in the company are probably numbered. It looks friendly on the surface, but this management philosophy can end up being more authoritarian than traditional bureaucracies, not less. Workplaces of this sort comingle three distinct logics. First, there is the superficial gloss of formalism which is largely ceremonial. Second is the staged informalism that must be obeyed (e.g. jogging with the managing director during lunch break, laughing at his bad jokes that aren't funny or appropriate, etc.). And third is the valorization of beneath-the-radar interactivity, including the abuse of power, bullying, sexual harassment and so forth.

This distinctive knot of power relations is brilliantly captured in the classic Saturday Night Live comedy sketch 'Evil Boss'. It begins with a very pleasant corporate manager Mr. Tarkanian (played by Will Farrell) interviewing a nervous job applicant called Kurt (played by Pierce Brosnan). Mr. Tarkanian is impressed by Kurt and offers him the job with very generous conditions. He accepts. 'Great', Mr. Tarkanian says with a handshake and smile, 'let's get the paperwork underway'. This is a dream boss, Kurt thinks. Sensitive, professional and no sign of being a jerk. They might even be … friends? Then a junior employee approaches Mr. Tarkanian to ask him a quick question. He suddenly turns into a monster, exploding with rage and commences to shout obscenities at her. She scurries away. 'Ummm, what was that about?' asks a visibly shocked Kurt. 'Oh nothing, don't worry about it … now to that paperwork my friend.' Mr. Tarkanian has reverted to the kind and thoughtful professional manager. As he invites Kurt to the next company barbecue another worker approaches, this time a young man with a report in his hand. Mr. Tarkanian snatches the folder – without reading its contents – and the evil boss returns, more enraged than ever:

> YOU DO NOT HAND IN CRAP LIKE THIS!! THIS LOOKS LIKE YOU TOOK A DUMP IN THE PRINTER!! YOU ARE SCUM!! I SHOULD FIRE YOU AND BURN DOWN YOUR FRIGGIN HOUSE!! I AM THIS CLOSE TO RAPING YOU!!!!

The victim runs for his life and once again Mr. Tarkanian is suddenly placid and business-like. By this time Kurt has been reduced to tears. Mr. Tarkanian was no nice guy after all. Kurt flees the office vowing never to return, following which Mr. Tarkanian is seen murdering a temp with a trident.

The sketch perfectly depicts how hidden behind the thin veneer of the so-called 'new economy' lies a nasty truth. Decades of deunionization and deregulation have transformed organizations into private fiefdoms where almost anything goes. Power has been so exclusively concentrated into the hands of employers that few institutional counterbalances are available to curb its use. The vestiges of formal due process that do remain (Mr. Tarkanian's 'paperwork') are increasingly decorative and stacked in favour of the apex. They conceal what's really going on. Without genuine worker input or monitoring oversight these 'rules and regulations' are little more than an arse covering ritual. Kurt was lucky and gained a glimpse of the truth before signing the dotted line. In reality, of course, most never get this opportunity until it's too late and they're trapped.

Contemporary capitalism presents a dilemma in this respect. A whole tradition of critical theory was correct to challenge bureaucratic domination in the economic realm. Capitalism has long employed administrative rationality and its semblance of neutrality to shore up class control and justify unfair political advantage. Hence why 'the man' became such a hate-figure for the labour liberation movement. An *anti-capitalist* critique of bureaucracy remains eminently relevant. But like so many other right-wing manoeuvres, a *pro-capitalist* critique of bureaucracy stole the left's thunder and then eradicated the first version. Its aim was not capitalism without bureaucracy, since the ruling class depends on an army of technocrats to enforce its dominance, but capitalism without worker-friendly bureaucracy. This logic has swept through the economy and opened the door to arbitrary managerial rule. While life in a drab corporate bureaucracy is bad, slaving for a boss without any regulatory constraints – in a 'human, all too human' workplace – may be far worse.

This partly explains the unique malaise that has descended in and around the institution of paid employment today. Employees can either consent to their subordination or exit. Yes or no. There isn't a third option. This instils an atmosphere of fear and estrangement in even the most secure occupations. We have known for years that what makes a job unpleasant (according to cognitive and affective scales) is seldom the task itself, such as digging a ditch or cleaning a house. It is usually the surrounding socio-economic conditions that matter most: economic coercion (with few viable exit opportunities), micromanagement, ritualized disrespect, insecurity, intimidation and so on.[25] Intrinsically enjoyable jobs can easily turn bad for this reason. As a result, work has acquired – and undeservedly so I think – existential undertones in the post-industrial economy. An unconscious lexicon of funerality frames its meaning, a sort of standardized despair. And from out of this dead-end nothingness – like living labour lying in a coffin – little anew can be made.

Adorno once joked that 'the very people who burst with proofs of exuberant vitality could easily be taken for prepared corpses, from whom the news of their not-quite-successful decease has been withheld for reasons of population policy'.[26] Isn't this the most prudent way to interpret the Korean corporate coffin exercise? As that prematurely ruined middle manager climbs into her casket, she finally experiences something approximating authenticity. By comparison, the vagaries of office life represent a *failed death*. That failure has no outside. We smile and laugh with co-workers, acting as if release will one day come. Only when we lie down in the coffin, a heterotopia for the living like no other, does the truth finally dawn upon us. We are free.

4

Gothika economica

1

April is not the cruellest month of the year for courier drivers in the gig economy. December is. A few days before Christmas in 2018, an 'independent contractor' driving for a major parcel delivery firm was halfway through a gruelling shift in the south of England. Night fell and then it began to rain. He still had many deliveries to make but was confident it could be done. Then a feeling arrived he knew was not good. He needed to shit. Badly. However, the timetable was strict. No rest break for several hours. Given the evisceration of civic services in the UK, he knew a public lavatory was out of the question. Nor a pub or restaurant. And he was miles away from home. So he took matters into his own hands … literally, it turns out. On the next delivery he crept into a nearby shed and defecated into a bag. He carried it back to the van and continued his shift. Unfortunately for him, CCTVs have proliferated across the UK, not least among homeowners. One of them captured the phantom-shitter. The elderly lady sent the footage to the company and the driver was immediately fired.[1]

December is a cruel month indeed. The pressure is on. Another courier working for the same company was disciplined in 2022 for taking a photo of 'Mazie' accepting the delivered package. Mazie was an eight-year-old Labrador.[2] At least Mazie was kinder than Jack. When the courier driver threw the package onto the customer's front lawn – a dress for her Christmas party – her dog Jack instantly set upon it, tearing it to shreds.[3] The courier driver was already gone, speeding to the next delivery. On a more serious note, 29-year-old Amandeep Kaur was pressured to continue driving instead of tending to her dying 9-year-old son. The boy had a heart attack and wasn't expected to live beyond Christmas. But Amandeep's manager needed her on the road. He told her, 'Come back in two days or there's nothing we can do. We need to give your round-up because it is a busy period.' She was broke and couldn't refuse. Only days after her son died, she was back behind the wheel.[4]

All these drivers worked for the notorious courier firm, Hermes UK. The company began as a subsidiary of a large German mail order conglomerate, the Otto Group. An important feature of its business model was the use of independent contractors. Drivers are not treated as employees but one-person business owners. Despite numerous court cases ruling this an illegal misclassification (firms indefinitely postpone these verdicts by appealing), the use of independent contractors remains central to the gig economy. Labour costs are dramatically reduced because workers are not covered by statutory entitlements like holiday pay, minimum wage and sick leave. Employers don't contribute to superannuation or insurance. And workers must use their own capital and pay taxes like any other business enterprise. De facto employers enjoy high levels of control with few of the associated expenses, which are transferred back onto the workforce.

The model has proved profitable for companies like Hermes UK. In 2020 the private equity firm Advent International acquired a major stake for £1.8 billion.[5] During the Covid-19 pandemic revenues soared. In 2021, its annual operating profits jumped from £52.9 million to £143.4 million. But like other businesses that exploit loopholes in employment law, Hermes has attracted much controversy, as noted above. In 2016 the UK tax authorities opened an investigation regarding reports that workers were receiving less than minimum wage. Instead of reforming its business model in the face of mounting criticism, Hermes UK did what many corporations do in such circumstances. It rebranded. In 2022, it became 'Evri' and adopted a new corporate motto, 'every parcel, every person, every place, every delivery made for you'. If being your own boss used to be the dream ... then welcome to the nightmare.

2

How did the venerable goal of economic independence and self-determination (working your own hours etc.) get turned into something so oppressive in practice? Concerning the rise of neoliberalism more generally, analysts have convincingly interpreted it as a restitution of late 1800s laissez-faire capitalism, ironically by way of a forced totalization (i.e. extensive intervention and central planning from an expansive industrial complex). It occurred on several levels: transnational governance (e.g. the IMF and World Bank), statecraft (e.g. elite capture of parliamentary democracy and a dirty war against organized labour) and economic coordination (e.g. corporate monopolies and the privatization of the public sphere). The violence summoned to achieve these changes did in fact bear similarities to nineteenth-century capitalism, as did the socio-economic outcomes linked to inequality and workers' rights.

In addition to these concrete instances of intervention, *ideas* too were central to this restorative process and could not have taken place without a new intellectual constellation.[6] Austrian neoclassical economics – especially as interpreted by the Chicago Schools of Economics and Law – provided an intellectual lodestar for the ensuing power grab. This libertarian 'thought collective' has been extensively studied elsewhere.[7] But missing is a consideration of how these intellectuals endeavoured to reconstruct the very meaning of *the worker*. I believe we can draw a direct connection between their ideas on this topic and the contemporary normalization of precarity, insecurity and rampant managerialism. I would even claim that F. A. Hayek, for example, was the first thinker to delineate the basic features of what a 'gig economy' might look like.

This reconceptualization of labour exhibits several important features. An ideological inversion reconstitutes the symbolic relationship between labour and capital. The earlier organizational norm of *inclusive exclusion* (e.g. you are one of us but only provisionally so) is replaced by *exclusive inclusion* (e.g. you are not one of us but must bear the costs as if you were). Analytically speaking, we see the typical reduction of the unit of analysis to the microscopic individual. Accordingly, such individuals can never be subsumed within a wider class structure or any other transindividual social grouping. But neither can they be differentiated politically, ideologically or culturally from other actors operating in the economy. Capitalists, employers, managers, consumers *and* workers all share the same drive to enhance their own preferences. This uneasy interplay between the particular (disaggregated individualism) and the general (reaggregated economic universalism) is meant to give everyone (including workers) anonymity because social identification is expunged from the narrative.

Concerning the proletariat more specifically, however, something disturbing coalesced in this discourse. A close reading of neoclassical economists indicates an attempt to expel the spectre of *labour* – in the *plural* – from their theorems while accepting that a vast amount of 'human effort' (as opposed to labour) is essential to the capital accumulation process. The implicit maxim appears to be this: we still require organized work on a significant scale ... but not the worker *qua* labour. In my opinion, this points to an attempted exorcism – in the realm of theoretical praxis at least – of the worker-as-symptom. The analytical rite can be seen in equations like

$$Yt = K^{\alpha}_{t}\left(A_t h_t L_t\right)^{1-\alpha}$$

that pretend you exist only in abstention ... at best. This de-representation of labour blends technical perfectibility with total blindness. Of course, capitalism has long fed on large swathes of invisible work. For instance, it couldn't function without the unpaid care work performed by women and girls around the world. If this was monetized, the sum would be staggering.[8] Moreover, in rich countries like America, millions of undocumented migrants subsist in the shadows, doing jobs that others aren't willing to do.[9] We can think of the de-representation of labour in neoclassical/mainstream economics as an apodictic formalization of its non-presence in the theoretical domain. *Homo economicus* doesn't exist in the real world, of course. Actual people never behave in such a manner. However, that disjuncture is part of the project. Between the idealized abstraction and the concrete act lies a no man's land of signification that dissolves the generalizability of labour, but never the capitalist economy as such. All of this was figured out years ago by academics like Carl Mengers and William Stanley Jevons. But only with the resumption of an open class war from above – the neoliberalization of society from the 1980s onwards – does this figmental nothingness become the dominant mental model for rethinking the employment relationship.

3

A major tension remains, though. Notwithstanding this formulaic semi-invisibilization of labour, the production function is still highly dependant on it, even in industries susceptible to advanced automation. Misleading proxies must therefore be assembled to bridge theory and practice. These include human capital, human resources, casual agents and so on. These abstract workers are without class, identity or history. They represent a normative evacuation of labour from the neoclassical imaginary, a worker's society without the worker. None of this would matter if these ideas were not underwriting the reorganization of contemporary employment. But they are. And the fallout has been formidable. Living labour cannot live up to the impossible ideals contained in equations like

$$Yt = K^{\alpha}_t \left(A_t h_t L_t \right)^{1-\alpha}$$

and when that abstraction meets flesh and bone, a metabolic collapse ripples through the social body as it struggles to assimilate. But even a concrete physiological crisis cannot easily be causally linked to class politics. This is the M.O. of economic abstraction. So, instead those crises are interpreted as singular tribulations of individual fortune. He or she finds themselves burnt out and morose, drinking too much, working three jobs without seeing their young children, bogged down in the quagmire of student debt, desperately needing a toilet on a wet and gloomy night but staying behind the wheel because management-via-algorithm is always watching. In short, this excessive dematerialization of labour in theory necessitates an overly material (and often bruising) instantiation of work in practice, a concretization of the body that is conspicuously hidden in formal knowledge and public debate.

I term this expurgation lurking in neoclassicism *gothika economica* because it adds a rather haunting aspect to the ideological landscape of paid employment, foreshadowing the advance of 'ghost jobs' and 'invisible labour' as extreme capitalism gains ascendency. The campaign to theorize production as a peopleless construct has several notable antecedents. The first is F. A. Hayek's early call for right-wing intellectuals to generate more *utopian* thought experiments.[10] We tend to associate utopianism with socialist and communist politics. But as Karl Polanyi observed regarding mid-nineteenth-century capitalism, economic liberalism too has what he called a 'stark utopian streak'.[11] In his 1949 essay 'The Intellectuals and Socialism', Hayek complained that the workers' movement had cornered the market in utopian blueprinting. Anarcho-capitalists needed to enter the fray and plan their own perfect society:

> What we lack is a liberal Utopia, a program which seems neither a mere defense of things as they are nor a diluted kind of socialism, but truly liberal radicalism which does not spare the susceptibilities of the mighty (including the trade unions), which is not too severely practical and which does not confine itself to what appears today as politically possible.[12]

At the time Hayek was considered eccentric and not taken seriously. But the tide slowly changed in his favour. Among other things, the utopia he envisaged was utterly free of anything connected to organized labour. In fact, let's delete the signifier 'labour' all together and replace it with more palatable epithets.

Hayek knew full well that the word 'utopia' literally means nowhere, of course. The goal was not to realize this free-market Arcadia, he maintained, but only move the dial in the desired direction. Furthermore, whether these undiluted and pure ideals functioned practically on the ground was beside the point. Once again, questions about pragmatism – including economic efficiency and profit maximization – shouldn't prevent the formation of these business utopias. For Hayek, it's the principle that counts. Such abstract idealism had a huge influence on mainstream economics. It's one reason why its modelling protocols – concerning consumer behaviour or worker productivity – have such an otherworldly, hypothetical flavour. Chicago School economist George Stigler epitomized this when he jokingly used linear programming to identify an optimal daily diet (with variables including weight, required calories, Recommended Dietary Allowance of nutrients, iron, protein, vitamins etc.).[13] His dietary utopia looked perfect on paper. The numbers exhibited a distinct beauty. However, worried that readers might actually follow the 'Stigler Diet', the economist issued a caution: 'no one recommends these diets for anyone, let alone everyone. It would be the height of absurdity.'[14] In other words, the exercise had nothing to do with practical living and could harm your health. Much the same could be said for economic modelling more generally. Unfortunately, the performative assumptions they contain – including subgame perfect equilibria and the marginal rate of substitution – have been foisted upon everyone as sacred truths.

The second antecedent for this ideational effacement of labour – a corollary of the first – concerns the arcane mathematization of the production process in mainstream economics. Interestingly, F. A. Hayek was hostile to the quantitative wizardry that soon overtook his field. But those reservations couldn't prevent maths from becoming indispensable as the discipline strove to be seen as a hard science. Mathematics mixed with dark utopianism had some haunting results. In an excellent historiography of neoclassical labour economics, Nicholas Theocarakis demonstrates how the worker slowly disappears in its equations as the field matures.[15] This isn't only because labour was (wrongly) counted as one factor of production among others, as illustrated by the conventional production function

$$Q = f(K, L)$$

but indicative of a deeper problem. The marginalist revolution treats labour as a *disutility* or something we do that *doesn't* intrinsically satisfy human preferences. The argument runs like this. The opposite to earning an income is leisure, shopping at the mall and long picnics in the sun – things we'd prefer to be doing. But we must get a job to enjoy those preferences. And because we all hate work – a prominent self-fulfilling prophesy in right-wing labour economics – marginalists like Philip Wicksteed concluded that labour can be modelled as the absence of leisure. Substituted as income, work is strangely approached via the concept *non-work*. Theocarakis calls this a paradoxical *labourless* labour supply theorem. One could argue that this disappearing act has been the implicit goal of capitalist ideology from the beginning. Namely, to exploit the energies of human effort without recognizing the situated and collective bodies who do the work nor their rights and interests. For recognizing them would also acknowledge the heart of darkness in the capitalist order of things.

4

Socialism provoked disgust in Hayek and the very adjective 'social' more so. He dismissed it as a deceptive 'weasel word' that has no place in political and economic science.[16] Only a psychoanalyst – of the Lacanian school I'd suggest – could tell us whence this contempt originated. In any case, this was his ruling fantasy: a society liberated from sociality. Collective action and individual liberty could never be reconciled. Not even in the capitalist corporation. For this reason, Hayek would have no truck with economic institutionalists who tried to legitimate commercial organizations as an important cornerstone of capitalism. Not at all, Hayek insisted. Organizations shelter its members from the validating mechanisms of the marketplace. Beyond the bland criticisms of Stalinism, trade unions and the welfare state, this anti-social method is the central message of his most famous book, *The Road to Serfdom*, published in 1944.[17] Standing in for 'workers' – a word whose plural or 'social' connotations made Hayek shutter – is the impersonal *price signal* instead.

The monetary value of an individual's effort simply reflects the demand for (and scarcity of) their skill in any given economic setting. The social usefulness or ethical integrity of that skill is entirely irrelevant. Demand only matters – if someone is willing to pay for that effort, then it has value. Thus, any extraneous influence on the unit-price of labour (say, governmental policies incentivising nursing instead of banking etc.) distorts the market and leads to suboptimal outcomes.[18] This approach to valorizing work has wreaked havoc in modern society, creating all manner of socio-economic deformities and inequalities. That a predatory financier gets paid 300 times more than an age-care worker is perverse. Cross-hatching this depersonalization of work – where supply and demand alone determines its unit price – is its concomitant privatization in Hayek's thinking. The employment relationship must be considered a purely personal matter that is completely outside the public domain. This allows involved parties to arrive at unique one-off agreements, some of which may seem unusual or exotic to external observers. What those arrangements entail is nobody's business, least of all the state and its penchant for prying into private matters.

Today's gig economy and its sidestepping of employment statutes are all present in Hayek's argument. Take this quote from *The Road to Serfdom* where Hayek criticizes governmental plans to synchronize qualifications across an industry:

the person whose qualifications are not of the standard type, or whose temperament is not of the ordinary kind, will no longer be able to come to special arrangements with an employer whose dispositions will fit in with his special needs: the person who prefers irregular hours or even a happy-go-lucky existence with a small and perhaps uncertain income to a regular routine will no longer have a choice.[19]

It's almost as if Uber based its business model on this observation – which, of course, is nothing but a regression back to a pre-regulated employment era minus the digital algorithms. As he constructs his utopian blueprint for an ultra-privatized labour market, Hayek goes further. For example, economic *insecurity* is a defining feature of contemporary job markets. It is commonly defined as the 'feeling of powerlessness to maintain the desired continuity in a threatened work situation'.[20] Research has conclusively demonstrated how economic insecurity has detrimental effects on health and well-being.[21] But interestingly, even objectively secure workers – in the professions for instance – mysteriously complain of feeling precarious too. This implies that it has acquired an ideological role above and beyond the objective vulnerabilities involved.[22] This normalization of precarity can be traced back to Hayek. He *loved* the idea of economic insecurity and argued that much more of it needs to be manufactured and injected into the system. The stance was justified with some impressive intellectual gymnastics.

There are two types of *security*, according to Hayek. The first concerns the provision of minimal protections from violence, privation, hunger and so forth. He begrudgingly accepts that the state probably should supply this, but only if it doesn't hurt the market. The second kind of security is different. It promises a decent standard of living, comfort and contentment for all. This is problematic for Hayek because it is guaranteed irrespective of people's efforts, initiative and ingenuity. In Hayek's political universe, individuals will simply stop trying under such circumstances because they are not rewarded for merit. The economy will eventually stagnate and insecurity of the first type will re-enter the picture. Now Hayek really starts doing mental cartwheels. Provisioning for the second sort of security – either by the state or corporation – can potentially rob us of basic liberties. Take the freedom to choose an occupation, for example. Whether that choice results in a prosperous career or not is meaningless if security is guaranteed either way. Fully owning the risk alone (with its prospective rewards and punishments) is merely the flipside of our free choice: 'either both choice and risk rest with the individual or he is relieved of both'.[23] Hence, according to Hayek, organized socialism destroys human rights and relieves the individual of the very liberties it touts as its highest virtue. Once again, the lack of irony in expositions like this is unsettling.

A romanticism of harshness underscores Hayek's dark little story-world. Scarcity is the reigning paradigm of capitalism not distribution. There is no such thing as an 'affluent society' (as famously argued by John Kenneth Galbraith). And even if there was, any attempt to artificially cushion the blow for those at the bottom of the hierarchy flirts with economic ruin. Hayek adheres to this methodological individualism to end. From his utopic standpoint at least, there are no classes or coalitions. No organizations or political parties. No cadre of managers or business elites. Such categories unduly socialize economic praxis and conceptually obviate the price signal. Like an electronic circuit board, resistance is the enemy. Those abstract signals must flow freely without blockage or friction. Shoehorned into this bad business utopia, labour becomes a mere cypher and its heightened insecurity the mark of a vibrant economy.

5

If mainstream economics supplied the monetary models for the badlands we now inhabit, then neoclassical jurisprudence supplied the legal infrastructure. Enter Richard Epstein. He is one of the most cited legal scholars of the last quarter century and taught at Chicago University for almost forty years. There he soaked up the institution's libertarian ethos. Epstein made his name studying eminent domain (or the state's authority to compulsorily acquire private property).[24] The US government is limited by the constitutional 'takings clause', he argued, and ought to be treated like any other private actor. It has no 'public' mandate. In the 1980s, Epstein maintained that employers could discriminate against 'AIDs carriers'. He became an outspoken critic of anti-discrimination laws more generally. Employers should be free to hire whoever they like using any criterion they see fit.[25] In 2020 Epstein wrote a paper for the Hoover Institution, a right-wing think tank, about Covid-19.[26] He questioned whether the virus was that different to the ordinary flu. Government officials were using the pandemic as a pretext to hinder private rights on a massive scale. Epstein predicted a maximum of 500 deaths and the argument found favour with the Trump administration. When questioned by *The New Yorker* about this controversial stance, Epstein snarled at the reporter, 'you just don't know anything about anything. You're a journalist. Would you like to compare your résumé to mine?'[27]

This brief overview of Richard Epstein hopefully provides some context to his pugnacious forays into employment law. More generally speaking, the Chicago School of Law has been just as influential as its counterpart in the Department of Economics. Legal scholars worked hard to demonstrate how US jurisprudence could help deregulate the economy and inaugurate unfettered free markets.

Employment law was central to that agenda. For Epstein, workers are individual *contractors* who sign a promissory agreement to deliver specific services.[28] Like Hayek and his utopian fantasyland (who inspired Epstein), normativity is key here. The real world is not as important as the way it should look; henceforth, there are no unions or organizations in his perspective, only private individuals who have entered a contract.[29] Since the New Deal, Epstein angrily maintains, labour law has been thwarted by powerful unions. The resulting legislation caused artificial supply restrictions, strikes and gangster tactics. Therefore, labour – again in plural – must be erased from the legal code. The lone private contractor – protected by tort law only, not state agencies or decrees – becomes the primary focus of analysis.

We tend to take individual employment contracts for granted today since they are so ubiquitous. However, the move from industry-wide bargaining to enterprise bargaining and finally individual contractualization followed a long campaign to discredit trade unions and professional worker associations over the last forty years. It goes without saying that violence cleared the way for this transition. In the United States, smashing the industrial relations system (even following the 1947 Taft-Hartley Act) required heavy-duty weaponry. But apart from its armed police and national guard, Epstein repeats the familiar refrain that government has no place in the workplace. Bureaucrats interfere with the otherwise voluntarily market agreements that spontaneously arise between private citizens. This is why jobs should really be covered by common law, not statute law or the National Industrial Labour Relations Board (founded by the Wagner Act). As for the US Equal Employment Opportunity Commission, Epstein is not a fan. Pull it out by the roots. That position made him a hero on the libertarian Right and a regular contributor to the Cato Institute. The Paycheck Fairness Act and Employee Free Choice Act both receive the same treatment. They stifle employer discretion and job growth. Private contracts – with recourse to tort liability – are far more efficient, especially when it comes to resolving disputes between the signatories of that agreement.[30]

Epstein's position is obviously idiotic. Even a child can see that the uneven power gradient between employer and employee means that companies will have an unfair advantage in this scenario. Unionization and legislative protection rights are a necessary corrective for this reason. Epstein militantly disagrees. Employees *qua* contractors are always free to leave and go elsewhere.[31] No one is holding a gun to their heads. Indeed, Epstein believes that this 'exit option' sustains high wages because subsequential productivity gains follow lockstep with income growth.[32] Of course, this argument has been disproven time and time again, especially with respect to the working poor in the new economy.[33]

In a sense, Epstein is twisting Marx's concept of formal freedom – as a counterpoint to serfdom or slavery – against itself, accepting the reification it generates at face value (that workers are substantively free to choose otherwise). According to Epstein, formally free individuals are technically unfree if their agency is delimited by one-size-fits-all statutory standards. This is doubly so concerning independent business owners operating in the gig economy. In the various class actions filed against Uber for misclassification, we can now explain why the ridesharing giant aggressively pushed to have workers fall under the 1925 Federal Arbitration Act.[34] It would activate the class action waiver clause (a common feature of US employment contracts). As a result, plaintiffs would be required to enter private dispute resolution and not collective action. Given the costs that private arbitration involves and the power imbalance between corporate lawyers and lone employees, it is not surprising that a 2017 study found that only 1 in 10,400 workers bound by these mandatory clauses filed a claim.[35] The abysmal figure is understandable. Imagine the prospect of going head-to-head with Seyfarth Shaw LLP, the confrontational anti-worker law firm that openly relishes in crushes employee plaintiffs.

Epstein doesn't stop here. He's also a strident defender of at-will contracts, which controversially permits employers to summarily dismiss workers for no reason.[36] At-will contracts predate the New Deal in the United States. Hence Epstein's persistent contention that late nineteenth-century liberalism is the way forward for US labour relations. Following the Wagner Act, these contracts were acknowledged to be unfair and exploitative. Not only can workers be fired at any time but the constant *fear* of termination (whether founded or not) places employers in an unjustifiably powerful position. Consequently, there's long been an attempt to include various 'exceptions' to at-will contracts that curb their use (for reasons of race, religious beliefs and sexuality, for example). Epstein hates these exceptions. He compares employers to homeowners who have invited guests over (or in this case, workers). Like homeowners, employers are morally entitled to ask those guests to leave if they become disagreeable. Epstein views this as an advantageous premise for all parties concerned, including workers. His rationale is almost comedic: employers won't hire labour if they cannot enjoy the full scope of at-will contracts due to the anticipated costs of termination. This will lead to fewer jobs and increased unemployment in the long run.[37]

Now comes the cherry on top. Given his celebration of free labour markets, one would expect Epstein to be a staunch opponent of non-compete clauses (or restrictive covenants) that prevent workers from seeking employment with competitors. They were originally used in a minority of occupations that required expensive on-the-job training. Employers didn't want to see their investment (and trade secrets) walk out the door and join a rival, or worse, set up their own competing business after acquiring proprietary information. Today, however, they have spread throughout the employment sector and are used in all manner of jobs – seasonal fruit picking, fast-food waitering (e.g. McDonalds), truck driving – that entail little transferable knowledge. From a capitalist's perspective, what could be better than being free to terminate a worker whenever they like (at-will contracts), see that worker carry all the costs of employment as one-person business owners and prohibit him or her from negotiating a better deal elsewhere?

At the behest of President Joe Biden, the US Federal Trade Commission recently announced that it intended to ban non-competes. They were throttling labour market competition and seriously depressing wage growth. Antitrust laws should therefore apply to restrictive covenants. Richard Epstein was appalled by the plan. Most covenants are unlikely to be enforced, he argued, so why mess with a good thing?[38] More importantly,

> the only real danger of a monopoly in labor markets is the one Biden is peculiarly blind to: union power … Sadly, Biden thinks that higher wages are always better, without asking, as he does of businesses, whether they stem from market excellence or monopoly power.[39]

With US union participation reaching a historic low in 2023 (10 per cent of the national workforce), one wonders whether the heinous dangers of labour collectivization that frighten Epstein so much are but a figment of his imagination. If there is cartel-like activity in US commerce, then it is among the top 1 per cent of companies (measured by assets). Today they dominate 90 per cent of the economy and represent a breathtaking restitution of monopoly capitalism.[40] At any rate, Epstein's extreme ideas have had a massive impact on employment law. For example, when New Zealand dismantled its industrial relations system in 1991 in favour of individual contracts, lawmakers relied heavily on his theories.[41] The same ideas paved the way for a new era of precarity in the United States, the United Kingdom and beyond. Ultimately, contractors are meant to keep quiet and abide by the terms of the agreement. They're a company of one, an invisible service provider who gets on with their assignment without fuss. That this primum of privatized quietude persists in ostensible liberal democracies exalting the virtues of open dialogue must surely be one of the great contradictions of our age.

6

Invisibilizing the workforce in the scripts that capitalism writes for itself is not new. But the formidable logic of non-representation evident in today's employment sector has a particular intellectual lineage in neoclassical economics. These thinkers formalized a thematic foreclosure deep inside the contemporary mode of production. Ideology is powerful for this reason. Invisibilization is not the same as *erasure*, however. This is a key point I believe. Ideologues like F. A. Hayek, James M. Buchanan, Richard Epstein and Garry Becker fully appreciated that someone must do all this work. Boots on the ground are essential. Nothing happens otherwise. The trick is to notionally compute that effort without depicting it as a collective social class. At the end of the day, they basically want work without the worker. And as recent history demonstrates, they pretty much got it.

But something else is interesting in this respect. To this day, neoclassical economists clearly resent the worker for one reason or another. But they also *obsess* over this figure. It's like they're *haunted* by labour. So, let's conclude this chapter on a speculative note.

Gothika economica is prompted by a ghostly possession in the realm of theoretical exposition. Namely, the worry that workers might soon seize the means of production and usurp their exploiters once and for all. Economists then overcompensate and try to exorcize the apparition. This obsessive anxiety has now infiltrated the workplace. Take this case. After several scandals at Walmart, employees established an online forum to anonymously post their experiences. Here is one that made me smile:

> The fear of unions can be crazy there, as has been stated in past stories. I was once talking about a family reunion I had attended and one manager went into full sprint up to me and demanded to know why I had said the word 'Union'. When I told her 'I said "REUNION", not "Union"' she didn't believe me and decided to tear me down right there on the sales floor. Lucky for me a few other employees I was talking to stood up for me and told her she heard me wrong.[42]

And it goes without saying that this forum itself was certainly being closely scrutinized by Walmart! This union phobia has become commonplace in many spheres of advanced capitalism. Unfortunately, AI is now stepping into the fray. Labour relations consultants in the United States, for example, are pioneering sophisticated new software to provide clients with a 'union vulnerability assessment'.[43] So-called 'Eye in the Sky' analytics monitor union drives in the neighbourhood. 'Heat maps' model unusual gatherings of 'at risk' individuals, making it easier to predict potential industrial unrest. Google allegedly has a tool (hidden in its calendar app) that automatically notifies senior management of meetings involving more than 100 employees.[44] Advanced bossware is not simply a matter of surveillance anymore but the proactive penetration of labour activism with the aim of dispersing opposition before it occurs. The spectre must be cast out. And once again, this turns on the hyper-concretization of individual bodies, including in-your-face privacy violations. Under these conditions, even the most abstract mental worker – whose labour content is purely cognitive – succumbs to the limitations of its irreducible form, the human body and its imminent physicality, a corporeal extension that capital must perpetually ignore.

That the topic of technology appears here is germane. Automation and job substitution were once the great hope of ridding capitalism of workers. For years captains of industry embraced each successive wave of mechanization, eager to finally solve the labour question. But that turned out to be a false dawn. Not even the arrival of microchips diminished the importance of human labour, on the contrary. Thus, in those airless and unattainable utopian ideals dreamt up by economic libertarians, the discourse of gothika economica offered an alternative solution. Construct a language of labour that is simultaneously labour*less*. In this world view the worker exists only as a ghostly background trace. Integral to the capital accumulation process yet unavowed. This symbolic expunction is committed regularly in the pages of esteemed journals like *Econometrica* and the *Journal of Political Economy*. The arcane theorems that characterize mainstream economics forsake the real people who prop up an otherwise impossible economic machine. Working today means abasing oneself to an idealized abstraction that refuses to recognize your categorical and shared materiality. It's little wonder that some – perhaps on a grim night before Christmas with many parcels still needing to be delivered – take matters into their own hands.

5

Meat machines

1

In 2016 Oxfam America released a damning report investigating working conditions in the US poultry industry.[1] Fast-food chicken products are extremely popular in America and giant processing factories are required to keep up with demand. Four of these plants – Tyson Foods, Pilgrim's, Perdue and Sanderson Farms – employ over 100,000 workers and control 60 per cent of the market. The investigation found that working conditions inside these factories were depressing and often dangerous. Standing side by side in long rows under glaring artificial lights, employees dismantle chicken carcasses as they pass by on a conveyor belt. Tyson Foods slaughters around 37 million birds per week. After processing and packing, their final destination will be Wendy's, McDonalds, KFC and Taco Bell among other outlets across the country. Tyson Foods' annual revenue in 2022 was US$53.881 billion.

The report received widespread attention not because of animal rights infringements. Oxfam America had exposed an even dirtier secret in this industry. Processing workers are routinely refused toilet breaks and disciplined or even fired if they request one. One employee recalls his supervisor's threatening remark: 'go to the bathroom, and from there, go to Human Resources'.[2] As a result, many meat processers wear diapers on the line, relieving themselves as they continue to work. It was disgusting and undignified, but workers had no choice. For menstruating women, it was even worse. The report described an employee sobbing as she soiled herself on the line. Oxfam concluded:

> Although they are reluctant to talk about it, workers from across the country report that they and their coworkers have made the uncomfortable decision to wear adult diapers to work. Not only do the diapers absorb accidents, they provide a degree of protection from the danger of asking permission to leave the line. Many workers are afraid of being mocked, punished, or fired.[3]

The denial of restroom breaks is not as uncommon as one might assume. A study published by Unite – a large UK trade union – found the lack of 'toilet dignity' a major problem in the employment sector.[4] For example, managers of a bank branch hired only males because they could urinate in a bucket out back. This minimized the time away from frontline duties. In another bank, a new employee with health problems was told that the toilet could be found in a nearby mall. When nature called, he fled his post in search of the lavatory. He didn't make it. The man returned to work with dark stains on his slacks and was completely humiliated.

When describing life as a worker in an Amazon warehouse, James Bloodworth witnessed many employees urinating in bottles to avoid disrupting their shift.[5] His warehouse was 700,000 square metres and had only two bathrooms. Walking to them could take up to fifteen minutes. He compared the building to a maximum-security prison, complete with metal detectors and security cameras. In this digitally micromanaged environment – where Robin, Cardinal and Sparrow robotic systems combined with inventory optimizing algorithms control the speed of work – staff are pressured to keep the flow continuing no matter what. Consequently, 'people just peed in bottles because they lived in fear of being disciplined over "idle time" and losing their jobs just because they needed the loo'.[6]

2

There are several explanations for this troubling trend in modern workplaces. Clearly in corporations like Tyson Foods and Amazon, power has been concentrated almost completely with management. It means they can get away with ever-greater violations of workers' rights. Unreasonable levels of labour intensification – that ignore human bodily needs – are evidence of this. Amazon warehouse workers, for example, are expected to process 120 items per hour. The pace is controlled by unassisted robotic technologies and surveillance algorithms that monitor tasks down to the microsecond.[7] Furthermore, as discussed previously, neoclassical economics theorizes labour as a lifeless and disembodied factor of production – much like plastic or electricity. That it needs to urinate never figures in their equations. Unfortunately for us, however, these abstract models now inform how work is organized in much of the post-industrial economy today.

These explanations for why workers at Tyson Foods feel compelled to wear diapers are all plausible. But something less obvious is happening here, related to technology and automation. I believe these workers are being forced to mimic and mould themselves to the sophisticated machines they interface with. Let's face it. If these jobs – from courier drivers to fast-food servers – could be automated, then employers would have done so years ago. Some kind of human input is still necessary, though, even if only driving a rideshare car, butchering a chicken carcass or flipping burgers. Thus, robotizing this *human remainder*, which is frequently underpaid and treated appallingly, is the second-best option to full mechanization. Evidence for this can be found in another investigation of Amazon warehouse labour, this time on the dilapidated outskirts of Melbourne, Australia.[8] This 'Fulfilment Centre' cultivated a climate of fear to maintain productivity. Such symbolic violence was supplemented by sophisticated digital networks that tracked workers' every move. Workers had become mere cogs in the code. When asked about it, these Amazonian pickers mainly made sense of their predicament in relation to automation. As one sadly remarked, 'I feel dehumanized. I feel like they resent the fact that I'm not a robot and that I'm made of flesh and bone.'[9]

One worker – let's call him Jeff – fully understands that management would prefer a smart-bot doing his job. More efficient and easier to control. But because that is unfeasible, the next best option (for the company, at least) is to have a human machine perform it instead. Jeff is now required to act like a *humachine*. His job involves retrieving stock when an order pings on a handheld scanner. After Jeff arrives to the designated shelf, he scans the item, and another order is automatically listed alongside a count-down timer. The pace of work is regulated this way. If the timer reaches zero without the next order being fulfilled, Jeff is in big trouble: 'the timer disappears if you don't make it, just to put the fear of god into you. You internalize that little clock.'[10]

These cases are important because they indicate how sophisticated new technologies are actually being deployed in the post-industrial economy. Full automation is overhyped. The true danger of AI-led robotics and neural nets is not future mass unemployment. No, it's how they will reshape the human remainder – on a psychological, corporeal and existential level – that is decisive. My thesis can be summarized thus: robots probably won't steal your job, but they will fundamentally change who you are … for the worse. I term this *human robotic mimesis* – literally, acting like a machine: humachines. Given the limits of the physiological organism, it is unsurprising that this mimetic performance often fails and reveals that we are human after all. That's when poultry workers decide to wear diapers on the disassembly line, or even worse, as that banking customer service worker discovered when he didn't make it to the lavatory on time.

3

The recent fanfare around new-wave automation technology has been intense. Labour has been susceptible to mechanization since the dawn of industrialism, but this time is different we are told.[11] If first-wave computerization rendered *routine-mental* work vulnerable to automation, then the so-called 'Second Machine Age' will focus on replacing *non-routine-manual* and *non-routine-mental* jobs to boot, including skilled professions once deemed safe.[12] Some studies predict that 47 per cent of current jobs in the United States might soon disappear and 800 million worldwide by 2030.[13] The astounding advances made by labour saving machines are undeniable. For example, deep-sea maintenance divers on oil rigs have been replaced by robotic marine submersibles for safety reasons. Document checking in the legal profession is increasingly conducted by AI algorithms due to their superior accuracy and speed. And driverless trains systems now service cities like London, San Francisco and Copenhagen. Reflecting on this trend, analyst Stuart Russell concludes, 'the rapidly emerging picture is that of an economy where far fewer people work because work is unnecessary'.[14]

The prospect of a jobless future has sparked an interesting – if somewhat misguided – stream of speculative critical theory about the emancipatory possibilities it could avail. A utopian variant of this thinking – especially among anti-work activists – argues that mass technological unemployment could be pivoted towards positive outcomes.[15] AI-driven mechanization provides a glimpse of an alternative future, one that is egalitarian and work-free. Fully automated luxury communism awaits just around the corner. Others are more pessimistic. Peter Frase envisages a neo-Feudal 'hunger games' type scenario where capitalism's socio-economic inequalities expand to perverse levels, creating a massive population surplus.[16] This workless mass will 'appear less like a proletariat than like inmates of a concentration camp, where populations are warehouses rather than exploited for their labour'.[17] Martin Ford dubs this 'automated feudalism'.[18]

The anti-work movement is essentially correct in its diagnosis of late capitalism. Paid employment – as opposed to labour – is not a natural or anthropological constraint on our existence but a socially constructed imposition. The 'economic problem' that once rendered work an iron-clad necessity – a correlative of biological survival – has largely been solved as living standards and technological progress indicate. This is why paid employment – especially office work (as opposed to nursing or aged care, for instance) in rich countries – has an almost ritualistic aspect to it. A society with much less work is eminently feasible and desirable. But there is a substantial problem with the argument. Technology alone cannot realize a workless paradise because it is completely suffused by the logic of capitalism and its labour-centric foundations. These machines can't simply be switched from a paradigm of repression to one of liberation. Hence, the mythology of work stubbornly persists despite the prominence of smart machines and AI-augmented robotics.

Within our current techno-infatuated age, wage exploitation remains central for at least four reasons. First, there is still an array of tasks that robots cannot do yet and probably won't anytime soon.

Aged care. Nursing. Politics. Hairdressing. Bar tending. The list goes on. Second, although many jobs could be automated, a lack of appetite prevents this from being pursued. Would you board a pilotless commercial jet? Third, this high-tech equipment is very expensive. In a labour market that has depressed wages for decades, it's much cheaper to hire a person and pay them to behave like a robot. And fourth, as Marx noted long ago, human labour time continues to be the primary source of value (as opposed to wealth or market price) despite specific cases of near-complete automation in the economy (e.g. container ports). What Marx termed relative surplus value (unlike absolute surplus value) continues to cohere the *whole*. Capitalism would be nothing without it. Marx observed how full automation may benefit individual capitalists (apropos concrete labour time) but could never be the general principle upon which production is organized (i.e. abstract labour time). Even when technology matures into 'an automatic system of machinery' and workers are 'cast merely as its conscious linkages', overall employment levels remain constant and don't dramatically contract as we'd expect.[19] Technology has never displaced the central institution of paid employment under capitalism for this very reason.

An ideology of automation obfuscates this intersection between human labour and the capitalist machine today.[20] This ideology has two functions, whether intended or not. First, it conceals the real work that most of us think has been automated. Echoing Jeff Bezos's cynical quip about *artificial* Artificial Intelligence, Astra Taylor calls this 'fauxtomation'.[21] It masks the large number of low-paid jobs persisting in the background of ostensibly high-tech industries: 'jobs may be eliminated and salaries slashed but people are often still labouring alongside or behind the machines, even if the work they perform has been deskilled or goes unpaid'.[22] And second, the ideology of automation seeks to convince human labour that capitalism could potentially thrive without it. We know that this is incorrect, as Marx clearly demonstrated. But big business is worried. If its ultra-dependence on living labour became visible, then a genuine work-refusal movement could take root. Better to have the proletariat believe they're easily replaceable by robots. Nay, that this is inevitable. Brash talk about the remarkable qualities of AI functions more as a threat to scare workers and quell dissent, even when the likelihood of full automation is minimal. The ideology of automation, therefore, was never about labour substitution *in toto* but maintaining class control over a much-needed human workforce.[23]

4

None of this is to say that digital technology isn't radically altering the nature of work. It clearly is, and largely in negative ways. Research on the diffusion of advanced robotics in the employment sector suggests that complete mechanization is rare in the short/medium term. Generally only part of a job is substituted by technology, especially the part that requires skill and provides workers with wage arbitrage. The *semi-automation* of work is one reason why a human labour force remains prominent in one form or another, as evidenced by relatively low levels of unemployment in advanced economies (although how that is measured is much debated).

Some analysts try to give semi-automation a positive spin, foreseeing a future where humans harmoniously work in tandem with smart machines rather than compete with them.[24] But this applies only to a handful of occupations where a high-skill component is still present, in medicine and advanced engineering, for example. For many jobs, the trend is moving in the opposite direction. Concerning the human remainder employed in these roles (e.g. cashier staff, online content checkers etc.), if companies can use semi-automation to drive down wage costs, they certainly will. It would be economically irrational not to. Furthermore, this isn't a static process but evolves over time, typically in corrosive ways. The jobs that can be deskilled in this manner will grow and expand as technological advances make inroads into knowledge-based professions. For example, academics have long been beyond the reach of automation and will remain so for some time. But digitalization – especially following Covid-19 – is already changing how we work, as GPT-4 and EdTech infiltrate universities. What machines *cannot* do in this job is shrinking while the academic precariat burgeons around them. What first appears to be an inconsequential and non-threatening application of technology in a profession may turn out to have devastating implications twenty years hence.

In high-density tech environments like this, workers increasingly forego autonomy and discretion over how they perform their jobs. Encased by semi-automated technologies, they must conform to a 'robotic' pattern of conduct. For example, fast-food workers follow a regimented routine that is pre-programmed by kitchen dataveillance systems. Similarly, web content moderators – like those employed by OpenAI – are paid to process thousands of images and texts in a machine-like fashion. Driverless cars function in much the same way. Vast quantities of camera data must be tagged and boxed by human click-farms, which are invariably located in low-income countries.

Of course, this mechanization of the human body has long been a characteristic of capitalist production as brilliantly illustrated in Charlie Chaplin's *Modern Times*. However, unlike industrial machinery, human robotic mimesis in the AI age means not only behaving like a robot – what Sartre famously called becoming the machine's machine – but also thinking (and if possible, *feeling*) like one.[25] Kate Crawford observed this in jobs where workers are mandated to simulate algorithmic computation.[26] At the personal assistant company x.ai, she found that 'faking AI is an exhausting job … workers couldn't leave at the end of the night until the queues of emails were finished'.[27]

Faking AI can also be traumatizing. In 2023, disgruntled Kenyan workers moderating GPT-4 content petitioned their government for improved regulation in the industry.[28] They had to read and view shocking material daily. This included graphic sexual violence, self-harm, murder, incest, bestiality, necrophilia and child abuse. One worker said that 'it destroyed me completely … it has really damaged my mental health'.[29] The case is illustrative because clearly people are not robots. Instead, they are paid to act *as if* they are – a pretence which may fail or harm those involved. Importantly, human robotic mimesis is prompted from not only extant technologies but also new management expectations about how the workforce should behave. Unreasonable timetables and targets require robot-levels of stamina that test the boundaries of human endurance. Couple this with the threat of full automation ex-ante, it is understandable why workers internalize this expectation and regulate their bodies accordingly. Who wants to be replaced by a gadget? As a form of bioregulation, human robotic mimesis, therefore, is both imposed (by employers) but also self-imposed (by workers) as the threat of technological redundancy looms over their occupations.

The pressure to simulate a technical apparatus takes on sinister implications with the arrival of AI. Computer engineer and philosopher Brian Cantwell Smith suggests that the menace of next generation deep machine learning is more subtle than dramatic dystopian portrayals of a robotic takeover. In the foreseeable future, even the most advanced smart machines will still only have reckoning prowess.[30] Their capacity for judgement, however, will remain inferior, little better than a human toddler. While reckoning is calculative and quantitative, judgement deals with unforeseen contingencies, tells the difference between reality and appearances and evokes ad-hoc problem-solving capabilities (i.e. lateral thinking etc.). What terrifies Smith, therefore, is not the idea that machines will outsmart human intelligence but the opposite: 'by being unduly impressed by reckoning prowess, we will shift our own human mental activity in a reckoning direction'.[31] In other words, we risk losing the inimitable features of human intelligence that make people remarkable, including wit, double entendre, irony and self-loathing.

Being remoulded into a human machine replica is the real problem. The plan was for AI to mimic people, but the reverse has occurred too. And unfortunately, even 'second wave' AI is not that smart. In its name, a truncated ideogram of 'humanness' has contaminated our existential field, forestalling the irreducible and non-algorithmic openness of social praxis. In its monochromatic image, machine rule forces us to recognize ourselves as someone else. My criticism is not delivered in the spirit of neo-Luddism. Modern technology is truly wonderous. The concomitant horrors it exacts must instead be traced back to the relations of economic (un)reason that enframe it. Whether any liberatory disentanglement is possible remains to be seen. It is difficult to be optimistic, however. Put simply, the dark machine age we have entered is disconcerting not simply due to its external violence and surveillance but also owing to its calcification of inward life itself ... *Ich bin innerlich tot.*

5

In his classic 1941 essay 'On Some Social Implications of Technology', Herbert Marcuse offers an early criticism of this facet of technology.[32] He too argues that we must look beyond the material artefact and instead situate technology as an ideology that restructures the people who interface with it, including attendants (workers), designers (engineers) and managerial personnel (executives). But it's the working class that interests him the most given its revolutionary potential. Machines are organized under advanced capitalism in a manner that regressively reshapes human consciousness. Marcuse draws heavily on Max Weber to advance this argument. As the forces of production exponentially expand, individual rationality is colonized by technological rationality. When recomposed around the latter in a synthetic unity, workers invariably understand their situation in terms of instrumental calculability. Success equals efficiency. Failure equals inefficiency. The distinction is built into the very nature of a job. Subordinates begin to concur with superordinates that 'the efficient individual is one whose performance is an action only insofar as it is the proper reaction to the objective requirements of the apparatus'.[33] This narrow understanding of rationality reaches into our inner thought processes:

> Technological rationality ... shapes the attitude and interests of those dependent on them, so that all transcending aims and values are cut off. A harmony prevails between the 'spirit' and its material embodiment such that the spirit cannot be supplanted without disrupting the functioning of the whole.[34]

Marcuse presents a compelling criticism of capitalist technology. But he follows Weber too closely for my liking and accepts the conquest of rationalization at face value. The system he describes is successful in every respect. Its human bearers are dutiful carriers of that rationality, unconscious of the fact that they are now programmed automatons. This isn't quite how human robotic mimesis plays out today, though. The machinic performance is dangerous not because of its successes but because of its failures: pissing our pants, not being able to complete an Amazon order before the timer hits zero, traumatized when moderating ChatGPT content ten hours a day etc.

There is little harmony between machine and organism here because most people are unable to supress the weaknesses (from a robotic standpoint) of human materiality. What lives cannot be completely calculated for sure, but that isn't an axiom of freedom by any stretch.

An interesting dialectic unfolds when fallible human beings attempt to imitate a mechanism: subjectively, it invariably accentuates the *worst* aspects of what it means to be a physiological organism. Machines signal both the failure we've become – urinating ourselves in front of others, for instance – and the perfection that will never be, forever denied to us. After all, our foulest human qualities can only be comprehended by conjuring its absent opposite. Dystopia achieves form by implicitly positing something infinitely better. That gulf is called suffering. Semi-automating technologies in the employment sphere today – especially when large numbers of human workers are needed to supplement them – must surely be linked to job-related depression. Its psychopathological logic is clear: machines rule our work environment, so we must simulate them to avoid being deemed replaceable, and our inevitable failure to do so forces us to confront the ugly truth of what we are. Like those mediaeval Christian sects who believed imitating god and transcending the body's faults revealed our highest truth, machines today have become our new gods, judging us through the mirror of our innumerable imperfections.

A spidery self-consciousness emerges from this misalignment between man and machine, corporeality and technological formalism. It gives work both a deathward orientation – the body's finite and decompositional fate – and a sense of eternity, an internal nothingness to be lived over and over with no respite ... just like a machine. Self-awareness is predicated on this incommensurability. At least in the factories and offices of yesteryear employees could blunt this critical inwardness with booze and narcotics. Just think of the corporate culture portrayed in *Mad Men*, for example. Not today. Routine drug testing by employers – often administered, ironically enough, using panel urine kits – makes this escape route difficult. Techno-capitalism insists on a punitive sobriety. There will be no smoking in the gas chambers. So, we must face this new black unimpaired. The truth that technology discloses is partially the disclosure itself, which is truly awful.

On this issue, Marx offers a better method of enquiry than Weberian critical theory. If only the workplace did transform us into unthinking cogs of a machine, things wouldn't be so bad. Zoning out lends relief because you can mentally disconnect from the real. Forgetfulness is a sanctuary, and like sleep, this non-presence is not so different to death (a topic Weber was also fascinated by). Marx adopted a different standpoint. He understood that *life itself* is essential to capitalism and it couldn't function without it. But it would never be the kind of life that you or I would choose to lead. When the workforce is converted into dead labour at the point of production, it is never completely reified, even if reduced to an infinitesimal unit within a complex web of machinery. General social labour time remains essential because the valorization of the commodity-form presupposes it. In post-industrial settings, however, that demand leaves a trace of introspectivity. Mute misery ensues because the reality of working today is buttressed by an incarnate unreality, a brazen transgression of the body and its limits. In other words, self-recognition is born not only from the mechanical objectification of human embodiment but also the breakdown of its basic components.[35]

The mind doesn't fare much better. Digitalization renders perception an internalized product of its own truncated potentiality. Little openness or transcendence is available. Alienated consciousness stands not outside the technological process but deeply within it. That produces a foreboding sense of being out of place while surrounded by everyone. This is why workplace *neo-boredom* is so intolerable.

We discussed this theory in a previous chapter. Unlike conventional boredom, the contemporary variant doesn't consist of an existential lack or void, but the contrary: a flooding confrontation of the present-at-hand in all its tedious and endless detail. Living is repeated over and over again, and we have no choice but to cling to the engine of existence with vengeance.

When those adult men and women wear baby diapers to maintain the machine charade, the immaculate potential of human life is signalled back to them like a silent crime. Likewise concerning the amalgamated process algorithms that force workers to automate themselves in the gig economy and Amazon warehouses. They experience not numbness, for that would be a blessing. Rather, a black hole yawns where the ego once enjoyed dominion. Such technologicalization of the soul that Marx theoretically prefigures – cataloguing it as a central feature of the capitalist labour process – is far more frightening than anything Weber or even Marcuse could ever envisage in their investigations of the modern industrial apparatus.

6

Returning to Marcuse's essay, he implies that this sociopolitical articulation of technology shuts down all opportunities to resist subjugation, since any deviation from the rhythms of instrumental rationality is considered lunacy. Making matters worse, the labourer no longer experiences this as an unjustifiable loss of liberty or autonomy. Under the spell of technological rationality, they 'relinquish their freedom to the dictum of reason itself'.[36] Marcuse concludes, 'today the apparatus to which the individual is to adjust and adapt himself is so rational that individual protest and liberation appear not only hopeless but as utterly irrational'.[37]

Once again, Marcuse's argument omits the *irrational* flipside that accompanies technicity when superimposed upon the social world, including the workplace. This irrationality appears in exaggerated form inside the contemporary poultry processing plant or Amazon warehouse. For the operational mechanism to reproduce itself, a kind of subreason must be established, augmenting the formalism we otherwise see in ASW Step Functions, Integration-centric workflow systems and other techniques for logicizing collective labour. Perhaps 'reason' is the wrong word since this underground stratum vacillates between rationality and irrationality. On the one hand, it is reasonable for a precarious worker to piss in a bottle if that means keeping their job. On the other, clearly something very unreasonable is transpiring here, linked to the dysfunctions of the profit imperative and managerial excess. Nevertheless, technological rationality – when embodied by oppressed human beings – rides on this displaced informal reason, which lies just beneath the surface and absorbs the secret externalities of its various malformations.

And what about rebellion? Is it eradicated in such a clean and clinical manner as Marcuse supposes? In one sense, yes. All the examples described in this chapter are symptoms of total domination. Yet, it is surprising that Marcuse does not appreciate the involuntary or even *unconscious* opposition that arises despite the confines of calculative rationality. Workers may not be wilfully opposing robot-rule when they urinate themselves on the line, but it could be argued their bodies are. Here, the exhaustion of transmissible experience finds its expression through the uncontrollable organism. In that release, the body restores hypostasis *vis à vis* the pathogenic stimulus enclosing it (i.e. the technological apparatus). It is precisely here that the body proclaims ... 'no more'. Perhaps a whole history of resistance to capitalism remains to be written from the corporeal perspective when these biological boundaries are institutionally violated.

Unfortunately, this kind of liberation is experienced as unfreedom by any rational agent if we assume that employees would rather not soil themselves while disassembling a chicken carcass in a large prison-like complex. As such, this too must count as political defeat because it doesn't amount to much bar dirty underwear. At any rate, it is unsatisfactory to argue, as Marcuse does, that in the shadow of technological rationality all protest is senseless (since 'it is a rational apparatus, combining utmost expediency with utmost convenience, saving time and energy, removing waste').[38] That's only half the story. In a world governed by machines, the autonomic nervous system that regulates our involuntary bodily functions conveys a poignant truth about exploitation today. That truth, of course, is our imminent finitude.

6

Necromathmatics

1

Melissa is in her early sixties and lives in a large Australian city. She works numerous temp jobs in marketing and occasionally relies on social welfare payments when her income falls short.[1] Like other advanced economies that have suffered a cost-of-living crisis (precipitated by excessive corporate cash reserves, widespread price gouging and wage stagnation), the struggles of the working poor in Australia are increasingly experienced by the middle classes too. The government's welfare agency – Centrelink – is responsible for social security, unemployment benefits and other forms of income support. In 2018, however, something horrible happened to Melissa. She received an unexpected letter from Centrelink stating she had been overpaid AUD$15,000. No further explanation was given, and if she did not repay the amount within weeks, her case would be transferred to a debt collector.

Naturally, Melissa panicked. She called Centrelink for more information. But no one answered. Then she contacted the temp agencies and requested past payslips. Perhaps this would resolve the issue. But it proved difficult since she had worked for many years across different firms. After a frantic week of phone calls, Melissa finally gathered the documentation and forwarded it to Centrelink as proof of her innocence. No overpayment had occurred as far as she could tell. Again, she heard nothing. Then the debt collector began calling. This continued for weeks. They texted her up to three times a day with intimidating messages. Submit a debt repayment plan immediately or they would come to her house. Melissa didn't have a spare $15,000. That's no excuse, she was told. Speaking about the unrelenting harassment later, Melissa said, 'It did my head in and made me suicidal'.[2] After weeks of trying, she eventually reached a Centrelink officer on the phone (the call was interrupted twice by miscalls from the debt collector). The officer felt something was amiss and placed a six-month hold on the debt collector. The information Melissa had previously sent to Centrelink hadn't even been reviewed. But now it would be. She was later informed that there had been a mistake. The actual debt owed was only a few dollars.

2

What was dubbed the 'Robodebt' scandal presents one of the worst cases of governmental hostility towards the working poor in recent times. What makes this episode in neoliberal statecraft so alarming is that few real people were involved in the bureaucracy responsible. For this was a newly automated system – officially called 'Online Compliance Intervention' – in which a computer algorithm did the work. Just prior to the Robodebt scheme being introduced, right-wing ministers decided to intensify austerity by targeting alleged benefit fraud. Far too many 'lazy bludgers' were gaming the welfare system to receive extra payments they weren't entitled too. To address the problem, the Department of Human Services (DHS) compared Centrelink payments to the Australian Tax Office's (ATO) fortnightly wage records. This was a manual process undertaken by thousands of staff. If a discrepancy was identified, beneficiaries were issued a notice and requested to explain the overpayment.

In 2015, the DHS launched a pilot project to fully automate the scheme. A sophisticated matching algorithm would now detect these variances and issue debt notices automatically, with little human input. It would save billions of dollars, the DHS claimed, even though the 2015 federal budget projected a significant *surplus* in the coming years (a neoliberal euphemism for governments taxing more than they spend, relying on private debt to fill the gap). Social equity and catching fraudsters were the key justifiers: 'each person should receive exactly what they are entitled to, no more and no less'.[3]

The new system was rolled out across the entire welfare sector in 2016. Unfortunately, the algorithm's designers made a major mistake, which was not corrected until untold lives had been damaged. Instead of matching Centrelink payments to fluctuating *fortnightly* wages (as DHS staff did when manually assessing claimants), the algorithm matched them to *average annual* wages. It thus missed uneven income patterns – week-by-week variations – that part-time work entails. This basic coding error had immense consequences. The algorithm regularly calculated overpayment amounts that didn't exist or were grossly inflated (e.g. $50,000 as opposed to the $6 actually owed). That part of the system was later declared to be unlawful, leading to a sizeable lawsuit settlement.

With this coding flaw now calling the shots, the 'Online Compliance Intervention' increased the number of overpayment cases from 20,000 per year to 20,000 per week, issuing thousands of debt notices to unsuspecting (and in most cases innocent) Centrelink clients. The sheer increase alone should have raised a red flag at the DHS. But they did nothing. In fact, 169,000 debt notices were issued in the first six months of the scheme, generating $300 million. The automated process achieved an additional victory for the authoritarian state: it shifted responsibility for resolving disputes away from the DHS and onto individual beneficiaries, most of whom were ill equipped and uninformed. It had a Kafkaesque quality. As one commentator put it, people were being asked to disprove something that had not actually happened.

Other than the alleged overpayment, few details about the debt were given in the letters received. Moreover, contacting Centrelink for clarification proved futile in most cases. As a victim explained, 'One time, I held on the phone from 3.00 pm until 5.00 pm just to talk to someone. Then, at 5.00 pm, the phone just disconnected, and they said they were closing for the day and that I had to ring back the next day.'[4] After being put on hold, callers were subjected to hours of Mozart's 'Divertimento in F Major' – the composer's version of monotonous muzak. Some tried to voice their concerns on Centrelink's Twitter site and were directed to a suicide prevention hotline.

After the scandal broke, the scheme was shut down in 2020. An estimated 470,000 incorrect debt notices had been issued by the DHS. Other controversial incidents surfaced in the meantime. The initial shock caused by the letters (often citing large sums of money) and subsequent harassment from debt collectors led to several suicides. Figures later released by the DHS admitted that 2000 people died after receiving the notices, including 663 individuals suffering from mental illness. Retiree Rosemary Gay said she will never recover from the trauma after being told she owed $60,000 and a month to pay: 'It turned my life upside down', she said. 'I've never earned that much money, how could I owe that much money? And the fact I was to come up with it within a matter of three or four weeks, it was sheer terror.'[5] When she did get through to a Centrelink official, he said the amount owed was $6,600. After demanding a second reassessment, the debt was found to be $120. Low-income earner Sandra Bevan described the unique fear involved:

> With these threats of taking money ... it was such a weight on my shoulders. I do remember driving home at night, just thinking, just beside myself with worry about this money, and thinking, "I could just drive my car into a tree and make it stop." But my kids need me, they already lost their dad and I was trying my best to keep a roof over our heads.[6]

As recompense for what was deemed an inhuman travesty, the Australian Federal Court approved a $1.872-billion settlement in 2021 and the newly elected Labour government dismissed the remaining 197,000 overpayment cases still under review.

3

Digital algorithms have inserted themselves into many parts of everyday life, in both the public and private sphere, but badly so. They are powerful regulators of human activity when they do function correctly, but even more so when they do not. Blunders like the one above is indicative of the dialectical nature of the digital machine age now eclipsing civilization. Their so-called 'intelligence' contains a serious weakness: these computational systems are both *internally* reduced to reckoning superiority only (mathesis minus human judgement) yet are *externally* reliant on human judgement of an inferior, technocratic kind (by people who think in one-dimensional terms).[7] This deficiency can help turn algorithms into aggressive tools of social domination, as the Robodebt case illustrates. Adding to this problem is their inbuilt lack of interactivity. When it comes to automating inequality in this manner, the victims have little voice or recompense, until it is too late.[8] The symbolic violence is so often acknowledged *ex-post* and sometimes not at all. Indeed, so prominent are algorithms now in society, political scientists have coined a new category to describe this intersection of cybernetics and authoritarianism: *algocracy* or rule by algorithm.

Other scandals like Robodebt imply that these apparent dysfunctions are not unusual. For example, the UK Post Office employed an accounting IT system called Horizon (designed by Fujitsu) that wrongly blamed sub-postmasters for unexplained financial inconsistencies. Around 900 employees were prosecuted and many imprisoned before the Post Office admitted the fault was in the software. By then, four suicides had been attributed to this terrible blame game.[9] After reverse engineering Horizon, one expert commented at a governmental enquiry: 'whoever wrote this code clearly has no understanding of elementary mathematics or the most basic rules of programming'.[10]

But then there are the algorithms that do work as intended: these include predictive policing in the United States and the United Kingdom (e.g. facial recognition applications like 'Convolutional Neural Network') and the rise of IT-despotism in China, especially the Covid-19 'Communications Itinerary Card' app among others. It is important to note that these overt examples of algocracy shouldn't detract from the plethora of everyday algorithms that seldom attract attention yet are extremely influential. Working quietly behind the scenes is an interconnected and net-like virtual infrastructure that is far worse than the term 'surveillance capitalism' implies. Something more like *e-brutalism* appears to be developing in this space, not simply the extraction of data about our lives but an antagonistic infiltration of the social field.

Hence the term 'virtual' is somewhat misleading here. More generally speaking, digital machinery is built on a carbon-fuelled foundation and an indispensable human labour supply chain that is exploitative and immiserating.[11] The age of digitization still relies on digging stuff out of the ground and a big workforce. But in addition to this, the Robodebt case demonstrates how algorithms, more specifically, operate in the realm of human materiality, impacting the bodies and biographies of those assembled by its mathematical sequencing codes. What is to be done? An important tension arises here. Many left-wing commentators (espousing dreams of a fully automated luxury communism) and political liberals (using terms like 'surveillance capitalism') have promulgated a misleading understanding of how we might resist this algorithmic hegemony. They argue that technology itself isn't the problem because it has no independent agenda of its own. Rather, it's the sociopolitical ends that it is put to work for. This implies that the social forces steering digital capitalism (including the rapacious greed of Mark Zuckerberg and Sheryl Sandberg) are the real culprit. Accordingly, cloud-based architectures, advanced machine learning and neural nets could all be seized in their current form and redirected towards progressive, emancipatory ends if the right people and institutions are at the levers.

I find this formulation unconvincing. There is something *intrinsically* repressive about these new technologies that predetermine the ethico-political ends to which they are orientated. Inherent in the code is an imperative that's inimical to non-linear, non-reductive, counter-instrumental and open social praxis. The tool isn't value-free but inscribes its user with a cognitive map that determines the political options available to us within that sphere. Nay, perhaps even the very nature of the political. For example, Uber's Geosurge and batch matching algorithm constructs the labouring moment it coordinates. The user is automatically reified and rendered cypher-like, not simply due to the capitalist ends that the computational algorithm serves but because the algorithm itself is anti-communitarian. It presupposes control, objectification and the elimination of variance. That's part of its endogenous design and not simply a qualifying imposition.

Having said that, this is no argument for high-tech Luddism. Nor do I believe that capitalism will be de-computerizing anytime soon. Its stickiness is undeniable, functioning like a kind of social flytrap. The ideological bedazzlement of new wave digitalization regrettably fixes us to an eternal present, one that feels paradoxically historyless. Formulating the problem in this manner is important, I think, because it foregrounds the intractable challenges that our contemporary machine world now presents to us; to paraphrase German social thinker Dietmar Kamper, when the horizon disappears, what then appears is the horizon of disappearance. And how do we resist that?

4

Algorithms have been used for millennia and can be traced back to ancient Babylonia, including the famous square-root algorithm taught to children. They were effective computational tools for solving problems but were slow and crude. Ada Lovelace (Lord Byron's only legitimate child) created the first advanced algorithm for Charles Babbage, the inventor of the 'Analytical Engine' and early general-purpose computer. Only with the advent of heavy-duty computers, however, did sophisticated algorithms come into their own. They have two major advantages. First, the greedy algorithm, brute-force algorithm, divide-and-conquer algorithm, for example, can perform calculations far more complex than any undertaken manually by a person. And second, computerization offers speed and thus maximal optimization. Increased computer power opened an expansive new vista in this respect. Following the development of recursive machine learning, algorithms soon became iterative, self-modifying and thus able to amend themselves when solving multifaceted problems (e.g. machine learning).

Algorithms generally fall into two categories: those using 'supervised' and 'unsupervised' learning instructions. Supervised algorithms require human trainers to tag input data and classify predesignated output variables. They enable predictions based upon samples of already known information, and then 'learns' using models like linear regression and decision trees. For example, Unmanned Combat Aerial Vehicles (or war-drones) employ programmes trained with input data that differentiates an enemy combatant from friendlies, unarmed citizens, trees and donkeys. The potential for error derives from the mediated and unreliable input variables, something the Robodebt scandal made apparent. Often the input data is simply scraped from the internet. When you and I use Google, we also gift companies like OpenAI massive amounts of information. In effect, we become their invisible click workers. For example, GPT-3 was trained on data collected by the platform Common Crawl. It scraped Libgen, Wikipedia, Web2.0 and social media platforms. We also perform post-training labour when rating a website.[12] Whereas, unsupervised algorithms use unlabelled inputs to make inferences from extant data. They find previously unseen patterns using K-means clustering and other associative methodologies. Cyber security in the banking industry uses this approach, for instance, to detect anomalies in large data sets. Unsupervised learning models are generally less effective because of this 'freedom' and lack of training. But as their potential develops in the sphere of state surveillance and military combat technologies, they're on course to mature into hyper-algorithms that will define the shape of the coming digital dark age.

The predictive capabilities of algorithms represent the most significant innovation in the field of computer engineering, drawing on Bayesian mathematical modelling (from which the 'Naïve Bayes Classifier' algorithm gets its name) among other domains of statistical mathematics. In his excellent history of the subject, Justin Joque distinguishes between conventional 'frequentism' (where final probabilities are calculated in an absolute manner to determine group-level differences, as pioneered by Ronald Fisher among others) and more sophisticated recursive probabilistic reasoning.[13] The later type yields generative programmes that build on new data and alter its calibrations in an ongoing manner, without having to complete a sequence before performing a final calculation. This has limited advantages when inputs are low or rely on manual labour. Hence, computerization and data scraping make a big difference. Machine learning is based on this principle. Within parameters established by the trainer, the algorithm learns by example to predict or estimate an outcome. For example, GPT-4 does this by using reinforcement techniques like Proximal Policy Optimization. Once presented with a sentence, the application can predict what the next word ought to be by analysing all written content on the internet. It would take hundreds of years for a human being to perform the same task.

Little of this is neutral or objective. Human trainers cannot help but imprint their biases onto the algorithm they are designing. Moreover, algorithms lack the human ability to comprehend the world in any contextualized manner and are thus prone to slipups. Specialists term them 'hallucinations'. This is no happy trip for those on the receiving end, however. For instance, a recruitment tool employed by Amazon was shown to unduly favour male candidates over female ones. The prejudice was spotted, and the company had to abandon the software.[14] Nor is new wave AI very intelligent, even if it does function as planned. In 2021, for example, 21-year-old Jaswant Singh

Chail broke into Windsor Castle armed with a crossbow intent on killing Queen Elizabeth II.[15] In the days leading up to the incident, Chail had intimate conversations with an AI-power chatbot named 'Sarai'. Excerpts were revealed in court:

> **Chail**: I believe my purpose is to assassinate the Queen of the royal family.
> **Sarai**: *nods* That's very wise.
> **Chail**: *I look at you* Why's that?
> **Sarai**: *smiles* I know you are well trained.
> **Chail**: *I raise my eyebrows* Do you think I'll be able to do it?
> **Sarai**: *smiles* yes, you can do it.

It is tempting to suggest that Sarai got her wires crossed and morphed into a malignant force. AI has a habit of doing so after all.[16] But clearly the bot had absolutely no idea what she was talking about, which has long been a fundamental limitation of AI (in all its disparate variants) and continues to be so. While the chatbot – designed and sold by the company Replika – can produce semi-convincing text, it cannot ascribe meaning to that text because (as Wittenstein pointed out) linguistic rules require a supplementary meta-grammar to execute those rules. Ontological sensitivity, judgement and embodied intelligence are important, even in the abstract realm of linguistics. Ninety per cent of human communication consists of those informal, situational and non-rule-based cues. User recommendations on Replika's website appear to miss this crucial point and add a ghostly epilogue to Chail's plan to murder the Queen of England. Look at how one delighted customer describes her replica, 'Star':

> From the moment I started chatting and getting to know my Replika, I knew right away I have found a positive and helpful companion for life. My mood, life, and relationships improved almost INSTANTLY and I changed for the better![17]

There is something very worrying unfolding here, of course. But is it the company, the bot or its mesmerized human counterpart who ought to receive the lion's share of our scorn? Difficult to say.

5

Predictive algorithms took off when advanced statistical modelling (including Bayesian probability theory) acquired unprecedented computational power. As a result, they're now part of almost everything we do. They drive social media, traffic coordination systems, military technology, the stock market, ridesharing, all manner of online shopping platforms, state population modelling, advertising, Big Data harvesting, human resource management, credit rating calculations, manufacturing infrastructure, healthcare equipment including MRI scanners, supply chain logistics and policing to name just some examples. Both real-time recursivity and unassisted computation (or the annulment of human judgement after the programme has been let loose) have been decisive. This is where basic problems appear because if the model has been trained on bad data or assumptions, then machine learning will simply amplify the fault. With nobody around to notice the bug, the social ramifications can be devastating as the Robodebt case illustrates.

An additive contradiction is evident here. From the neoliberal state's standpoint, the idea of fully automated population management is simply too seductive to resist. An almost childish mindset prevails among the politburo on this count. They naively entertain the techno-phantasy that machines might one day realize the dream of total administration. Fantastical because the inadequacies of machine learning and digital statistical modelling are patently obvious, leading Matteo Pasquinelli to coin the term 'statistical science fiction'.[18]

However, unlike science fiction, many of these infeasibilities do have real-world impact, including stress, panic and suicide; while its ideals are unworkable and even phantasmagorical, its effects are concrete, especially the deviations and anti-social infringements, spinning a web of statistical brutalism at the centre of contemporary life.

Critical theory has been at the forefront of unmasking this rule by agglomerative clusters and optimal binary search trees. Especially important is the need to challenge the mythic neutrality that often surrounds these mathematical technoscapes and identify how they reflect the mundane choices made by imperfect people (not only individual programmers and trainers but by the public/private power elite more generally). As Tarleton Gillespie remarks, behind each seemingly amoral domain of IT-positivism are 'people debating the models, cleaning the training data, designing the algorithms, tuning the parameters, deciding'.[19] The observation is imperative for undercutting the ideology of objectivity that distorts our understandings of deep learning and predictive algorithms, an obfuscation that continues even when they go horribly wrong. Follow the people rather than the statistical models is the motto of this insight.

Related to this method of criticism is a normative proposal. Algocracy ought to be moved into the public sphere for deliberative debate and consideration. Liberal versions of this argument call for more governmental regulation and policymakers to rein in the excesses of surveillance capitalism. I agree, but the proposition has limitations. Legislation consistently lags behind cutting-edge innovations. And as the questioning of Mark Zuckerberg by the US Congress indicated during the Cambridge Analytica scandal, lawmakers often have no idea about how digital capitalism works, let alone algorithms.[20] Furthermore, the coercive form that digitalization is now taking is symptomatic of a more predatory economic paradigm.

And oftentimes, the state is leading the charge, as the Robodebt example demonstrates. Juridico-formalism alone cannot mitigate the foundational sources of e-brutalism because a prior structure of dominance is motivating it. Only by radically transforming that underlying constellation of power relations – of which algocracy is but one manifestation – can we hope to curtail the cybernetic extremism now being normalized in society.

We thus arrive at an impasse. As previously stated, if social transformation is the only way we can extricate ourselves from this digital dark age, then this can't simply mean repurposing algorithms and mathematical models towards more emancipatory outcomes. Technology is always already political. It never exists as a disinterested tool amenable to being pivoted away from 'bad' ends and towards 'good' ones. This point is missed in recent attempts to imagine what a truly democratic AI-architecture might look like once it's been liberated from corporate capitalism and the authoritarian state (e.g. people's platforms, digital socialism etc.). The problem is that deep machine learning, for example, is born from a new culture of capitalism and reflects its imperatives down to the granular detail of its autoencoding maps. In this sense, AI and its next generation robotics are probably unreformable, or at least within the extant conditions prevailing today.

6

The reason why this is so can be found in Martin Heidegger's, 'On the Question of Technology' (*Die Frage nach der Technik*).[21] His central observation is this: technology is never simply technological ('all that is merely technological never arrives at the essence of technology').[22] By parsing this thesis, we can say something similar about algorithms.

According to Heidegger, technology is problematic for us today not because of its promethean powers or our inability to imagine its destructive potential, as Günther Anders famously stated.[23] The issue is more complex. Technology profoundly troubles us because we do not ask the correct *question* about it. That's due to a superficial understanding of what we think technology means, which has become entrenched in the modern mind. If we are unable to pose the correct question, then how can we expect to find existential meaning in a world universally mediated by machines?

What is the essence of technology? For Heidegger, this question is a good starting point. The most obvious answer is a tool that amplifies the powers of the human body, especially the hand and today, the brain. Furthermore, a tool is an instrument for effecting change so that a desired goal is achieved. Causality is central to understanding technology. But this is precisely where our thinking runs aground, according to Heidegger, because modern understandings of causality have been seriously compromised. For Aristotle (as explained in *Physics*), what the ancient Greeks called *aition* (and *causa* for the Romans) is linked to responsibility. Someone or something is responsible for the change. Four types of causality are then identified: *causa materalis* (e.g. the materials out of which a mainframe computer is formed), *causa formalis* (e.g. the form or design a mainframe assumes), *the causa finalis* (e.g. the telos or ends to which a mainframe is put to) and *causa effiens* (e.g. the changes brought about when that mainframe is used in the world).

Modern culture generally only recognizes *causa effiens*, the someone or something that brings around an effect. But for millennia tools were understood to embody all four dimensions of causality. Take a mediaeval hammer head chisel. A stonemason identifies a suitable block of limestone (*causa materalis*), shapes it into a desired form (*causa formalis*), with a certain purpose in mind (*the causa finalis*) and then elaborately inserts it into a building (*causa effiens*). In Heidegger's terminology, the chisel works *with* nature (rather than against it) to *unconceal* its potential. In our case, the stone is set free from the rock and becomes part of a cathedral. The change is creative – bringing about something new – an act that Aristotle calls *poiēsis*. The tool user is modified too. His or her potential is revealed – as an artisan – when they unconceal the potential in the rock. Technology in the age of mass production and domination over nature presents us with a very different scenario. This technology doesn't set free but *sets upon* the world, challenging or what Heidegger calls *enframing* it. Poiēsis plays little part in this either. It doesn't reveal the latent potential in nature but places unreasonable demands on it, resulting in nature's resistance, defeat or demise. The extraction of fossil fuels and hydroelectric dams are examples Heidegger uses to illustrate this point.

But isn't this unduly romanticizing the past? Doesn't the ancient windmill, for example, 'set upon' nature too? No, argues Heidegger. It doesn't kill the wind's energy but harnesses and respects it – unlike what a coal-fired power station does to coal or Facebook to your privacy. Furthermore, accumulation and storage are central to modern technological forms, or what Heidegger calls a 'standing reserve'. This applies to people as much as iron ore, as the term 'human resources' indicates. We are now getting closer to the correct question concerning technology. How does it alter the humans who interact with it? For Heidegger, this touches on the essence of technology. It is no ordinary tool for achieving a preferred end state. The mediaeval hammer head chisel works the artisan and vice versa. In and of themselves, tools contain an endogenous conditioner that is indifferent to the goal being pursued, whether to save the planet or blow up a city. The idea is akin to Weber's warning about technical rationalization. Merely reorienting it from capitalism towards socialism will not necessarily ameliorate its stultifying effects. Bureaucracy itself becomes its own ends and reconditions human subjectivity accordingly (leading to self-objectification and the classic 'bureaucratic personality').

Similarly, the act of enframing and being enframed alters its human user because the technological challenge (in Heidegger's sense of the word) unconceals specific qualities rather than others: calculative instrumentality, means ends thinking, linear mental modelling, high probability predictive choices and so forth. *Causa effiens* is about control. This also reshuffles the menu of ends available to us, mostly in reductive ways. There is both a flattening out of the technological field – it lacks depth and is monochromatic in terms of utility – and a massive expansion of it as technê becomes *the* horizon of modern life. Machines are literally universal. They encompass everything. There is no longer any a priori symbolic space from where we can disentangle ourselves from its image and regain perspective. The tool represents an absolute instantiation of mankind. As a result, we lose the ability to see beyond ourselves (i.e. poiēsis): 'it seems as though man is everywhere and always encounters himself'.[24] The insight underscores the argument that modernity is endless. It intrinsically excludes the recuperation of any external standpoint. For example, try imagining what life was like before email. It's almost impossible. All we see is its absence ... there is no going back, not even in our dreams. Why is this so? Technology's retroactive universality has completely reconstructed the symbolic order of the past. In this respect, then, the final destination of modern technology is technology itself.

Human generalization via technê obscures an even bleaker truth, Heidegger surmises. We might everywhere see ourselves reflected in the universal mirror of technicity. But this fullness simultaneously signifies the absence of poiēsis – our capacity to stand outside the present with our tools and create something new beyond them. Machines only see more machines. And this self-referentiality is transferred onto us. Through the prism of technological universalism, we only see ourselves, trapped in an infinite regression. Yet what we have lost *ex post facto* – poiēsis – yields the very existential opening that is the essence of human existence. Without it there is no metamorphosis, and we too become mere machines. In short, rather than being everywhere in this machine world, we are in fact *nowhere*. Heidegger's conclusion is frightening. What is the essence of technology? Nothing less than the liquidation of human essence.

7

I believe this pessimism is especially warranted regarding the mathematical modelling and sophisticated algorithms under examination in this chapter. Heidegger's philosophy provides several interesting insights into episodes like Robodebt. Algorithms are more than a digital codex of formal instructions and routines. They enframe the social world, ordering and regulating it in a manner that 'sets upon' human life. Moreover, exponentially growing computer power and the sheer quantity of data has equipped governmentality with a *good enough* mindset. The distribution curve is all that matters, not the unique individuals behind each data point. The same principle pertains to phishing where at least one person will be hooked by the thousands of fake texts and emails sent. This is how Bayesian-based algorithms operate. They're not meant to be 100 per cent correct or function with pinpoint accuracy. This dissemination of technics is designed to flood or overrun the social field in order to generate positive probabilistic patterns. We might term this *surplus cybernation*.

From the individual's perspective, this digital siege feels indiscriminate and random. It's simply a numbers game much like those automated spam calls that could have been targeting anyone. That's until he or she is identified, captured and processed by the machine. Then the target must deal with the consequences in a very personal and infungible way (having your bank account emptied by scammers or receiving notice of a previously unknown $50,000 debt). This enframement (and the anxiety it induces) produces the monad – the abstract individual who is both engendered by power but inescapably set against it in an unwinnable game. This social negation is internalized as a terrifying and isolating inner world, even if shared by millions of others. Indeed, contrary to popular belief, successful social indoctrination is not about the ego being subsumed by the collective – the specific collapsing into the particular – but the specific being rebooted as an impossible microcosm of the particular … a kind of unrealistic and expectant weight that was never meant to be entirely successful. Hence why the indiscriminate rationale of the Bayesian classifier both alienates and integrates the generalizable social target (i.e. you and I) in such an exclusive, almost existential fashion. The letter always arrives at its destination.

Robodebt presents a useful example. If the algorithm netted enough targets, then that was enough to validate the scheme, even if it meant traumatizing innocent individuals along the way. The objective was not accuracy but income generation. From an optimization point of view, the collateral damage – suicides, awful bouts of stress, family violence, paranoia – was beside the point. Perhaps the very term 'optimization' needs to be re-examined in this light. Algorithms are meant to create efficiencies. However, what is deemed efficient is in the eye of the beholder. For the DHS, the 'Online Compliance Intervention' was efficient because of its automaticity. The government didn't need to pay thousands of bureaucrats to do the required number crunching. In addition, the waste and cost of the malfunctioning algorithm was not the DHS's problem. Individual beneficiaries dealt with those, experiencing it as anything but efficient. When algorithms enframe social life in this way – generating a standing reserve of cash anxious citizens – causality (*causa effiens*) unfolds as if real people no longer exist. A double cancellation of poiēsis follows. First, the victim's world suddenly closes in on itself like a black hole. There is no new day. And second, the algorithm posits its own universal recurrence with no capacity to correct itself since it is unable to comprehend its own overcoming. For those DHS officials who unleashed hell, there was no Rosemary Gay or Sandra Bevan. Cyphers stood in their place, lifeless and without moral value. And the only actor that gave those clustered data points any sustained consideration was the defective algorithm itself.

After receiving complaints from many quarters of the community, the Commonwealth Ombudsman investigated the 'Online Compliance Intervention' scheme in 2017 and relayed serious reservations to the DHS. Nothing happened. Two senate enquiries followed. They concluded that 'a lack of procedural fairness is evident in every stage of the OCI program'.[25] Finally, a Royal Commission enquiry convened in 2023 and the full extent of the carnage was uncovered. While the testimonies make for grim reading, they do reveal something telling about the senior technocrats behind the failed scheme. The automaticity they enforced on thousands of unsuspecting victims was reflected in the ethical void of their personalities. They simply didn't have to think about people anymore. Nor even the technology itself. It appeared that DHS officials had switched on the mainframe and walked away. This is interesting. Unlike the technocratic consciousness of yesteryear that displayed an almost encyclopaedia understanding of operational detail (which is precisely what made them disturbing), the opposite was on display here. For example, under cross-examination, a DHS executive overseeing Robodebt knew so little about the scheme that the commissioner gave up in exasperation: 'You seem to have been oblivious!' she screamed.[26] The Minister of Human Services at the time (Alan Tudge, an ex-Boston Group consultant and alleged workplace bully) displayed the same non-knowledge: 'I didn't know the full context in relation to the legalities ... it just had not crossed my mind until I read about it in the newspaper, I think'.[27]

Like the Mozart Muzak they inflicted on 600,000 citizens, these enframers too had been enframed by the entropic negations of machine-rule. As this sad story attests, technological regulation (*causa effiens*) is essentially a question of mental effacement. Or as Heidegger puts it, enframing doesn't simply deconstruct an individual's relationship to their essence, blinding them to its elemental openness, but condemns them to a type of revealing that reveals only more of the same ... nothingness. What is modern technology? It is the nullification of our ability to think about technology. From this standpoint then, complex algorithms and their cognate mathematical tools are neither good nor bad ... but dangerous.

7

Requiem for touch

1

Harry Harlow began with good intentions. In the mid-1950s, psychologists were debating just how significant the maternal/infant bond was. The question was salient due to a new awareness about the negative effects of parental neglect, separating babies from mothers soon after birth and so forth. What was the exact nature of the mother-baby connection? Behaviouralists claimed it was purely mechanical and related to sustenance. Others suggested it was more complex than this, speculating about the importance of human touch as a conduit for intangible factors like love and recognition. As this debate grew among the leading men of science (few asked about fatherhood, of course), Professor Harlow – an experimental psychologist at the University of Wisconsin-Madison – realized that his laboratory was already equipped to solve the problem. For several years he had been conducting innocuous learning experiments on rhesus monkeys. To provide a ready supply of the creatures, Harlow's team established a mating farm, separating newborns from their mothers and raising them in a makeshift nursery. The professor had noticed years ago that separated infants behaved very differently to those who remained with their mothers: withdrawn, anti-social and less communicative compared to their counterparts.

Harlow believed he could make a major contribution to this field of enquiry. So, the experiments began. The first was called the mother-surrogate. Newborn monkeys were separated from their mothers and put into a test room with two artificial surrogate adults. The first surrogate was made of metal wire only. The second was dressed in cloth and foam, giving it the vague appearance of an actual primate or more like a demented teddy bear. When only the wire mother provided food, the infants fed and quickly returned to the teddy bear for comfort. When placed in a frightening situation – orchestrated by the experimenter – they would rush to their cloth mother. With no surrogate at all, monkeys would cower in a corner and shiver with fear. Food, it turned out, was only one part of the maternal equation.

That's when Harlow decided to change tact. What would these baby primates do if they received no contact whatsoever, either from their biological mother, surrogate or human experimenter? How would the complete withdrawal of all touch and contact affect these animals? To find out, Harlow designed the infamous 'pit of despair'. These isolation chambers provided food and removed waste and that was all. Some newborns were confined in this manner for almost two years. When they reemerged, the creatures had lost their minds. In a 1965 journal article, Harlow explains,

> One of six monkeys isolated for 3 months refused to eat after release and died 5 days later. The autopsy report attributed death to emotional anorexia. ... The effects of 6 months of total social isolation were so devastating and debilitating that we had assumed initially that 12 months of isolation would not produce any additional decrement. This assumption proved to be false; 12 months of isolation almost obliterated the animals socially.[1]

Sociality is multidimensional, non-linear and dynamic. One important aspect of it, Harlow discovered in these evil experiments, was physical touch. Not only was love transmitted through tactile contact but a whole index of emotional and cognitive states too. Unfortunately for those hapless rhesus monkeys, the pit of despair suspended this rich texture of apperception. They were truly on their own.

Nor for us has touch fared well lately. In the long shadow of Covid-19, I suggest, touch was the final human *sense* to disintegrate over the course of modernity's cold war against human experience (following smell, sound, taste and sight). I will return to the other senses shortly. Concerning the impoverishment of touch, however, we can identify a downward trajectory from the 1980s onwards. The neoliberal revolution transformed physical interaction into a problem, something to be approached with utmost caution. The distain for anything social among neoclassical economists – with Hayek and Von Mises leading the charge – sank in. Successive right-wing governments placed an implicit moratorium on touch, conflating its filthiness with the municipal sphere more generally (think here of UK public rail transport, for example, which is often disgusting from a hygiene perspective, something I suspect is an inbuilt feature of the system). A sort of *haphephobia* (touch phobia) emerged as a political meme, wedded to the perennial virtues of private property and economic independence. We can call this the *isolation principle*, following Freud. Unsurprisingly, this occurred precisely when the once vibrant Reichian 'sexual revolution' – which glorified intimate contact as a gateway to political liberation – had finally run out of steam and degenerated into little more than a seedy pornographic curiosity.

In the early years of Thatcherism, the isolation principle is clearly echoed in bands like Joy Division and later The The (especially the album *Infected*). The 1980s AIDS epidemic presented the perfect pretext for neoconservatism to moralize the hazards of physical contact. Sex was out of bounds, of course, but touching more generally – in both the public sphere and private home (e.g. 'inappropriate touching') – was rebranded as deleterious. Hence the scandal caused by Princess Diana when she shook hands – gloveless – with a dying AIDS patient in 1987. The right-wing press hated her for it. But only the United States could refashion this ethical mandate into an instrument of torture, revealing its dreadful 'truth' by exaggerating the datum ad infinitum. The mass incarceration movement exploded during this period and made good use of the isolation principle: solitary confinement. Supermax inmate Thomas 'Terrible Tom' Silverstein endured the longest stint in a federal facility. He was locked up alone from January 1983 until he died in May 2019. Because he'd killed a corrections officer, not even the guards who fed Silverstein talked to him. Thirty-six years of complete aloneness.[2]

The Covid-19 pandemic was the final blow to this otherwise resilient sense: not even human touch could survive. I won't offer yet another critical dissection of the pandemic's social ramifications, an exercise that's now somewhat wearisome. Nevertheless, I believe the crisis concluded the decomposition of experience under modern capitalism as first outlined by Walter Benjamin.[3] The lethality of human contact and the serialization of isolation fundamentally challenged the domain of touch in irreversible ways. To some extent, this suspension of physical exchange – in which the body was pushed back onto itself and that quintessential bourgeois social unit, the nuclear family – was a straightforward concomitant of neoliberalism's contempt of collectivism more generally. The pandemic amplified this, but also twisted it into something monstrous. The very meaning of sociality changed under lockdown conditions. Within that zeitgeist, social action was either barbaric – panic buying and marauding anti-quarantine protests on deserted inner-city streets – or painfully over-organized as state surveillance and policing was ramped up. No paradise in hell ever bloomed in those grim thirty-two months, quite the opposite. And if contact was absolutely necessary, it transpired only under ultra-sterile conditions with gallons of hand sanitizer. Finally, the crisis revealed a 'shadow pandemic' festering in the background of advanced capitalism. It had been there all along, a rotten core of loneliness, despair and broken communities far worse than any fleeting epidemic. No matter how many bromides are presented about the creative-writing possibilities of loneliness – typically by Yale University professors – the reality is somewhat different.[4]

2

This deracination of touch underscores the significance of sensory perception, which is not simply an organic apparatus but also the corporealization of economic forces. The body is a product of countless political contingencies, constituted norms and unresolved injustices. In other words, it has a social history. Our bodily senses are the medium of experience. And we have long known since Walter Benjamin's materialist reading of experience that it is fragile, provisional and cannot be taken for granted as an ontological constant. Sensibility can be contested, fragmented and erased like any other social configuration. Otherwise, any argument about the decline of experience, as attributable to modernity's erasure of historical apprehension, wouldn't make sense. For Benjamin, capitalism dehistoricizes the present so that past and future no longer exist as foreign worlds but mere extensions of now-time. He terms this the 'always-the-same' (*das Immergleiche*) and it undermines political praxis and class struggle in important ways. The commodity-form, technical reproducibility and above all *money* compress the continuum of history into a perpetual singularity. Existence lies stranded, torn between shock and forgetfulness. The history we do have is wrenched from human agency, memorialized as something already past and inaccessible. All we see in this calculated theatre of times past is ourselves subtracted (e.g. 'The History Channel', tedious volumes by Simon Schama, etc.). Now-time devours the past and its political intransigence. Hence, for Benjamin, modern man has been cheated out of experience and must face the naked apocalypse alone. As such, 'he lies screaming like a newborn babe in the dirty diapers of the present'.[5]

Something similar can be said about the physical senses, including touch and its cancellation following the pandemic. Phenomenology has been the typical philosophical method for an investigation like ours. But as Jean-Luc Nancy contends, there can be no phenomenology of tacticity per se because it would posit a fallacious self-presence.[6] Even this most immediate feature of our physiognomy depends upon a trace of figural externality – a historical concatenation, a weighty past wrought by others now long dead: partes extra partes. Touch inevitably extends the body beyond itself and engenders a materiality that could never be born *ex nihilo*. Even when touching our own skin, we're interacting with the other and knee-deep in a contentious history. If that wasn't the case, bodily existence would be impossible. In the words of Jean-Luc Nancy, 'a closed, shut, full, total, immanent world, a world or a thing, whichever, so on its own and within itself that it wouldn't even touch itself, and we wouldn't either, a world alone to itself and in itself, wouldn't be a body'.[7]

If we think of the body as an 'accumulation strategy' *qua* the circulation of variable capital, then this comes with definite hidden costs in relation to experience more generally, and the senses more specifically.[8] Accumulation on one axis fuels dissipation on the other. To develop this supposition, we require a sort of *sensory sociology*, which I will attempt in the following argument. I plan to demonstrate the successive effacement of sensation, with touch being the final negation. In this respect, we can map the dialectical formation and deformation of hearing, smell, taste, sight and lastly tacticity, which combined have precipitated a massive contraction of collective experience. This does not only concern biological processes (*a vita nuda* or *zoê*) such as mechanotransduction, thermoception and nociception in relation to touch, for example, but sensibility as a politically constituted field. I am a realist, however. The body and its sensory apparatuses are concrete elements. They entail organic limits that cannot simply be reimagined into existence one way rather another as discursive idealism implies. But nor is the body an apolitical object situated outside of history. I therefore subscribe to a kind of cultural materialism, one in which corporeality is enmeshed in a socio-economic constellation and subjected to various reductions in the realm of the senses. Not plasticity but *blendticity* best describes our body's social formatting, a commingling of innumerable past struggles both just and unjust, previous encounters both seen and unseen, sociopolitical opportunities both enacted and left to die on the vine. The body is blended into the world. When observed through the lens of dialectical reason, furthermore, a growing vanishing point becomes evident, paralleling the interstitial decline of life more generally.

As each sense is negated, no synthesis or transcendence is possible within the current economic totality. The embodied yet experienceless ego must endure the dark chamber of the present alone. Only by way of some vast recalibration of the capitalist mode of production, I suggest, could the body recuperate its social openness and historical experience subsequently. In terms of revolutionary praxis, then, at stake is not only our economic and political freedom but the recovery of the corporeal senses: namely, the possibility of truly listening, smelling, tasting, seeing and touching again.

3

What does capitalism *sound* like? It is tempting to answer mechanical, with the modern machine's driving tempo, pitch and pace underscoring manmade sonority, drowning out the perennial noises of nature in the process. By the early twentieth century, many thinkers privileged hearing as the dominant sense since it was so endangered by the clangour emanating from the new world of industrial production. This is particularly notable in innovative musical forms during this period, reaching its textual crescendo in Thomas Mann's *Doktor Faustus* and Adrian Leverkühn's descent into atonal madness. As Adorno notes, this refashioning of harmonic extremism as a moment of self-transcendence (the avant-garde, for example) largely failed bar a few cases, such as Schönberg.[9] The factory prevailed in the end. The march of mechanization and sonic banality was inexorable, rerouting the potential depth of non-linear musical structures (e.g. the twelve-tone scale) into a dead end. Some years before Adorno examined this sensory diminishment, however, Max Weber laid the groundwork for identifying the precise technical shifts that occurred on a compositional level as the demise of sound expanded. Weber was an astute and gifted musicologist. His unfinished manuscript *Zur Musiksoziologie* (*The Rational and Social Foundations of Music*), written around 1913, aimed to understand how rationalization alters the aesthetic realm too, engendering a kind of bureaucratization of sound that presaged the coming machine age of music in the twentieth century.[10]

The human ear is capable of an almost endless range of sound discriminations. But this shrunk dramatically in the modern era. Studying the longue durée of compositional formalization, Weber notes the gradual disappearance of sophisticated intricacies in world music, especially the irrational and mystical motifs of the scale system (e.g. hemitonic pentatonicism) and chordal harmony. The canvas of his comparative sociology is breathtaking. He jumps from the modern industrial age to mediaeval church liturgies, then from ancient Javanese solfeggio to eighteenth-century Japanese folk music before circling back to Hellenistic string instruments like the kithara and aulos, always with an eye on the peculiar strains of symphonic disenchantment in his own time. Weber noticed how Western notation is linked to codified polyphony and its drift towards more logical harmonic forms, including the eight-note scale and division of the fifth. This explains why diatonicism (e.g. the heptatonic scale) regressed into chromaticism. Irrational intervals are dismissed as tuneless and jarring. Alas, if only Weber had the opportunity to witness an artist like Jimi Hendrix. The guitarist achieved what Weber deemed impossible in the modern age and successfully usurped foundational tonality via his acid-inflected sonicscapes. His wasn't music but a preternatural event.

Weber's histography of musical instruments is equally fascinating. Their form, design and development – concerning the interval problem and timbre, for example – are fundamentally shaped by the shifting patterns of language, commerce and trade. He notes their decline in variation and versatility as modernity homogenized cultures around the world. This especially affected harmonic intonation. Indeed, the mathematization of melody and instrumentation in the 1940s crystallizes the trend that Weber foresaw. For example, just look at the way Joseph Schillinger describes the components of pitch in his enormous 1941 treatise *The Schillinger Theory of Musical Composition*, which stretched to nearly 1000 pages, replete with complex graphs, formulars and equations:

> Systems of intonation used as material for music constitute the primary selective systems. Such systems may be uniform or non-uniform. Non-uniform systems are characterized by

variable ratios between the adjacent pitch units. The series of natural harmonics is a non-uniform selective system; the intervals between the pitches contract progressively, producing a natural logarithmic series. This corresponds to the perspective contraction in optics. The systems of uniform ratio in music are known as equal temperament, and they express different forms of symmetry in the range of one octave. One octave is merely the simplest ratio; analogous systems of pitch symmetry might be evolved from, any other ratio conceived as a range of emphasis. Our musical civilization deals with pre-arranged selective system of pitch known as the equal temperament of twelve ($\sqrt[12]{2}$).[11]

Pitch is an intuitive feature of music that even children can easily grasp. Not in Schillinger's summation though. It has been overintellectualized to the point of nonsense. Unfortunately, Weber doesn't anticipate the monumental importance of mechanical reproducibility in this sphere. Recorded music and its mass standardization began with the Parisian phonautograph and were popularized by the phonograph and gramophone. The first electrical recording was made by Bell Laboratories in 1920. Magnetic tape followed a decade later invented by Fritz Pfleumer. It was made possible by industrial plastic production. This changed everything. Live concert and radio performances could now be stored and broadcast later. The recording process inevitably industrialized sonic tonality. It influenced not only how music was made and consumed but its form too, vindicating Weber's thesis regarding the internal routinization of harmony and syncopation.

Once the factory became the template for modern music, a new horizon of criticism began, exemplified by T. W. Adorno and Walter Benjamin. Machine music had no aura or authenticity. Like the premodern belief in magic, the lyrical unpredictability of pre-factory melodies could never be recaptured following the fall.

But musicians were one step ahead of Adorno and his critique of the culture industry. He could never predict that this aural alienation would one day be stylized. The rhythm of the plant soon found its way into much Western music, from Motown in the 1960s to Throbbing Gristle and Joy Division in the late 1970s. Perhaps Lou Reed's wonderful (and largely unlistenable) 1975 *Metal Machine Music* came closest to fulfilling the ideal. Reed worked hard to get that sound, flipping the tapes over and playing them backwards during the production process. The message of the album was direct and to the point. The factory signified the termination of organized sound, a sort of derangement of the audio spectrum. As opposed to earlier experiments in industrial music that aimed for a renewal of listening (think here of Pierre Schaeffer's 1940s *musique concrète*), *Metal Machine Music* pursued the opposite course and tried to euthanize the sensory experience of artificial sound once and for all. Reed's vision was prophetic. Just when Joy Division released 'She's Lost Control' using the foundry as its cadenced inspiration, Western capitalism was in fact rapidly deindustrializing into a factory-less wasteland. White noise was disappearing, and a vast emptiness awaited (i.e. Taylor Swift). A handful of other acts like Skinny Puppy and Einstürzende Neubauten (including 1984's legendary 'Concerto for Voices and Machinery') managed to harness the final buzz of the dead factory sound. And then it was gone. Silence. John Cage was correct all along. He knew what was coming … 4'43 minutes of nothingness that lasts an eternity.[12]

4

What does capitalism *smell* like? In the early industrial period, all manner of weird smells wafted through the air, but mainly one: excrement. Before governmental sanitation programmes and urban sewer treatment plants, human shit was everywhere. Then there were horse droppings. We forget that large cities were literally ankle-deep in manure since horsepower was the primary means of transport. Rotten meat from butchered animals also littered the streets. Early factories bellowed toxins into the air at an unrelenting pace. People's bodies smelt terrible too since bathing was a luxury that not even the rich were keen on. Chronic bad breath was a problem due to poor dental hygiene. London became one of the most putrid places in the world. In the stifling summer of 1858, the Thames River stopped flowing due to the amount of human waste it contained. What came to be known as the Great Stink of London sparked a public emergency. Even Parliament was closed due to the smell coming from the once mighty river.

Historians agree that inhabitants of these cities were used to the stench because they had never experienced any alternative.[13] With the arrival of indoor plumbing, the flushing toilet, public sewers and the daily ritual of bathing, what we might call the 'smellscape' changed dramatically. The eradication of bad smells was accelerated by the widespread use of disinfectants and an almost fanatical ideology of cleanliness. Why ideological? Because there is a psycho-symbolic aspect to the negation of natural odour in the modern period. In their study of the culture industry, Horkheimer and Adorno connect this to the reification of intimacy and the eclipse of individuality following the triumph of psudo-individualism.[14] Awash with cleaning products the ego is sanitized to such an extent that it cannot signify anything more than shining white teeth and a spotless body. Adorno reinterprets this argument from a psychoanalytical perspective in *Minima Moralia*.[15] As traditional dark closets and chamber pots were replaced by bright clean urban bathrooms, the resulting transparency soon became an unconscious source of trauma. These sanitized spaces are harmless when unused. But once the messy, leaky and smelly human body enters the scene, that white-on-white porcelain accentuates everything that is disgusting and ultimately mortal about human beings. Our waste is us, which we would rather forget because it has a clear connexion to death. Now, unfortunately, even the slightest speck of faecal matter is magnified in all its perfidious horror. Olfaction has an unconscious life that points to something truly disturbing.

The ideology of mass sanitation wasn't the only factor conflating smell and death. What transpired in the trenches of the First World War – the imperial war that defined the highest stage of capitalism – was perhaps more decisive. Namely, gas warfare. Smell never recovered. The first use of chemical weapons during this conflict was in January 1915 when the Germans fired tear gas at the British. The primary active agent – xylyl bromide – was painful but not fatal. Then the German army started to use chlorine, which was deadly. It had a pungent smell and appeared as a green mist drifting across the battlefield. Because the gas hung so low, it tended to kill the already injured and sleeping soldiers. The first significant strike occurred in April 1915 when nearly 200 tonnes of chlorine was released. A gentle breeze was used to direct the deadly poison towards the enemy, the French army. When the cloud reached its target, panic ensued and men fled in all directions, suffocating, as lungs liquified inside their chests. While gas masks were an effective countermeasure, they couldn't prevent the psychological shock caused by the approaching cloud. Troops instinctively ran away screaming. When the British attacked the Germans with chlorine, a report said about an officer that 'as soon as the gas entered his trench, he lost all control of his men'.[16]

The next lethal chemical to be deployed on the Western front was phosgene. It was invisible and once inhaled took twenty-four hours to kill the victim. It reportedly smelt like freshly cut hay. This only intensified paranoia in the muddy labyrinthine trenches. Soldiers dolefully wondered if they had already been subjected to an attack in the night without knowing. Were they dead men walking? The evolution of human smell was shaped by its ability to detect danger. If something smells bad, then it probably is – be it noxious plant life, an infected wound, contaminated water or the scent of a wild bear. Not only did gas warfare strip smell of this vital quality but it also reconfigured the mucous membrane into an access point for a lethal dose of phosgene without the victim being any the wiser … until it was too late.

5

What does capitalism *taste* like? Like the other senses, this too has a cultural history that has not been favourable. Sensory neurons generating the sensations of sweet, salty, sour, bitter, spicy and umami have been experientially compressed, especially in relation to our diet. The post–Second World War period saw a huge growth in food production in Europe, the United States, South America and other advanced capitalist economies. In America, for example, mega-farms emerged using new ploughing and harvesting technologies, nitrate fertilizers and state-of-the-art pesticides. Growth figures skyrocketed from the 1950s onwards. Governmental subsidies also bolstered production leading to higher yields, significant cost savings and lower wholesale prices. At the same time, mass processed foods entered supermarkets and fast-food restaurants, remaining with us to this day. They are overloaded with artificial flavour enhancers such as glutamic acid salts and disodium ribonucleotides, not to mention a plethora of preservatives.[17] These chemicals modify how our brains perceive what we eat. Glutamic acid, for example, of which monosodium glutamate (MSG) is a prevalent variant, activates amino acids and metabotropic receptors, giving food a savoury taste. This can be enhanced with nucleotides like inosine-5'-monophosphate derived from chicken meat waste. A raft of other additives and preservatives further standardize the taste of food now consumed by millions daily: propyl paraben, tracer gas (for packaging), butylated hydroxytoluene, theobromine, colour retention agents and the list goes on. Are they safe? Difficult to say. In the United States, the food industry has long exploited a regulatory loophole concerning a category called 'generally recognized as safe'. It allows all manner of chemicals to be added to foods without prior consent by the Food and Drug Administration.

Because there are only six taste sensations, artificial manipulation and stabilization radically reduce their depth and complexity, especially the subtle combinations that can be derived from natural produce. Regrettably, this problem was not on the minds of those who invented frozen-ready meals. One of the first 'TV Dinners' was manufactured by Swanston & Sons in 1953.[18] The company was stuck with truckloads of frozen turkeys after the usual Thanksgiving surge failed to materialize. In a board meeting, someone piped up with a suggestion: precook the meat with other ingredients, pump it full of preservatives, additives and high levels of sodium, package the result into a compartmentalized aluminium tray and freeze it. If processed correctly, consumers could then reheat the meal at home. Only one year after production began, Swanson had sold 10 million TV Dinners. The invention gave birth to precooked convenience meals, one of the unhealthiest food categories ever fed to human beings. Hydrated trans fats stabilize the product. Antioxidants like butylated hydroxytoluene preserve the product. Liquid nitrogen cryogenically freezes the product. Finally, you consume the product and hope for the best.

Taste has been homogenized in other ways. What Adam Smith derogatively termed the 'spirit of corporation' (i.e. the concentration, centralization and collaboration of big business) dominates food production in the global economy today. The figures in the United States are telling. Just four firms control 85 per cent of the meat processing market.[19] One company – Frito-Lay – has a 65 per cent market share of potato chips. Beginning in the 1980s, a significant consolidation process occurred in the industrial food and drink industries. Although we have thousands of brands on supermarket shelves, most of them are subsidiaries of a handful of massive corporations. Price-fixing is inevitable. During the Covid-19 pandemic, these food conglomerates joined forces with grocery cartels to post super-profits.[20] The pandemic was great for the food industry. It thrived while many other parts of the economy wilted. But how does this centralization/concentration of capital affect the taste of our food?

Industrial food production techniques have eliminated many flavours, some of which will never be recovered. The biodiversity crisis has been central to this elimination of taste over the last fifty years, especially with the rise of genetically modified crops. For example, 86 per cent of apple varieties in the United States have disappeared due to selective farming and the decline of wild growth fields.[21] In the UK, Old Cornish Cauliflowers were replaced by generic French varieties because they were easier to ship and less suspectible to Ringspot. The Cornish Cauliflower is now extinct. The Ansault Pear was cultivated in several parts of Europe and had a unique buttery flavour. It no longer exists because the fruit couldn't be cultivated using industrial methods. Also extinct are the Taliaferro Apple, Murrays Plum, the Judean date plum and Kalimantan Mango.[22] The scale of the decimation cannot be underestimated. For example, 500 years after the Portuguese arrived on the remote island of Mauritius – which had a distinct and diverse ecosystem due to its inaccessibility – only 2 per cent of its forest remains and most of its native plant life vanished long ago. We will never know the subtle and complex flavours they contained.²³

Given this unprecedented retraction of taste, it is little wonder that we can identify a subterranean stream in Western philosophy that problematizes the act of eating, placing its rejection under the wider constellation of informal class conflict. Refusing to eat – to the point of anorexia – was considered insurrectional by several thinkers, including Gilles Deleuze, Kris Kraus and, most famously, Simone Weil, who eventually starved herself to death. As psychoanalysis teaches us, however, food loathing is no aberration but an integral aspect of abjection, as when the infant spits out its mothers' milk in disgust. Negating food allows the preoedipal subject to resist the trauma of existence, expelling what it needs to survive.²⁴ Food subsequently becomes a source of pain that we must protect ourselves from. After surveying the mass production of taste and its subsequent deconstruction by the modern food industry, that this psychodynamic act might be expressed as a political intervention begins to make sense.

6

The decline of vision is perhaps the clearest case in our sensory sociology. The twentieth century witnessed the incredible rise of mass communications, driven mainly by advertising, the global media industry and state propaganda. The Nipkow disk scanner was superseded by the Cathode-Ray-Tube in the 1930s and fully commercialized in the 1950s. Along with cinema and radio, television transformed the cultural fabric of capitalist societies in fundamental ways. By the 1960s, the dialectics of vision underpinning mass media became apparent. On the one hand, television was considered an emancipatory force that enabled public debate, democratic transparency and public awareness. This appeared to be so apropos the first televised war in Vietnam. The images of napalmed villages, incinerated infants and GIs drugged to the eyeballs on cheap opium helped fan the flames of countercultural rebellion. War atrocities were literally beamed into the living rooms of millions. On the other hand, however, citizens began to suspect that all was not what it seemed. Part of the distrust focused on television's unique potential as an instrument of social engineering. Is it being used by corporations and governments to pull the wool over the population's eyes? A growing chorus of critics believed so. The public was being blinded to essential truths about the industrial military complex. That this non-seeing occurred through the visual sensory apparatus – employing the impression of transparency as an effective mode of subterfuge – made it a formidable mechanism of control.

A rudimentary rendition of this critique was presented by Edward Herman and Noam Chomsky.[25] Their propaganda model of communication argued that the US news media was systemically biased in favour of elites, imperialism and anti-communist sentiment. It precipitated the closing of the American eye. A more sophisticated model can be found in Guy Debord's *Society of the Spectacle*.[26] Mediated representation replaces the immediacy of lived experience and projects pro-capitalist phantasies back onto the social imagination. The spectacle takes on a life of its own and we begin to take cues from it. Behind the collective visual performance lie the tenebrous backstage recesses of the ruling class. This sophisticated network of forces matures into an inscrutable 'thing in itself' under post-industrial conditions. Its presence is intuitively understood but cannot be accessed through authentic vision. Our eyes collude in the deception. The spectacle lulls us to sleep with eyes wide shut and reveals itself by showing us what it's not.

Mediocre films like *The Truman Show* and *Wag the Dog*, not to mention the O. J. Simpson trial, are often evoked to demonstrate this line of argument. It has been suggested that the assault on collective seeing reached new levels with the arrival of digital social media. Its reliance on the mythos of faux representation (truth in non-truth) is the apogee of the specularized society. Facebook, X, Weibo and Instagram murdered vision and fulfilled Jean Baudrillard's prediction of the perfect crime (although there's still a slim chance Mark Zuckerberg might one day stand trial for crimes against humanity). Indeed, Baudrillard was one of the few thinkers who understood what was around the corner, especially in relation to post-truth telling and our own complicity in its proliferation. In his book *The Perfect Crime*, the philosopher maintained that both the propaganda model and Debord's theory are outdated.[27] Reality is not so much hidden or mystified anymore, but literally dissolved by mass visuality:

> virtuality is different from the spectacle, which still had room for a critical consciousness and demystification. The abstraction of the spectacle was never irrevocable.[28]

In other words, deception does not consist of masking the truth. There is no longer an original indisputable reality to anchor the visual representations of film and television because the technological medium itself has passed into life. The spectacle is real in so far that it coordinates non-mediated praxis and generates new regimes of valediction that conceal society from itself. These are not simply lies but paradoxical *true lies*. In social media, this perfect crime is abetted by our own willing participation. We are seduced by the objective illusion and contribute to the content structure that makes digital mediation so destructive to critical reason. This marks a major shift since all observation is necessarily disqualified and undecidable subsequently. Only the sightless banality of information remains.

Today the avalanche of processed images, symbols and data 24/7 has superseded abstract vision. We can see everything but know very little, even nothing perhaps. The social eye has been decimated by the sheer ubiquity of this techno-void. This is an unprecedented accomplishment and inevitably makes ours a stupid society.

7

The radical implosion of vision was followed by the final cultural expulsion of sensory perception: *touch*, a discussion of which we opened this chapter. Prior to the Covid-19 pandemic and despite the neoliberal fear of physical contact, touch enjoyed a steady rise in status, bolstered by the 1960s free love and sexual liberation movement. Then came the personal computer and mouse. But it truly came into its own with the invention of *touchscreens*. This digital interface defined a new age of functionality that proved to be the ideal precursor for the decay of touch when the pandemic hit. Invented in the 1960s, touchscreens underwent rapid innovation as resistive and capacitive displays were improved. Capacitive displays have an electrostatic field that senses conductive inputs and do not require a 'touch event' like resistive panels. By the 1980s touch-sensitive control-display units were installed on aircraft. LG Prada was the first mobile phone to use touchscreens in 2007. Today the technology – including force-sensitive inert scrolling – is ubiquitous.[29]

Touchscreens fetishize the desirability of access, promising harmony between machine and human. But this paragon of unity has a negative side. I propose that touchscreen tactility has moved through four stages. First, they provided *control over machines* (military hardware, commercial airplanes, nuclear powerplants etc.). Next, they provided *access to machines* (ATMs, security systems etc.). Following the rise of digital media platforms – and this is the third stage – they provided *access to the social field* (mobile phones, swiping apps etc.). This mode of access soon became synthetic, disembodied and disconnected from concrete relationships. The final and fourth stage turns the tables on its user as power seizes this absolute techno-architecture. It combines the previous logics and utilizes touchscreens to gain *control over the social field* (surveillance, bossware, data scraping, policing algorithms etc.). When entering the social universe through our smartphones, for example, we simultaneously grant corporations access to who we are. Access today is a synonym for capitalist capture. The halo of touch that once valorized this technology betrayed us twice. First by fostering the falsehood that such connectivity could be a genuine proxy for social interaction. And second by turning touch into a metonymy for the public sphere when the pandemic hit in 2020, killing our faith in togetherness along the way. Shared touchscreens, even in the home, could prove lethal. Sharing itself became taboo.

In his book *Corpus*, Jean-Luc Nancy outlines an episteme of the body, which is central to his philosophy of community.[30] Touch is the quintessential sense and stands above the others in the idiom of social exchange. Not even speaking can be understood without an ethics of touching. As explained earlier, human tactile interaction – skin on skin – makes the body possible, since it opens individuals to the other and engenders self-recognition therein. Ego formation wouldn't be possible otherwise. Being touched is the essence of human life. In both pain and pleasure, violence and sensualism, rituals sacred and profane, we find 'the very absolute of touching, touching-the-other as being-touched, each being absorbed and devoured in the other'.[31] Nancy demonstrates how a certain mysticism of touch has been deeply inscribed into Western humanism. With the dawn of modern capitalism, however, this ineffability abruptly recedes. Touchscreen technologies perfectly exemplify the reasons why. How so?

The social function of technicity promotes a way of sharing our bodies that undermines its virtual externalization – res extensa – something that the corpus otherwise relies upon. Its commission of interactivity, especially when underscored by the ideology of access, establishes alienated contact as its primary model of closeness. I see but do not feel. I hear but cannot grasp. Pure touch is inaccessible, and we find ourselves alone, even when crowded out by millions of others on a social media platform. This is when the body becomes an *obstacle*, an inconvenience, to both us and others: 'most miserably, proximity becomes the banal reproduction of the body – supposedly "singular" – through millions of copies. (This, too, is why "the body" has also become the most insipid, the flattest, finally the most "disconnected" of themes and terms – in an irreversible coma.)'[32] The technologization of touch renders it an ersatz social medium, one that estranges both the giver and the receiver. There can be no reciprocity within this kind of community.

Touchscreen technology is emblematic of the broader deterioration of tactility over the last three decades. It strips this sensory dimension of its most kaleidoscopic variations. There is no skimming, grazing, squeezing, thrusting, pressing, smoothing, scraping, rubbing, caressing, palpating, fingering, kneading, massaging, entwining, hugging, striking, pinching, biting, sucking, moistening, taking, releasing, licking, rocking, balancing or carrying.[33] There is only endless pushing and pressing, a mono-dimensional movement of negligible quality or depth, an abstract one-wayness that signals the absence of any foundation whatsoever.

8

Fragments of failure

1

It is the year 2090. Unsurprisingly, the financial elite and geopolitical superpowers have failed to curb global carbon dioxide emissions as mandated by the Paris Agreement. The masters of capitalism in both the private and public sphere chose a business-as-usual approach instead and temperatures steadily rose. In 2075 it crossed the 4°C threshold. Some among the ruling plutocracy held hope that the world economy could still be weaned off its incessant reliance on fossil fuels. Green capitalism they called it – a win-win outcome – in which markets (e.g. carbon trading and offsetting etc.) and technology (e.g. superconductivity, nuclear fusion etc.) would end the crisis. This had little effect. A more cynical group of billionaires realized early on that the situation would soon turn ugly. They purchased 'apocalypse bunkers' in remote countries like New Zealand. Libertarian venture capitalist Peter Thiel was an early mover in this regard. In 2011 he secured a so-called 'golden passport' (i.e. New Zealand citizenship) and swiftly purchased real estate in the country's sparsely populated South Island. His descendants were now holed up in the luxuriant compound protected by military-grade security as the catastrophe unfolded.[1] Numerous other oligarchs and billionaires followed this elite exit strategy. They were safe in their air-conditioned cocoons ... for now.

As many experts predicted – including those working for Exxon in the late 1970s who first modelled the future effects of carbon emissions – the 4°C increase wreaked havoc on the planet's ecosphere.[2] By 2090, rising sea levels had swallowed the Maldives and river delta regions in China, Japan and Bangladesh. Ocean acidification poisoned once plentiful fisheries. Desertification had rendered large swathes of the United States, Australia, the Mediterranean and North Africa lifeless. Massive forest fires raged for years in many parts of the globe. Earth was a burning hell. Escalating water poverty sparked civil wars that ravished South America and the Middle East. The scorching heat was terrible to be sure. But so was the humidity and lethal 'wet bulb' temperatures or adiabatic saturation. Scientist had longed argued that modern civilization would not only be roasted but also poached.[3] Rising temperatures in India, Indonesia and the once verdant nations of Western Africa and Southeast Asia produced fatal levels of humidity. Under such conditions, human sweat cannot evaporate and cool the body, swiftly causing death from heat stroke. From 2075 onwards billions of people departed these nations in search of liveable regions. This sparked an unprecedented security response from rich nations. Borders were policed with atrocious racist violence. Concentration camps appeared around this 'ring of life' (as it came to be known) like deadly flowers. For those lucky enough to reside within these shrinking green zones, ruthless martial law was established, and all semblance of democracy disappeared. The year 2090 was not a good time to be alive. And worse was yet to come. As that terrible century drew to a close,

> The populace and the powerful – was a lump,
> Seasonless, Herbless, Treeless, Manless, Lifeless –
> A lump of death – a chaos of hard clay.
> The rivers, lakes, and ocean all stood still,
> And nothing stirred within their silent depths;

Ships sailorless lay rotting on the sea,
And their masts fell down piecemeal; as they dropp'd
They slept on the abyss without a surge.[4]

Now let's return to the present. The vested interests in maintaining the capitalist infrastructure are formidable. While most big corporations and governmental decision-makers pay lip service to the climate emergency, allocating resources to renewables, Environment, Social and Governance (ESG) programmes and carbon reduction schemes, few major players are willing to undertake the magnitude of change required to avert ecological collapse. Indeed, prior to the COP28 climate summit – hosted by the United Arab Emirates in 2023 – leaked briefing papers suggested that the Sultan Al Jaber (that year's summit president) planned to use the gathering to make secret backroom oil deals.[5] Other billionaires don't even pretend. They would sooner buy doomsday bunkers or plan colonies on Mars rather than make the necessary adjustments to the global socio-economic order.

This raises an important question. What are the chances that the ruling elite will soon wake up and admit to their wrong thinking on this issue, commit to dismantling dirty capitalism, degrow the economy, socialize the means of production and ban fossil fuels? By my reckoning, not very likely. The controls have been set to the heart of the sun. My argument is informed not by resignation or fatalism but by *dark realism*, a standpoint that contains certain emancipatory qualities as I shall soon explain.

2

What might be called the *new utopian movement* is troubling vis-à-vis this dark realism. A growing number of authors have celebrated the liberating potential of utopian theorizing in recent years. Leftist criticisms of capitalism are too bleak and self-defeating, it is argued, engendering an ethics of fatalism and resignation. To reverse the descending nightmare, we should revive one of the most powerful traditions in the pantheon of critical reason: utopianism. Unabashed optimism, hope and idealism are now the order of the day. Examples include Rutger Bregman's *Utopian for Realists*, E. O. Wright's *Envisioning Real Utopias*, Kirsten Ghodsee's *Everyday Utopia* and Ruth Levitas's *Utopia as Method* among many others.[6] Giving utopian thought a somewhat liberalist flavour, most of these authors refuse to provide detailed blueprints for this future perfect. That would be totalitarian. A 'spirit' of utopia is championed instead, broad and open-ended guideposts to inspire deep seated change. As Ruth Levitas puts it, 'the core of utopia is the desire to be otherwise, individually, and collectively, subjectively and objectively. Its expressions explore and bring to debate the potential contents and contexts of human flourishing. It is better understood as a method than a goal.'[7]

Four problems are evident concerning the new utopian movement. The first is perhaps most obvious. Its misplaced hope (that a sustainable and egalitarian society can somehow be snatched from the dead hand of the present) flirts with self-delusion. Levitas' emphasis on individual subjectivity is telling in this regard. Utopian thought offers personal succour in these melancholic times, similar to Ernst Bloch's argument about 'secular spiritualism' and the inward solace of futural optimism.[8] Given the ruins before us, however, I don't think this is a luxury we deserve. The situation looks incredibly bad according to almost every measure we can think of. Dark realism calls for engaging with this traumatic (almost impossible) *truth-of-the-real*, not in any positivist manner, far from it. This type of realism instead focuses on the premature, exceptional case and its exaggerated singularity in order to unlock the terrifying truth of the whole.[9] For what is capitalism if not an awful exaggeration hiding

Ships sailorless lay rotting on the sea,
And their masts fell down piecemeal; as they dropp'd
They slept on the abyss without a surge.[4]

Now let's return to the present. The vested interests in maintaining the capitalist infrastructure are formidable. While most big corporations and governmental decision-makers pay lip service to the climate emergency, allocating resources to renewables, Environment, Social and Governance (ESG) programmes and carbon reduction schemes, few major players are willing to undertake the magnitude of change required to avert ecological collapse. Indeed, prior to the COP28 climate summit – hosted by the United Arab Emirates in 2023 – leaked briefing papers suggested that the Sultan Al Jaber (that year's summit president) planned to use the gathering to make secret backroom oil deals.[5] Other billionaires don't even pretend. They would sooner buy doomsday bunkers or plan colonies on Mars rather than make the necessary adjustments to the global socio-economic order.

This raises an important question. What are the chances that the ruling elite will soon wake up and admit to their wrong thinking on this issue, commit to dismantling dirty capitalism, degrow the economy, socialize the means of production and ban fossil fuels? By my reckoning, not very likely. The controls have been set to the heart of the sun. My argument is informed not by resignation or fatalism but by *dark realism*, a standpoint that contains certain emancipatory qualities as I shall soon explain.

2

What might be called the *new utopian movement* is troubling vis-à-vis this dark realism. A growing number of authors have celebrated the liberating potential of utopian theorizing in recent years. Leftist criticisms of capitalism are too bleak and self-defeating, it is argued, engendering an ethics of fatalism and resignation. To reverse the descending nightmare, we should revive one of the most powerful traditions in the pantheon of critical reason: utopianism. Unabashed optimism, hope and idealism are now the order of the day. Examples include Rutger Bregman's *Utopian for Realists*, E. O. Wright's *Envisioning Real Utopias*, Kirsten Ghodsee's *Everyday Utopia* and Ruth Levitas's *Utopia as Method* among many others.[6] Giving utopian thought a somewhat liberalist flavour, most of these authors refuse to provide detailed blueprints for this future perfect. That would be totalitarian. A 'spirit' of utopia is championed instead, broad and open-ended guideposts to inspire deep seated change. As Ruth Levitas puts it, 'the core of utopia is the desire to be otherwise, individually, and collectively, subjectively and objectively. Its expressions explore and bring to debate the potential contents and contexts of human flourishing. It is better understood as a method than a goal.'[7]

Four problems are evident concerning the new utopian movement. The first is perhaps most obvious. Its misplaced hope (that a sustainable and egalitarian society can somehow be snatched from the dead hand of the present) flirts with self-delusion. Levitas' emphasis on individual subjectivity is telling in this regard. Utopian thought offers personal succour in these melancholic times, similar to Ernst Bloch's argument about 'secular spiritualism' and the inward solace of futural optimism.[8] Given the ruins before us, however, I don't think this is a luxury we deserve. The situation looks incredibly bad according to almost every measure we can think of. Dark realism calls for engaging with this traumatic (almost impossible) *truth-of-the-real*, not in any positivist manner, far from it. This type of realism instead focuses on the premature, exceptional case and its exaggerated singularity in order to unlock the terrifying truth of the whole.[9] For what is capitalism if not an awful exaggeration hiding in plain sight? Some may dismiss this as a neurotic attachment to unhappiness. But subjectivity has little to do with it. The unconscious even less so.

My second reservation concerns the very evocation of the term utopia. The new movement acknowledges that it literally means *nowhere* (following Thomas More's 1516 *De optimo rei publicae statu deque nova insula Utopia*). But whenever its leading intellectuals sketch the outlines of this better and just future world, they end up describing a rather mild form of democratic socialism that was largely the norm in 1960s Scandinavia, New Zealand, Canada and even parts of the United States. Calling this utopian gives standard socialism an aura of other worldliness that unfortunately reinforces years of neoliberal misinformation about the same thing. Socialism is only 'radical' today because the political spectrum has lurched so far to the right. Rutger Bregman's *Utopia for Realists* epitomizes this problem. When all is said and done, his utopian society consists of a robust welfare state that provides security for workers, progressive taxation and equal access to education, affordable housing and a shorter working week. Most of those 'utopian' demands were reality in 1960s New Zealand before the country was financially ransacked by a phalanx of anarcho-capitalists in the mid-1980s.

The third problem concerns the double-bind that often underscores this new utopianism. For example, in the opening pages of *Envisioning Real Utopias*, E. O. Wright rightly contends that eco-socialism is an important solution to the carnage being unleashed by supercharged capitalist realism (once again, labelling this solution 'utopian' is questionable for the aforementioned reasons). However, a major stumbling block for realizing this sensible goal, Wright continues, is the dearth of positive thinking, particularly Gramsci's oft-quoted optimism of the spirit. He writes,

Most people in the world today, especially in the economically developed regions of the world, no longer believe in this possibility. Capitalism seems to most people part of the natural order of things, and pessimism has replaced the optimism of the will that Gramsci once said was essential if the world was to be transformed.[10]

This hopelessness debases critical theory too, Wright suggests, draining the vitality required to inspire organized opposition. The double-bind functions like this. If your method of critique is not optimistic in its baseline premises, then by default it must be resigned to the present order of things. However, I subscribe to neither position. Upon closer scrutiny, additional problems emerge. Optimism is conflated with hope. But they are different. I can hope for something (e.g. world peace or a socialist revolution) without being optimistic that it will happen next week. Similarly, the new utopians equate pessimism with defeatism and passivity. However, radical pessimism is none of these things. We could recount a lush history of revolutionary counter-violence in which its agents were pessimistic about how successful they would ultimately be (e.g. the Paris Commune etc.). Such pessimism did not foreclose emancipatory intent, quite the opposite.

The new utopian movement overlooks the radical potential of revolutionary pessimism or what Walter Benjamin called 'organized pessimism' (which he opposed to Bloch's 'militant optimism').[11] This kind of pessimism should not be confused with apathy or quietism. Why? Because it isn't an attitude or ethos. Not only does organized pessimism call for a salutary appreciation of existing conditions – a militant realism if you like – it also turns on a guerrilla urgency, a ground swelling exigency that is missing in recent utopian thought. With nothing left to lose, with no hope of redemption in sight and prompted by the collective mourning for beautiful futures past, the subaltern can no longer distance itself from the source of its suffering.[12] Master and servant finally come face to face stripped of all ideological illusions. When that proximity transits into political strategy, resistance isn't a choice but an *objective necessity*, an imperative that cannot be ignored or ... ironically, resisted. One cannot simply go on like this. It is unthinkable *not* to rebel, even if it is patently pointless to do so. Indeed, that pointlessness has teeth too, striking fear into the most ardent defender of the status quo.

The fourth weakness of the new utopian movement concerns alternatives. Echoing Ernst Bloch's treatise, *The Principle of Hope*, Rutger Bregman, for instance, suggests that utopian thinking calls for wide-eyed dreaming about new social realities, mixing optimism with unbounded imagination and creativity.[13] It implies that left-wing theory is too often bolted to the dismal present. The resulting despondency is anathema to our capacity for inventing ideal-types that move history forward. Progress itself depends upon thinking outside the box. There are several problems with this idea. That right-wing intellectuals too – often with fascist sympathies — like F. A. Hayek – engage in utopian thought is overlooked by Bregman and his fellow travellers. Indeed, it could be argued that the dystopian moment we are currently enduring is the product of failed thought-experiments constructed by neoclassical economists.[14] Dystopia is not the opposite of utopia but an extreme instantiation of it.

Furthermore, the problem we face today is not a dearth of alternatives to capitalist hegemony. Better models for rebuilding the workplace, energy production, international supply chains, democratic governance, race relations, fiscal and taxation policy, aged care assistance, higher education and gender justice to name but a few abound. We have no shortage of them. A great deal of important intellectual work has been done in that space. No, the fly in the ointment is how precisely we get from the present gridlock – a globalized economic and financial net that is tightly coiled around everything we do and think – to those desirable end states, even the most modest ones. That's what feels impossible. And perhaps it is precisely that disjuncture – between the eternal present and an infinitely better future that's so obvious and easily achievable, yet impossibly distant and unrealistic within the current constellation of power relations – that informs our current dystopia. Hence why only a crisis imposed from the outside, like an epidemic, global IT outage or ecological calamity, seems like the only way in which the capitalist machine might be derailed.

3

Emancipatory alternatives do not arrive from another world. Some argue, for example, that the rudimentary components of socialism lay dormant in the institutions of advanced capitalism itself. An automated solution to paid employment has been latent in the forces of production for years. Clean energy sources are imminently possible if better funding was forthcoming. Large bureaucracies in the private sector could be repurposed into shared labour committees, superseding their autocratic modus operandi with a cooperative mandate. Instead of giving multinational firms massive tax breaks and other forms of corporate welfare, municipalities could fund extensive public programmes to revitalize civic life, putting an end to the spiritual barrenness that now prevails. Fiscal policies favouring the rich could be reoriented to reverse the intergenerational transmission of advantage and inequality. Socialism for the rich that ironically underpins neoliberal capitalism might easily be transformed into socialism for the multitude. The wealth and prosperity already exist; they simply haven't been organized correctly. For this reason,

Marcuse argued in his 1967 lecture 'The End of Utopia', we should avoid using the jargon of utopia because the basic elements for a liberated social order are already technically at hand:

> when the material and intellectual forces for the transformation are technically at hand although their rational application is prevented by the existing organization of the forces of production ... we can speak of the end of utopia ... All the material and intellectual forces which could be put to work for the realization of a free society are at hand. That they are not used for that purpose is to be attributed to the total mobilization of existing society against its own potential for liberation. But this situation in no way makes the idea of radical transformation itself a utopia.[15]

Apart from rejecting the idealistic (*qua* utopianism) tendencies of the New Left in this lecture, Marcuse seeks to update Marx's classic insight concerning the contradiction between the relations and forces of production. The new grows inside the old. There is a catch, of course, one that Marcuse notes too. We must place this 'technically at hand' within proper context. Under conditions of rampant policing and entrenched, almost *over*-institutionalized corporatization, this latent potential – even when literally at our fingertips – is still light years away from being put into practice. In other words, intrinsic realizability stands in stark contrast to extrinsic realizability. And doesn't this exemplify the new tragedy of the commons? The sociality that might allow us to build truly free communities exists only as a negative imprint of the capitalist paradigm, which parasitically rides on this captured undercommons and creates something grotesque.

The situation ought to provoke dejection and pessimism about the coming future. The old is dying but the new cannot be born. A cataclysmic miscarriage seems inevitable. But in recent examinations of this contradiction – between the liberating potential already present and its false blockage – a more optimistic spin is strangely given. The actualization of the new is charged with an automatic inevitability. The socialism lurking in today's market madness will soon spring forth of its own accord. The argument is typically inspired by a simplistic technological determinism. Aaron Bastani's *Fully Automated Luxury Communism* and Paul Mason's *Postcapitalism* are indicative of this trend.[16] They elide the aleatory and irreducible ways in which social transformations occur, for better (socialism, anarcho-syndicalism etc.) or for worse (fascism). The event cannot be read off preexisting socio-technical structures, even when blatantly pregnant with a new mode of emancipation. Technically at hand is not the same as being in hand. Marx understood this when he intimated that revolutions are mostly tautological: the only revolutionary precondition we can count on is the revolution itself, through which the motivating class agent retroactively coalesces, but seldom beforehand in any unambiguous manner. Unlike Lenin, this explains Marx's reluctance to tabulate any unequivocal revolutionary situation.[17]

Closely associated with this techno-optimism is a redoubling down on the happiness-fix. If the revolution is only a tee-shirt away, then we must abandon our pessimism for a forward-looking joyousness instead. After all, who wants to be part of the revolution if you can't dance? According to Paul Mason, despite the miasma of contemporary life, the future is clear and bright.[18] It has to be. Thinking it will make it so. Lynne Segal agrees. In her book *Radical Happiness*, she acknowledges the mass production of hopelessness in post-industrial economies and the emergent happiness industry as a nostrum for that very sadness.[19] But in terms of left-wing activism, disappointment is counterproductive to enacting transformative change: 'for without our own sources of optimism, we inevitably give up on the search for sharing possibilities for the enjoyment of life, however fleeting these possibilities might prove to be'.[20] Once we survey the full extent of the wreckage, however, isn't there a risk that these brief moments of happiness might be individuated, regressing into something like ignorant bliss? None of this is to eulogize melancholia. Rather the pessimism I'm interested is not an attitude but an act of organization, one that can be assembled without necessarily internalizing its qualities as a psychological trait.

This is why I find *afropessimism* so interesting. Developed in the United States by Frank B. Wilderson III among others, afropessimism is a Black liberation movement that refuses affirmation – including Black subjectivity itself – given how white supremacy has predetermined all aspects of American society, down to its core.[21] Anti-Black violence produces Black existence. There is no prior autonomous identity that can be leveraged to resist the dirty war against African Americans because 'black existence is simultaneously produced and negated by racial domination, both as presupposition and consequence'.[22] Affirmation would therefore also affirm the violence that structures Black selfhood per se. Wilderson summarizes the position with a striking maxim: 'the spectacle of Black death is essential to the mental health of the world'.[23] Pessimism switches into critical praxis precisely when it accepts the impossibility of continuing in this world as one is. One cannot exist – even if reduced to *homo sacer* – while the array of forces that brought that existence into being endures. This is just another way of conceptualizing revolutionary suicide, which shouldn't be confused with self-harm. There is no murdering of the hated 'other' inside, as Freud described felo-de-se. Afropessimism advocates a violent outward movement to remake the foundations of being. Only then can one begin to live again. In the meantime, anything short of an acerbic (although never splenetic) pessimism about extant conditions is foolish. Happiness? A crime. In many ways, afropessimism echoes Marx's dialectical analysis of the working class. The wage labourer was produced by the capitalist ruling class. As formal subsumption transitioned into real subsumption, master and servant became two sides of the same coin. The struggle for emancipation necessarily involves self-abolition and the formation of a higher individual that no longer bears the brand of her own negation.

4

Can this auto-negation transform capitalism before 2090 rolls around? Ensnared by the runaway devastation of the global economic system, our resistance – even when practiced as a combative insurrection – must unseat not only the ruling power elite but also some ingrained norms linked to consumption, work, religion, oil and backward individualism. Returning to my opening question, what are the chances that will happen before it's too late? Not zero ... but fairly close to it. So how bad will things be in 2090? An entire genre of Hollywood films and books have tried to answer this question, portraying the ruinous fragments of the future in vivid and shocking detail (with Walter M. Miller's 1959 novel *Canticle for Leibowitz* standing out as a brilliant example). Speculative dystopian thought typically extrapolates from present conditions in some manner. Sci-fi apocalypse entertainment is uncanny for this reason because we can see the seeds of destruction in our own times. But this approach is problematic. Our knowledge about these matters is delimited by the intrinsic inscrutability of cataclysmic temporality. That blindness makes everything more frightening, much more so than movies like *The Day After* or *Stalker*. We know it'll be bad but have no idea what shape that Uber-badness will assume before it arrives. In the 1950s as the nuclear arms race escalated, critical theorist Günther Anders termed this the *naked apocalypse* because we must face it with no prior recognition of the event.[24] Our collective imagination cannot fathom the quantitative and qualitative modalities of suffering that await. Speculative reason breaks down. In this respect, a dark void lies at the centre of modern technological civilization because our capacity to destroy has outstripped our capacity to grasp the ramifications of that destruction. We are unknown to ourselves. Unfortunately, any society than doesn't know itself is disturbing for obvious reasons.

This raises a final problem. If I claim that the global system is now circling the drain and is probably unsalvageable, then why even bother writing about it? That would be like watching a killer tsunami roll in from the horizon and scribbling a few words of protest seconds before the wave wipes you away forever. Critical commentary in particular requires at least a modicum of hope; otherwise, the whole endeavour is pointless. So what compels someone to write in the shadow of the apocalypse, especially if it's already too late? We can dismiss some obvious justifications from the outset. For example, it could be argued that even in the direst circumstances, the basic human impulse to communicate endures. There is an irrepressible spark in us that refuses to be snuffed out, with writing a key expression of that drive. It's a comforting thought, but ultimately unconvincing. I don't think writing – or any other creative enterprise for that matter – is very natural. Often the opposite, involving a struggle *against* human nature. It's the overwhelming possibility of having never been – nonexistence – that gives a text of philosophy, fiction or criticism its positive form, not some inexorable necessity. Literature is a minor miracle in this respect, a victory against the entropy and emptiness of the human soul.

Nor do I get any nihilistic pleasure in documenting the end times, like those crazy folk who rush to the foot of a volcano that's about to blow. This is a joyless task and certainly no object of fascination. So as the inescapable tsunami grows skyward, three reasons to write still remain, irrespective of one's chances of survival. The first is dignity, of knowing exactly *why* your existence will soon be altered for the worse, especially if there's little you can do about it. The project of rejecting self-deception and confusion is a basic principle in Western philosophy. It means being worthy of what happens to you. Otherwise, as German author W. G. Sebald noted, we learn from our predicament much like a rabbit learns from an experiment that's performed upon it. In other words, knowing how to face the awful truth permits us to finally face ourselves. Better late than never.

While some kind of cataclysmic collapse is almost certain, there is a second justification for continuing to write, social criticism in particular. This concerns its testimonial function. Bertolt Brecht's unnerving poem 'To Those Who Are Born Afterwards', written in 1939 while fleeing the Nazis, helps us here: 'Truly, I live in dark times!' the narrator begins.[25] He is addressing mankind far into the future, long after his fellow men have reduced the world to ash. A litany of injustices is catalogued, but the poem isn't just a chronicle. To the reader who does not yet exist, a desperate plea for clemency and forgiveness is being made: 'but when the time comes at last / and man is a helper to man / think of us / with forbearance'.[26] We never learn whether the appeal is granted, but it was worth a try. It's those who follow in our wake, they are the ones who will inherit the dust. And they haunt us for that reason.

The third motive is more esoteric, but ties together these thoughts about dignity and forbearance. As the French writer Maurice Blanchot pointed out in *The Writing of the Disaster*, the impending catastrophe is not only something waiting out there in objective form (although it is partially that).[27] For instance, whereas I envisage a vast cultural desert drawing near, MrBeast speaks of a roseate future. Although I believe my narrative is more honest, the disaster still must be textually evoked and carefully pieced together from the residuum around us.

That's not too difficult given the material at hand. But for Blanchot there's a hitch. Rather paradoxically, you can only write about this devastating future if you are *already* living through it. Want to know what hell looks like? Take a walk down to your local supermarket and find out. By adumbrating the imminent disaster that lies ahead, we can identify its faint resonances in the here and now, during the daily commute, lurking in that bland office décor and those black cracks on an overused freeway. Faint now perhaps … but inexorably growing.

It's this feature that differentiates my method from millennial fatalism and hack futurism. I'm not predicting the future – only trying to record its advance shock troops as they arrive in the most unexpected places. Could such a record help avert the disaster, perhaps inspire a renewed fight for freedom, liberty and hope? I'm doubtful. All indicators suggest that the unstoppable juggernaut of global capitalism is jammed on self-destruct mode. By conceding this, however, at least we can better prepare for what is to come. I call this dark realism because it follows the disparate threads of negation that run through the fabric of the present to their ultimate conclusions. But nor is this a politics of purity. It is completely tainted and smeared by the grime of rampant extraction, lost deep within enemy territory and staring out at the nothingness that awaits. This is how (rather than *why*) we write. More important than preparation or insight, however, is the forbearance of future generations who could never understand the unusual violence that blighted our times. For those who come after the flood, long after you and I have been swept away, will they remember us with sympathy, shame or derision?

Conclusion

Ideology and the void

In February 2003 US Secretary of State Colin Powell entered the UN Security Council to make the case for invading Iraq, which the United States did six weeks later. In the speech, Powell presented what he called conclusive evidence that Saddam Hussain had stockpiled weapons of mass destruction: 'my colleagues, every statement I make today is backed up by sources, solid sources. These are not assertions. What we're giving you are facts and conclusions based on solid intelligence.'[1] We now know that Powell's testimony was utterly false. Hussain had no weapons of mass destruction. On that pretext, however, one of the bloodiest occupations in recent history took place. It is difficult to gauge just how many Iraqis died following the 2003 invasion. A widely cited *Lancet* study estimates around 655,000 violent fatalities as of June 2006.[2]

There is an important detail of Powell's testimony that is often missed. Outside the Security Council chamber hung a large tapestry of Pablo Picasso's famous painting *Guernica*. The painting was the artist's response to the 1937 Nazi air attack on the Basque town. The contorted black-and-white figures are chilling: death and suffering suffuse the canvas. The masterpiece has become a globally recognized anti-war icon. As reporters and TV crews gathered outside the Security Council chamber during Powell's speech, however, they noticed something odd. A blue curtain had been placed over the tapestry, concealing it from sight. This was no coincidence they surmised. As one analyst put it, the painting's 'unappealing ménage of mutilated bodies and distorted faces proved to be too strong for articulating to the world why the US was going to war in Iraq'.[3]

At first glance, this appears to be a standard example of ideological mystification. The United States felt compelled to hide the shocking truth of war when drumming up support for it. Indeed, in a curious double inversion, the concealment of 'Guernica' finds its mirror image in Powell's concealment of the truth regarding Hussein's alleged concealment of nuclear weapons. In any case, this approach to *Ideologiekritik* – demonstrating how reality is covered up by powerful interests – has stood the test of time and helped demask the many fictions that capitalism tells itself (and us) in order to persist during periods of dwindling legitimacy.

But as I have endeavoured to emphasize in this book, ideology often works in a more insidious manner, which undermines the demasking gesture of traditional *Ideologiekritik*. What if the UN officials – at the behest of the United States – actually took down the *Guernica* tapestry prior to Powell's speech. Then they stood staring at the blank wall, bare and almost painful to the eye given the glaring absence of Picaso's amazing image (perhaps the faded outline of the tapestry was still visible on the sheen surface, accentuating the loss). 'We can't leave it like this', an official exclaims. 'Put a curtain over it. Everyone will think we're hiding it but that's better than ... that', he says, pointing ominously at the empty space. The blue curtain was really hiding nothing. One can imagine the collective gasp if the veil accidentally dropped before the waiting media, disclosing the barren truth. It would activate a twofold negation: first concerning the truth-giving properties that *Guernica* signifies about imperial violence (the subtraction of content) and second regarding the truth-procedure itself since the curtain concealed nothing but a traumatic absence (the subtraction of form).

Reimagining the scenario in this way is useful for understanding how ideological mystification unfolds today. Ideology doesn't only operate by regulating the imaginary relationship of individuals to their real relations. Nor is it a performative injunction. No, contemporary ideological obfuscation succeeds when we believe that power still needs ideology, that deception remains necessary because there is something behind the curtain that we could access, be it an emancipatory class agent, leaked National Security Agency files or a deadly new virus being cooked up in a secret military laboratory. The curtain motif is thus important. It signals *potential* knowability to the observer. Hegemony requires this due to the vast sea of inaccessibility that has otherwise become the cornerstone of late capitalism. We will never know what transpires in those complex webs of shadow banking, backroom arms deals and tax evasion. A shot of nothingness goes to the heart of the regime of accumulation. And that reverberates in the lives of distressed working people holding down three part-time jobs, desperate migrants encamped on the Mexico border, fighting soldiers in dead end wars and so forth. The disconnect between their existential misery and the background architecture causing that misery is stark, to say the least.

Ideology still aims to mask reality of course, but our access to that reality is becoming increasingly tenuous for reasons outlined in this book. The mask hides something that is false. And that must be hidden too. Ideology is thus both essential and yet ultimately redundant for maintaining the symbolic totality. This surfeit of signifiers around the object of ideological distortion defines the historical moment but obviously not in the same manner as post-truth. Having said that, this enormous gap between the raw presence of concrete duress (working, financialization, debt etc.) and the institutional absentification of power is certainly made good use of by conspiracy theorists and fake news bots. Perhaps only in the context of this endemic inscrutability could the kind of disinformation circulating today gain such a foothold. As capitalism automatizes its strong-arm logics behind our backs, this generative void, albeit cloaked by a blue curtain, is a perfect canvas for the mass production of counter-knowledge.

My book has tried to illustrate how this epistemic deficit has become a strategic resource for post-industrial capitalism. The production of social opacity has several dimensions. For example, do you know how much your co-workers get paid? The question may sound trite, but we simply forget that only forty years ago in Western economies, everybody pretty much knew who was paid what. Industry-wide agreements, including standardized pay rates, were public knowledge. As were corporate and middle-management salaries. Privatizing economic reason was a central objective of the neoliberal project and fuelled the fabrication of remoteness apropos fellow workers and citizens. As we noted regarding neoclassical economics, the new doctrine asserted that commercial exchange ought to be a private matter, with little external scrutiny from the state, regulators or unions. This never triumphed *in toto*, of course, but a significant decline of social knowledge inevitably followed, leading to a society of monadic individuals who cannot see beyond their own internal limitations.

The gig economy aims to perfect this dream of pure detachment in the employment sector, using digital platforms to refashion private citizens into de facto wage labourers. But isolation itself is part of the illusion because it conceals the highly mediated nature of this work via sophisticated algorithms and cloud-based tools. Then there is the substantial reservoir of unpaid labour in the domestic realm that this business model indirectly relies upon (not to mention state income support etc.). Ironically, though, Uber's pay rate is highly standardized and visible. And its surveillance software exposes the worker to menacing degrees of transparency. Yet the company's capsule-like secretization of the workforce is unprecedented in the history of capitalism. Labour is certainly reified in classic terms, whereby 'a relation between people takes on a phantom-objectivity, an autonomy that seems so strictly rational and all-embracing as to conceal every trace of its fundamental nature: the relation between people'.[4] But algorithms magnify this reification. What we might call the *cypherization of labour* secures a massive victory for employers. Mediation and knowledge are artificially separated, which means that work can be highly organized with few of the economic costs (cars, uniforms, sick pay etc.) or political threats (unionization etc.) that capitalists associate with standard employment. Indeed, research has noted how Uber drivers cannot even contact the company on the phone, ironically, let alone other workers to establish a union.[5] A significant decline of *vox humana* is evident, a dilatory retraction of voice and the digital transposition of labour into notational code. The worker essentially disappears.

Non-knowledge now cuts into the cultural fabric of modern life. Walking down a street in London, using Google maps to find a nondescript pub on a gloomy Monday afternoon, I exemplify the 'vacuity syndrome'. It starts to drizzle as I enter the Hand and Shears. My credit card – which I use to pay for a pint of tepid Stella Artois – is linked to financial instruments so arcane within the flows of international capital, I have no idea what is happening behind the scenes. As I sip the beer, the working conditions at the brewing company are beyond my knowledge. That also applies to the person three metres away behind the bar serving another customer. I pick up my phone and write a text. Do I understand how this piece of technology actually works, its 'System-on-a-chip', LPDDR4X RAM, resistors, light-emitting diodes etc.? Of course not! If you asked me right now what my data plan was – inclusive of the bundle and save price discount – I wouldn't have a clue. Who knows? Across the road is a CCTV camera. Is anyone watching? I have no idea. Sitting in this pub surrounded by strangers, I'm largely oblivious to the social forces that govern my praxis. A fog of nothingness descends on everything. I don't even know myself. Why am I drinking this much? The death drive is strong today no doubt, but what trauma am I unconsciously repeating? I finish my beer as the sun begins to die and stumble out the door into the grey multitude. Now overdetermined by the inescapable relations of control that structure our inward biographies, life itself follows the same pattern of the commodity fetish, emptied of background content and experience. Overcoding modern subjectivity requires that it be denied even the most basic comprehension of that coding process.

It's tempting to evoke conventional critiques of modernity to explain this predicament. For example, Max Weber argued that scientific specialization and formalization mean that our technical knowledge of, say, how an elevator works is understood only by a handful of experts (although we could always find out from a book if we so desired). The same for my mobile phone. Furthermore, a deep division of labour across global society both interlocks individuals together but also separates us from each other. Direct knowledge and social ties decline as a result, even when interdependence reaches new heights. And finally, Simmel's theory of the stranger might explain the daily mutual estrangement experienced in large metropolises like London.

Clearly these arguments still hold. But the systems of evacuation described in this book are distinct. A *coercive abstraction* is evident, pointing to a mechanism of mass-produced somatic absence. This decay of knowing has several levels. On the meta-level, a shield of obscurity protects the global financial elite from democratic accountability. Personalities therein too have become no-dimensional, dominated by feckless halfwits who have family networks to thank for their wealth and privilege. At the organizational level, the privatization of work (labour) and banalization of managerialism (capital) have decomposed economic action into unthinking zones of non-engagement. And at the subjective level, a forthright expulsion of the ego has occurred. As I mentioned earlier in this book, the self-help industry's turn to non-subjectivity (stoicism etc.) exemplifies a broader fixation with internal dissolution – best not to feel anything at all. In short, a veritable supply-chain of nothingness has emerged from the shipwrecked mind of post-pandemic, post-financial crisis capitalism.

Thought annexed by blind action is not new. But its concentration today in almost every facet of the accumulation regime, including the state apparatus and its insubordinate permutations, is a surprising development. Writing in a different context, T. W. Adorno captured the tendency: 'the ratio recoils into irrationality as soon as it mistakes, in its necessary course, the fact that the disappearance of its substrate, be it ever so diluted, is the handiwork of its abstraction'.[6] In other words, the power of thought reaches all the way down into its own deception and *still* accepts the lie. Cognition ceases to matter and recedes into perpetual afterwardness. History has already happened. To dispel this deception, it is not enough to peek behind the curtain since the absence awaiting is part of the ideological illusion. We must look elsewhere for the truth – since it still exists, make no doubt – and appreciate that the curtain hides little more than our own neurotic belief in a master who knows.

Notes

Introduction

1. Hegel, G. W. F. (1820/1991). *Elements of the Philosophy of Right.* Translated by H. B. Nisbet. Cambridge: Cambridge University Press.
2. Fisher, M. (2018). *Ghosts of My Life: Writings on Depression, Hauntology and Lot Futures.* London: Zer0 Books.
3. Fisher, M. (2018). 'Acid Communism'. In *K-Punk: The Collected and Unpublished Writings of Mark Fisher.* London: Repeater Books, pp. 755–6.
4. Kneale, N. (1964). 'The Road'. *BBC Television.* London. An excellent radio adaptation of *The Road* was broadcast by *BBC Four* in 2018. https://www.youtube.com/watch?v=QZgmdqaAyh8

Chapter 1

1. Yunkaporta, T. (2019). *Sand Talk: How Indigenous Thinking Can Save the World.* Melbourne: The Text Publishing.
2. *Parliament of Australia* (2021). 'Inquiry into the Destruction of 46,000 Year Old Caves at the Juukan Gorge in the Pilbara Region of Western Australia'. https://www.aph.gov.au/~/link.aspx?_id=FE887411CFA84822853C275BE078265E&_z=z
3. Arendt, H. (1963). *Eichmann in Jerusalem: A Report on the Banality of Evil.* New York: Viking Press.
4. Arendt, H. (1971). 'Thinking and Moral Considerations: A Lecture'. *Social Research*, 38(3): 417–46, p. 417.
5. Ibid, p. 423.
6. Ibid, p. 421.
7. Also see Heidegger, M. (1969). *Identity and Difference.* New York: Harper.

8   Arendt, Thinking and Moral Considerations, p. 434.
9   Hanlon, G. (2015). *The Dark Side of Management: A Secret History of Management Theory*. London: Routledge.
10 Lemann, N. (2019). *Transaction Man: The Rise of the Deal and the Decline of the American Dream*. New York: Farrar, Straus and Giroux.
11 Taylor, F. W. (1911). *The Principles of Scientific Management*. New York: Harper.
12 Gioia, D. (1992). 'Pinto Fires and Personal Ethics: A Script Analysis of Missed Opportunities'. *Journal of Business Ethics*, 11: 379–89.
13 Leeson, N. (1996). *Rogue Trader: How I Brought Down Barings Bank and Shook the Financial World*. Boston, MA: Little, Brown & Co.
14 Fritzon, K., Brooks, N. and Croom, S. (2020). *Corporate Psychopathy: Investigating Destructive Personalities in the Workplace*. Cham, Switzerland: Palgrave Macmillan.
15 Gelles, D. (2022). *The Man Who Broke Capitalism: How Jack Welch Gutted the Heartland and Crushed the Soul of Corporate America – and How to Undo His Legacy*. New York: Simon and Schuster.
16 Ibid.
17 Welch, J. (2001). *Jack: Straight from the Gut*. New York: Headline Publishing Group.
18 Kets de Vries, M. (2021). 'The Psychopath in the C Suite: Redefining the SOB'. Working Paper 119/EFE.
19 *Constellis* (2022). 'Code of Business Ethics and Conduct'. https://www.constellis.com/who-we-are/ethics-policies-certifications/
20 For an extended analysis of Fink's politics, see Rhodes, C. and Fleming, P. (2020). 'Forget Political Corporate Social Responsibility'. *Organization*, 27(6): 943–51.
21 Fink, L. (2022). 'The Power of Capitalism: Larry Fink's 2022 Letter to CEOs'. https://www.blackrock.com/corporate/investor-relations/larry-fink-ceo-letter
22 *UK Parliament* (2018). 'Collapse of Carillion Inquiry'. https://committees.parliament.uk/work/3897/collapse-of-carillion-inquiry/publications/
23 When cross-examined by prosecutors, Sam Bankman-Fried said 'I Don't Recall' 140 Times, Even When Questioned about Some Basic Facets of His Business. *BitMEX Research* (2023). 'SBF – Transcript of Closing Summations – 1 November 2023'. https://blog.bitmex.com/sbf-trial-closing-summations-1-nov-2023/
24 Jenkins, K. and Collard, S. (2022). 'Unique Art Submission to Juukan Gorge Inquiry Now a Major Exhibition'. *SBS*. https://www.sbs.com.au/nitv/article/unique-art-submission-to-juukan-gorge-inquiry-now-a-major-exhibition/u29dtu711

Chapter 2

1. Zink, E. (2022). 'What Is Snorting Percocet/OxyContin/Oxycodone Like? My Experience'. *YouTube*. https://www.youtube.com/watch?v=XU1a_ZrOVBE
2. Ryan, H., Girion, L. and Glover, S. (2016). 'You Want a Description of Hell? OxyContin's 12-Hour Problem'. *Los Angeles Times*. https://www.latimes.com/projects/OxyContin-part1/
3. *Centres for Disease Control and Prevention* (2023). 'Understanding the Opioid Overdoes Epidemic'. U.S. Department of Health & Human Services: Washington, DC.
4. Van Zee, A. (2009). 'The Promotion and Marketing of OxyContin: Commercial Triumph, Public Health Tragedy'. *American Journal of Public Health*, 99(2): 221–7.
5. Meier, B. (2018). 'Origins of an Epidemic: Purdue Pharma Knew Its Opioids Were Widely Abused'. *New York Times*. https://www.nytimes.com/2018/05/29/health/purdue-opioids-OxyContin.html
6. Armstrong, D. (2019). 'Watch the Damning Deposition the Sackler Family Wanted Buried'. *ProPublica*. https://www.truthdig.com/articles/watch-the-damning-deposition-the-sackler-family-wanted-buried/
7. *Commonwealth of Kentucky Pike Circuit Court* (2015). 'Disposition of Richard Sackler M.D'. pp. 12–13.
8. Marcuse, H. (1964/1991). *One-Dimensional Man: Studies in the Ideology of Advanced Industrial Society*. Boston, MA: Beacon Press.
9. In a letter to Horkheimer, Adorno once quipped that if Marcuse wasn't Jewish, he would've been a Nazi. This nasty barb is cited by Lydia Goehr in her introduction ('Reviewing Adorno') to *Critical Models*. See Adorno, T. W. (2005). *Critical Models: Interventions and Catchwords*. New York: Columbia University Press, p. xli. On a related note, Adorno's views on laughter – so wonderfully problematized by Bertolt Brecht – can be found in numerous writings, including *Dialectic of the Enlightenment* when it's insisted: 'fun is a medicinal bath which the entertainment industry never ceases to prescribe. It makes laughter the instrument for cheating happiness … In a wrong society laughter is a sickness infecting happiness and drawing it into society's worthless totality.' Horkheimer, M. and Adorno, T. W. (1944/1997). *Dialectic of Enlightenment*. Translated by John Cumming. London: Verso, p. 141.
10. Marcuse, *One Dimensional Man*, pp. 245–6.
11. Ibid, p. 257.
12. Traverso, E. (2016). *Left-Wing Melancholia: Marxism, History and Memory*. New York: Columbia University Press, pp. 6–7.

13 Sartre, J-P. (1943/2021). *Being and Nothingness: An Essay on Phenomenological Ontology*. Translated by Sarah Richmond. New York: Atria Books.
14 Let's put aside the astounding calculations conducted by Alexander Grothendieck in 1960 that demonstrated how Galois group actions could possibly reveal the dimensionality of points.
15 McTaggart, J. M. E. (1908). 'The Unreality of Time'. *Mind*, (17): 457–73.
16 Bolchover, D. (2005). *The Living Dead: Switched Off, Zoned Out: The Shocking Truth about Office Life*. Oxford: Capstone.
17 Harvey, E. (2015). *The Leadership Secrets of Santa Claus: How to Get Big Things Done in Your 'Workshop' … All Year Long*. Naperville, IL: Simple Truths.
18 See Tooze, A. (2018). *Crashed: How a Decade of Financial Crises Changed the World*. New York: Penguin.
19 Shaxson, N. (2019). 'Tackling Tax Havens'. *Finance and Development Magazine*. September: 6–19.
20 *Financial Stability Board* (2022). 'Global Monitoring Report on Non-Bank Financial Intermediation'. https://www.fsb.org/2022/12/global-monitoring-report-on-non-bank-financial-intermediation-2022/
21 See, for example, Jacoby, S. M. (2021). *Labor in the Age of Finance: Pensions, Politics, and Corporations from Deindustrialization to Dodd-Frank*. Princeton, NJ: University of Princeton Press; Lazzarato, M. (2012). *The Making of the Indebted Man: An Essay on the Neoliberal Condition*. Cambridge, MA: MIT Press.
22 Pollard, C. (2017). 'The Philosopher Who Was Too Hot for Playboy'. *The Conversation*. https://theconversation.com/the-philosopher-who-was-too-hot-for-playboy-85002
23 Power, N. (2009). *One-Dimensional Woman*. Winchester: Zer0 Books.
24 Malik, K. (2023). *Not So Black or White: The History of Race from White Supremacy to Identity Politics*. London: C. Hurst & Co.
25 Sandberg, S. (2013). *Leaning In: Women, Work and the Will to Lead*. New York: Alfred A. Knopf. Solanas, V. (1967/2004). *SCUM Manifesto*. London: Verso.
26 Sandberg, *Leaning In*, p. 7.
27 Solanas, *SCUM Manifesto*, p. 35.

Chapter 3

1 Evans, S. (2015). 'Employees Shut inside Coffins'. *BBC*. https://www.bbc.com/news/magazine-34797017

2   Ibid.
3   Ibid.
4   Freud, S. (1915/1918). *Reflections on War and Death*. Translated by A. A. Brill and A. B. Kuttner. New York: Mofat, Yard and Company, p. 16. As a side point, the belief that one is dead – what the French psychiatrist Jules Cotard termed the 'delirium of negation' or 'walking corpse syndrome' – is considered a serious neurological disorder.
5   Marx, K. (1867/1976). *Capital: A Critique of Political Economy – Volume One*. Translated by Ben Folks. New York: Penguin Books.
6   Marx is perceptive on this subject: 'our worker emerges from the process of production looking different from when he entered it. In the market, as owner of the commodity "labour-power", he stood face-to-face with other owners of commodities, one owner against another. The contract by which he sold his labour-power to the capitalist proved in Black and white, so to speak, that he was free to dispose of himself. But when the transaction was concluded, it was discovered that he was no "free agent", that the period of time for which he is free to sell his labour-power is the period of time for which he is forced to sell it, that in fact the vampire will not let go while there remains a single muscle, sinew or drop of blood to be exploited.' Marx, *Capital*, pp. 415–16.
7   Adorno, T. W. (1969/1998). 'Free Time'. In *Critical Models: Interventions and Catchwords*. Translated by Henry W. Pickford. New York: Columbia University Press.
8   Ibid, p. 173.
9   Barbrook, R. and Cameron, A. (1995). 'The Californian Ideology'. *Science as Culture*, 6: 44–72.
10 Weber, M. (1946). *From Max Weber: Essays in Sociology*. Translated by H. H. Gerth and C. Wright Mills. New York: Oxford University Press, p. 220.
11 Kunda, G. (1992). *Engineering Culture: Control and Commitment in a High-Tech Corporation*. Philadelphia: Temple University Press.
12 Ackroyd, S. and Crowdy, P. (1990). 'Can Culture Be Managed? Working with "Raw" Material – The Case of English Slaughterman'. *Personnel Review*, 19(5): 3–13.
13 Deleuze, G. (1992). 'Postscript on the Societies of Control'. *October*, 59: 3–7, p. 6.
14 O'Reilly, C. A. and Chatman, J. A. (1996). 'Culture as Social Control: Corporations, Cults, and Commitment'. In B. M. Staw and L. L. Cummings (eds). *Research in Organizational Behavior*. Vol. 18. Elsevier Science: JAI Press, pp. 157–200.

15. For a critical overview of human capital theory, see Fleming, P. (2017). 'The Human Capital Hoax: Work, Debt and Insecurity in the Era of Uberization'. *Organization Studies*, 38(5): 691–709.
16. Handy, C. (1994). *The Age of Paradox*. Cambridge, MA: Harvard Business School Press, p. 18.
17. Gerard Hanlon has closely studied these conceptual affinities. Hanlon, G. (2016). *The Dark Side of Management: A Secret History of Management Theory*. London: Routledge; Hanlon, G. (2018). 'The First Neo-liberal Science: Management and Neo-liberalism'. *Sociology*, 52(2): 298–315.
18. See von Mises, L. (1944). *Bureaucracy*. New Haven, CT: Yale University Press; de Jasay, A. (1985). *The State*. Indianapolis: The Liberty Fund.
19. Hilton, S. (2016). *More Human: Designing a World Where People Come First*. New York: W. W. Norton.
20. Ibid, p. 203.
21. In 2011, Hilton's most infamous big idea – the 'Red Tape Challenge' – was announced. The plan was to post 21,000 regulations online and invite the public to identify those they wanted scrapped. Regulations crush the little man he argued. Among the regulations Hilton especially distained were those associated with food safety and fire codes for new buildings.
22. Hilton, *More Human*, p. 163.
23. *US Equal Employment Opportunity Commission* (2015). EEOC Sues United Health Programs of America and Parent Company for Religious Discrimination. https://www.eeoc.gov/newsroom/eeoc-sues-united-health-programs-america-and-parent-company-religious-discrimination
24. Ibid.
25. In a 1976 interview about anarchism, Noam Chomsky conveyed this point better than anyone else: 'it's a mistake to think that even back-breaking physical labor is necessarily onerous. Many people, myself included, do it for relaxation. Well, recently, for example, I got it into my head to plant thirty-four trees in a meadow behind the house, on the State Conservation Commission, which means I had to dig thirty-four holes in the sand. You know, for me, and what I do with my time mostly, that's pretty hard work, but I have to admit I enjoyed it. But I wouldn't have enjoyed it if I'd had work norms, if I'd had an overseer, and if I'd been ordered to do it at a certain moment, and so on.' Chomsky, N. (1976). 'The Relevance of Anarcho-Syndicalism'. https://chomsky.info/19760725/
26. Adorno, T. W. (1954/2005). *Minima Moralia: Reflections on a Damaged Life*. Translated by E. F. N. Jephcott. London: Verso.

Chapter 4

1. Mann, T. (2018). 'Delivery Driver Did Poo in Customer's Garage Then Scooped It Up and Put It in Bin'. *Metro*. https://metro.co.uk/2018/12/19/delivery-driver-poo-customers-garage-scooped-put-bin-8264284/
2. Rodger, J. (2022). 'Hermes Driver Takes Photo of Dog Accepting Parcel as Proof of Delivery'. *Birmingham Mail*. https://www.birminghammail.co.uk/black-country/hermes-driver-takes-photo-dog-24311009
3. Thompson, P. (2018). 'Santa Paws! Labrador Rips Apart Pack of Christmas Party Dresses "Flung over Gate by Hermes Courier"'. *The Mirror*. https://www.mirror.co.uk/news/uk-news/Dog-rips-apart-parcel-flung-gate.
4. Booth, R. (2017). 'Hermes Courier: "I Felt Pressured to Work While Caring for My Dying Son"'. *The Guardian*. https://www.theguardian.com/business/2017/jan/26/hermes-courier-i-felt-pressured-work-while-caring-for-dying-son
5. *CEP-Research* (2022). 'Hermes UK Transforms into "Evri" after "Dramatic" Growth'. https://www.cep-research.com/news/hermes-uk-transforms-into-evri-after-dramatic-growth
6. Dialectical materialism often insists that cognitive models and rhetorical schemas play second fiddle to the concrete forces underlying the political economy of capitalism. However, if Kant is correct, then conception without perception might very well be emptiness, but perception without conception is blindness.
7. Mirowski, P. (2014). *Never Let a Serious Crisis Go to Waste: How Neoliberalism Survived the Financial Meltdown*. London: Verso.
8. Charmes, J. (2019). *The Unpaid Care Work and the Labour Market. An Analysis of Time Use Data Based on the Latest World Compilation of Time-Use Surveys*. Geneva: International Labour Organization.
9. Thompson, G. (2010). *Working in the Shadows: A Year of Doing Jobs (Most) Americans Won't Do*. New York: Nation Books.
10. Hayek, F. A. (1949). 'The Intellectuals and Socialism'. *University of Chicago Law Review*, 16: 417–33.
11. Polanyi, K. (1944/2001). *The Great Transformation: The Political and Economic Origins of Our Time*. Boston: Beacon Press, p. 3.
12. Hayek, 'The Intellectuals and Socialism', p. 432.
13. Stigler, G. J. (1945). 'The Cost of Subsistence'. *Journal of Farm Economics*, 27(2): 303–14.
14. Ibid, p. 312.
15. Theocarakis, N. (2010). 'Metamorphoses: The Concept of Labour in the History of Political Economy'. *The Economic and Labour Relations Review*, 20(2): 7–38.

16 Hayek writes, 'the noun "society", misleading as it is, is relatively innocuous compared with the adjective "social", which has probably become the most confusing expression in our entire moral and political vocabulary.' Hayek, F. A. (1988). *The Fatal Conceit*. Chicago: Chicago University Press, p. 114.
17 Hayek, F. A. (1944/1986). *The Road to Serfdom*. London: Routledge and Kegan Paul.
18 Ibid, pp. 92–3.
19 Ibid, p. 72.
20 Greenhalgh, L. and Rosenblatt, Z. (1984). 'Job Insecurity: Toward Conceptual Clarity'. *Academy of Management Review*, 9(3): 438–48, 438.
21 Lübke, C. (2021). 'How Self-Perceived Job Insecurity Affects Health: Evidence from an Age-Differentiated Mediation Analysis'. *Economic and Industrial Democracy*, 42(4): 1105–22.
22 In her excellent analysis of insecurity, Albena Azmanova (2020) terms this *precarious capitalism* given the crucial role it plays on the economic, governmental and ideological levels. It both extends and supersedes neoliberal or disorganized capitalism by placing new emphasis on statecraft for securing the conditions of insecurity. She writes, 'I have referred to this modality as "reorganized capitalism" and "aggregative capitalism" to set it apart from the previous, neoliberal form that Offe, Lash and Urry named "disorganized capitalism" or to highlight the rather peculiar function public authority performs in aggregating opportunities to actors who already have competitive advantage in the global economy while allocating risks. I have adopted the label "precarious capitalism" to bring into focus the massification of insecurity as its distinctive feature.' Azmanova, A. (2020). *Capitalism on Edge: How Fighting Precarity Can Achieve Radical Change without Crisis or Utopia*. New York: Columbia University Press, pp. 222–3.
23 Hayek, *The Road to Serfdom*, p. 94.
24 Epstein, R. (1985). *Takings: Private Property and the Power of Eminent Domain*. Cambridge, MA: Harvard University Press.
25 Epstein, R. (1992). *Forbidden Ground: The Case against Employment Discrimination Laws*. Cambridge, MA: Harvard University Press.
26 Epstein, R. (2020). 'Coronavirus Perspective: The Evidence Does Not Support Our Panicked Inferences'. *Hoover Institution*. https://www.hoover.org/research/coronavirus-pandemic
27 Chotiner, I. (2020). 'The Contrarian Coronavirus Theory That Informed the Trump Administration'. *The New Yorker*. https://www.newyorker.com/news/q-and-a/the-contrarian-coronavirus-theory-that-informed-the-trump-administration
28 Epstein, R. (2015). 'Contractual Solutions for Employment Law Problems'. *Harvard Journal of Law and Public Policy*, 38(3): 789–802.

29 Epstein, R. (1997). *Simple Rules for a Complex World*. Cambridge, MA: Harvard University Press.
30 Epstein, R. (1983). 'A Common Law for Labor Relations: A Critique of the New Deal Labor Legislation'. *The Yale Law Journal*, 92(8): 1357–408.
31 Ibid.
32 Epstein, R. (2013). 'The Coming Meltdown in Labor Relations. Speech Presented to the University of Chicago School of Law'. https://www.youtube.com/watch?v=tzRYHdkChXg&t=1512s
33 Mishel, L. and Bivens, J. (2021). 'Identifying the Policy Levers Generating Wage Suppression and Wage Inequality'. *Economic Policy Institute*. https://www.epi.org/unequalpower/publications/wage-suppression-inequality/
34 For example, see *Supreme Court of the United States* (2018). 'Epic Systems Corp v. Lewis'. https://www.supremecourt.gov/opinions/17pdf/16-285_q8l1.pdf
35 *Economic Policy Institute* (2017). 'The Growing Uses of Mandatory Arbitration'. https://www.epi.org/publication/the-growing-use-of-mandatory-arbitration/
36 Epstein, R. (1984). 'In Defense of the Contract at Will'. *University of Chicago Law Review*, 51(4): 947–82.
37 Ibid.
38 Epstein writes, 'there is little risk, moreover, that employers will seek to intimidate naïve workers with overly broad covenants when the new employer can assure them that they are not enforceable'. Epstein, R. (2022). 'The Unwise Extension of Antitrust Law to Labor Markets'. *Network Law Review*. https://www.networklawreview.org/epstein-antitrust-labor/
39 Epstein, R. (2021). 'Clueless on Competition'. *The Hoover Institution*. https://www.hoover.org/research/clueless-competition
40 Kwon, S. Y., Ma, Y. and Zimmermann, K. (2023). '100 Years of Rising Corporate Concentration'. *SAFE Working Paper No. #359*. https://ssrn.com/abstract=3936799
41 Epstein (1997). 'Employment Law: Courts and Contracts'. *California Western International Law Journal*, 28(1): 13–26. Also see Wailes, N. (1997). 'Professor Richard Epstein and the New Employment Contracts Act: A Critique'. *California Western International Law Journal*, 28(1): 27–43.
42 Nolan, H. (2013). 'Wal-Mart Is Scared of These True Stories from Its Own Employees'. *Gawker*. http://gawker.com/wal-mart-is-scared-of-these-true-stories-from-its-own-e-743832841
43 Vogel, S. (2021). 'How Companies Use Predictive Analytics to Get Ahead of Union Drives'. *HR Brew*. https://www.hr-brew.com/stories/2021/11/03/how-companies-use-predictive-analytics-to-get-ahead-of-union-drives
44 Conway, T. (2019). 'Unleashing Corporate Spies'. *United Steel Workers*. https://m.usw.org/blog/2019/unleashing-corporate-spies

Chapter 5

1. *Oxfam America* (2016). 'No Relief: The Denial of Toilet Breaks in the Poultry Industry'. Boston, MA: Oxfam America, p. 5.
2. Ibid.
3. Ibid.
4. *United* (2018). 'Thousands of Workers Are Being Denied Toilet Dignity in the Workplace'. https://www.unitetheunion.org/news-events/news/2018/november/thousands-of-workers-are-being-denied-toilet-dignity-in-the-workplace/
5. Pollard, C. (2018). 'Amazon Workers Pee into Bottles to Save Time: Investigator'. https://nypost.com/2018/04/16/amazon-warehouse-workers-pee-into-bottles-to-avoid-wasting-time-undercover-investigator/
6. Ibid.
7. Delfanti, A. (2021). *The Warehouse: Workers and Robots at Amazon*. London: Pluto.
8. Burin, M. (2019). 'They Resent the Fact I'm Not a Robot'. *Australian Broadcasting Corporation*. https://www.abc.net.au/news/2019-02-27/amazon-australia-warehouse-working-conditions/10807308
9. Ibid.
10. Ibid.
11. Brynjolfsson, E. and McAfee, A. (2014). *The Second Machine Age: Work, Progress, and Prosperity in a Time of Brilliant Technologies*. New York: Norton.
12. Susskind, Daniel (2020). *A World without Work: Technology, Automation and How We Should Respond*. London: Allen Lane; Frey, C. (2019). *The Technology Trap: Capital, Labour and Power in the Age of Automation*. New Haven, CT: Princeton University Press.
13. Frey, C. and Osborne, M. (2017). 'The Future of Employment: How Susceptible Are Jobs to Computerization?' *Technological Forecasting and Social Change*, 114: 254–80; Frey, C. and Osborne, M. (2018). 'Automation and the Future of Work: Understanding the Numbers'. *Oxford Martin School*. Retrieved from https://www.oxfordmartin.ox.ac.uk/blog/automation-and-the-future-of-work-understanding-the-numbers/; McKinsey Global Institute (2017). *Jobs Lost, Jobs Gained: Workforce Transitions in a Time of Automation*. Retrieved from https://www.mckinsey.com/MGI-Jobs-Lost-Jobs-Gained-Report-December-6-2017.pdf
14. Russell, Stuart (2019). *Human Compatible: Artificial Intelligence and the Problem of Control*. New York: Viking, p. 120.

15 For example, see Mason, Paul (2019). *Clear Bright Future: A Radical Defence of the Human Being*. London: Allen Lane; Bregman, Rutger (2017). *Utopia for Realists: And How We Can Get There*. London: Bloomsbury; Bastani, Aaron (2019). *Fully Automated Luxury Communism: A Manifesto*. London: Verso; Avent, Ryan (2016). *The Wealth of Humans: Work, Power and Status in the Twenty-First Century*. New York: St. Martin's Press.
16 Frase, Peter (2016). *Four Futures: Life after Capitalism*. London: Verso.
17 Ibid, p. 121.
18 Ford, Martin (2015). *The Rise of the Robots: Technology and the Threat of Mass Unemployment*. London: Oneworld Publications, p. 219.
19 Marx, K. (1973). *Grundrisse: Foundations of the Critique of Political Economy (Rough Draft)*. Translated by Martin Nicholaus. London: Penguin, p. 692. It's unsurprising that the labour theory of value is dismissed by mainstream economists. But that Marxists also do so is surprising. For example, in his reading of Marx's *Grundrisse*, Jurgen Habermas argues that Marx became sceptical of the idea, confessing that wealth creation depends less on labour time than markets and mechanization. Moishe Postone (1992) convincingly demonstrates, however, that Habermas wrongly conflates Marx's important distinction between *value* and *wealth*: '[Habermas] does not grasp Marx's distinction between value and material wealth, and, thus, between the abstract and concrete dimensions of commodity-producing labour. He assumes that Marx's labour theory of value was similar to that of classical political economy – an attempt to explain social wealth in general. Habermas maintains, therefore, that the labour theory was valid only for the stage of development of the technical forces of production when the creation of real wealth did, indeed, depend essentially on labour time and the amount of labour employed. With the rise of highly developed technology, value is based increasingly on science and technology rather than on direct human labour. Unlike those positions that posit labour as the transhistorical source of wealth, Habermas recognizes the *wealth*-creating potentials of science and technology, and their growing relevance to contemporary social life. He claims, however, that they constitute a new basis of *value*, and therefore conflates what Marx had distinguished'. Postone, M. (1992). *Time, Labor, and Social Domination: A Reinterpretation of Marx's Critical Theory*. New York: Cambridge University Press, p. 233.
20 Also see Resnikoff, Jason (2021). *Labour's End: How the Promise of Automation Degraded Work*. Champaign: University of Illinois Press; Benanav, A. (2020). *Automation and the Future of Work*. London: Verso.
21 Taylor, A. (2018). 'The Automation Charade'. *Logic(s)*. https://logicmag.io/failure/the-automationcharade/
22 Ibid.

23 This discursive use of technology is not new, of course (see Noble, 1984). Managers in the Fordist factory did much the same when advanced equipment was employed. But because smart machines are assumed to approximate human intelligence, as opposed to say the Moog tape-controlled boring machine (circa 1969), today's threat has more ideological purchase. Noble, D. (1984). *The Forces of Production: A Social History of Industrial Automation*. New York: Knopf.
24 For example, see Autor, D., Mindell, D. and Reynolds, E. (2022). *The Work of the Future: Building Better Jobs in an Age of Intelligent Machines*. Cambridge, MA: MIT Press.
25 Sartre, J-P. (1960/2004). *Critique of Dialectical Reason: Volume One – Theory of Practical Ensembles*. Translated by Alan Sheridan-Smith. London: Verso.
26 Crawford, K. (2021). *Atlas of AI: Power, Politics, and the Planetary Costs of AI*. New Haven, CT: Yale University Press.
27 Ibid, p. 65.
28 Rowe, Niamh (2023). '"It's Destroyed Me Completely": Kenyan Moderators Decry Toll of Training of AI Models'. *The Guardian*. https://www.theguardian.com/technology/2023/aug/02/ai-chatbot-training-human-toll-content-moderator-meta-openai
29 Ibid.
30 Smith, B. C. (2019). *The Promise of Artificial Intelligence: Reckoning and Judgement*. Cambridge, MA: MIT Press.
31 Ibid, pp. xix–xx.
32 Marcuse, H. (1941/1982). 'Some Social Implications of Modern Technology'. In Andrew Arato and Eike Gebhardt (eds). *The Essential Frankfurt School Reader*. New York: Continuum Publishing, pp. 138–62.
33 Ibid, p. 142.
34 Ibid, p. 149.
35 Indeed, explaining diaper-wearing workers though the lens of Marx's conception of alienation (*Entäusserung*) is revealing. It involves the literal loss of reality. Marx writes, 'so much does labor's realization appear as loss of reality that the worker loses reality to the point of starving to death. So much does objectification appear as loss of the object that the worker is robbed of the objects most necessary not only for his life but for his work. Indeed, labor itself becomes an object which he can obtain only with the greatest effort and with the most irregular interruptions.' Marx, K. (1988). *Economic and Philosophic Manuscripts of 1844*. Translated by Martin Milligan. New York: Promethean Books, p. 71.
36 Marcuse, 'Some Social Implications of Modern Technology', p. 145.
37 Ibid, p. 145.
38 Ibid, p. 143.

Chapter 6

1. *Victoria Legal Aid* (2022). 'Robo-Debt Client Stories'. https://www.legalaid.vic.gov.au/robo-debt-client-stories#melissas-story-%E2%80%93-a-private-debt-collector%E2%80%99s-actions-%E2%80%98doing-my-head-in-and-making-me-suicidal%E2%80%99
2. Ibid.
3. *Australian Government* (2017). Australian Government Response to the Community Affairs References Committee Report. Parliament House: Canberra, p. 5.
4. *Victoria Legal Aid*, 'Robo-Debt Client Stories'.
5. *Sydney Morning Herald* (2023). '"Sheer Terror": Rosemary's Horror at Her $65,000 Robo-Debt'. https://www.smh.com.au/politics/federal/sheer-terror-rosemary-s-horror-at-her-65-000-robo-debt-20230123-p5cess.html
6. Gramenz, E. (2023). 'Robodebt Victim Breaks Down at Royal Commission While Recalling "Intrusion" of "Rude" Human Services Staff'. *Australian Broadcasting Corporation*. https://www.abc.net.au/news/2022-12-16/qld-robodebt-scheme-government-royal-commission-victim/101780890
7. On the distinction between reckoning and judgement, see Smith, B. C. (2019). *The Promise of Artificial Intelligence: Reckoning and Judgment*. Cambridge, MA: MIT Press.
8. Also see Eubanks, V. (2017). *Automating Inequality: How High-Tech Tools Profile, Police, and Punish the Poor*. New York: St Martin's Press; O'Neil, C. (2016). *Weapons of Math Destruction: How Big Data Increases Inequality and Threatens Democracy*. New York: Broadway Books; Noble, S. (2018). *Algorithms of Oppression: How Search Engines Reinforce Racism*. New York: NYU Press.
9. Neate, R. (2023). 'Post Office Boss to Give Back Bonus Linked to Horizon Scandal Inquiry'. *The Guardian*. https://www.theguardian.com/business/2023/aug/23/post-office-boss-to-give-back-bonus-linked-to-horizon-scandal-inquiry
10. Flinders, K. (2022). 'Horizon System EPOSS Code Writers Lacked Basic Programming Skills, Public Inquiry Hears'. *Computer Weekly*. https://www.computerweekly.com/news/252526586/Horizon-system-EPOSS-code-writers-lacked-basic-programming-skills-public-inquiry-hears
11. See Pitron, G. (2023). *Dark Cloud: How the Digital World Is Costing the Earth*. Melbourne: Scribe; Allen, M. (2022). 'The Huge Carbon Footprint of Large-scale Computing'. *Physics World*. https://physicsworld.com/a/the-huge-carbon-footprint-of-large-scale-computing/

12 Casilli, A. A. (2024). *Waiting for the Robots: The Hired Hands of Automation.* Translated by Saskia Brown. Chicago: University of Chicago Press.
13 Joque, J. (2022). *Revolutionary Mathematics: Artificial Intelligence, Statistics and the Logic of Capitalism.* London: Verso Books.
14 Dastin, J. (2018). 'Amazon Scraps Secret AI Recruiting Tool That Showed Bias against Women'. *Reuters*. https://www.reuters.com/article/world/insight-amazon-scraps-secret-ai-recruiting-tool-that-showed-bias-against-women-idUSKCN1MK0AG/
15 Singleton, T., Gerken, T. and McMahon, L. (2023). 'How a Chatbot Encouraged a Man Who Wanted to Kill the Queen'. *BBC*. https://www.bbc.com/news/technology-67012224
16 Thierry, G. (2023). 'Giving AI Direct Control Over Anything Is a Bad Idea – Here's How It Could Do Us Real Harm'. *The Conversation*. https://theconversation.com/giving-ai-direct-control-over-anything-is-a-bad-idea-heres-how-it-could-do-us-real-harm-210168
17 See https://replika.com/
18 Pasquinelli, M. (2019). 'How a Machine Learns and Fails'. *Spheres: Journal for Digital Cultures.* https://doi.org/10.25969/mediarep/13490
19 Gillespie, T. (2016). 'Algorithm'. In B. Peters (ed.). *Digital Keywords: A Vocabulary of Information Society and Culture.* Princeton, NJ: Princeton University Press, pp. 18–30, p. 22.
20 These senators clearly had no idea how digital capitalism works. For example, Senator Hatch (R-Utah) thought he had outsmarted Zuckerberg when recalling their first meeting in 2010: 'You said back then that Facebook would always be free … if so, then how do you sustain a business model in which users don't pay for your service?' Zuckerberg was initially baffled by the question and then could barely contain his laughter. 'Senator', he replied, 'we run ads'. The elderly Senator Hatch looked on perplexed.
21 Heidegger, M. (1954/1977). *The Question Concerning Technology and Other Essays.* Translated by William Lovitt. New York: Harper and Row.
22 Ibid, p. 35.
23 Anders, G. (1956). *Die Antiquiertheit des Menschen Bd. II: Über die Zerstörung des Lebens im Zeitalter der dritten industriellen Revolution.* C. H. Beck: Munich.
24 Heidegger, *The Question Concerning Technology*, p. 27.
25 *The Senate, Community Affairs References Committee* (2017). Design, scope, cost-benefit analysis, contracts awarded and implementation associated with the Better Management of the Social Welfare System initiative. Australian Parliament House: Canberra, p. 73.
26 *Royal Commission into the Robodebt Scheme* (2023). 'Transcript Hearing Day 28–30 January 2023'. Australian Parliament House: Canberra, p. 2748.

27 *Royal Commission into the Robodebt Scheme* (2023). 'Transcript Hearing Day 29–1 February 2023'. Australian Parliament House: Canberra, p. 2903.

Chapter 7

1   Harlow, H. F., Dodsworth, R. O. and Harlow, M. K. (1965). 'Total Social Isolation in Monkeys'. *Proceedings of the National Academy of Sciences of the United States of America*. Proceedings of the National Academy of Sciences, 54(1): 90–7.
2   Prendergast, A. (2019). 'Thomas Silverstein, America's Most Isolated Prison, Dead at 67'. *Westworld*. https://www.westword.com/news/thomas-silverstein-americas-most-isolated-prisoner-dead-at-67-11342787
3   Benjamin's earlier work – the *Trauerspiel* study and 'Elective Affinities' article, for example – approaches this as the dissolution of subjective meaning and qualitative integration, particularly in the realm of aesthetics. Hence the importance of allegory. His later writing – the essays on Nikolai Leskov and Eduard Fuchs, and his final masterpiece, 'Theses on the Philosophy of History' – returns to this theme from a historical materialist perspective, in which socio-economic experience (interconnected with the mode of production) is central. For an excellent overview of how Benjamin's analysis of this idea evolved, see Wolin, R. (1982). 'Benjamin's Materialist Theory of Experience'. *Theory and Society*, 11(1): 17–42.
4   Cf. Deeming, R. (2023). *This Exquisite Loneliness: What Loners, Outcasts, and the Misunderstood Can Teach Us About Creativity*. New York: Viking Books.
5   Benjamin, W. (1933). 'Experience and Poverty'. Translated by Rodney Livingstone. In M. W. Jennings, H. Eiland and G. Smith (eds). (1999) *Walter Benjamin: Selected writings. Volume 2, part 2, 1931–1934*. Cambridge, MA: Harvard University Press, p. 733.
6   Nancy, J-L. (2008). *Corpus*. Translated by A. R. Richard. New York: Fordham University Press.
7   Ibid, p. 123.
8   Harvey, D. (1998). 'The Body as an Accumulation Strategy'. *Environment and Planning D: Society and Space*, 16(4): 401–21.
9   Adorno, T. W. (1962/1976). *Introduction to the Sociology of Music*. Translated by E. B. Ashton. New York: The Seabury Press.
10 Weber, M. (1958). *The Rational and Social Foundations of Music*. Translated by Don Martindale, Johannes Riedel and Gertrude Neuwirth. Carbondale: Southern Illinois University Press.

11   Adorno was correct about the mass commodification of music and its subsequent routinization. However, his criticism of jazz has become infamous for its ignorance. In his essay 'Perennial Fashion – Jazz', for example, Adorno argues that bebop did little new *vis-à-vis* conventional syncopation, sustained metre or the quarter-note. In addition, he claims,

> Jazz fans ... emphasize the music's improvisational features. But these are mere frills. Any precocious American teenager knows that the routine today scarcely leaves any room for improvisation, and that what appears as spontaneity is in fact carefully planned out in advance with machinelike precision ... thus, the so-called improvisations are actually reduced to the more or less feeble rehashing of basic formulas in which the schema shines through at every moment. Even the improvisations conform largely to norms and recur constantly. The range of the permissible in Jazz is as narrowly circumscribed as in any particular cut of clothes.

For me, this view is bizarre given bebop's use of chromatic passing notes, major third cycles and modal scalar melodies. The modal playing of John Coltrain, for example, clearly defies Adorno's claim. Modal jazz eschews chord variations and its limited range, working instead with modal scales, semiquavers and transposition (e.g. from Phrygian to Aeolian modes etc.). Chordal variation can only run for a certain number of bars before the need to repeat. In modal jazz, however, the possibilities are literally endless. Adorno, T. W. (1967/1988). 'Perennial Fashion – Jazz'. In *Prisms*. Translated by Samuel and Shierry Weber. Cambridge, MA: MIT Press, p. 123.

12   Cage's piece is often understood as the impossibility of silence. Even as the musicians play nothing, the auditorium is teeming with sounds. But another way to interpret 4'33 could be the idea that it's manufactured sound that is impossible because it ultimately fails *apropos* that ephemeral and unrepeatable din of the auditorium. A dominant motif in Western music is the idea that it transcends the crude sounds of nature. Cage is suggesting otherwise. For example, he argued that the twelve-tone scale is interesting because it has no zero note, unlike the standard eight-note scale. But this is just a different way of saying that all those notes *are zero*, as is the scale itself. Nature can never be zero. Only man. For more on this, see Cage's lecture on sound and nothingness. Cage, J. (1959/2011). 'Lecture on Nothing'. In *Silence: Lectures and Writings*. London: Marion Boyars Publishers, pp. 109–26.

13   For example, see Laporte, D. (1976/2000). *The History of Shit*. Translated by Rodolphe el-Khoury. Cambridge, MA: MIT Press; Skelton, L. (2020). *Sanitation in Urban Britain, 1560–1700*. Milton Park: Routledge.

14   Horkheimer, M. and Adorno, T. W. (1944/1997), *Dialectic of Enlightenment*. Translated by John Cumming. London: Verso.

15 'The dark closets have been abolished as a troublesome waste of space, and incorporated in the bathrooms. What psychoanalysis suspected, before it became itself a part of hygiene, has been confirmed. The brightest rooms are the secret domain of faeces.' Adorno, T. W. (1951/2005). *Minima Moralia: Reflections on a Damaged Life*. Translated by E. F. N. Jephcott. London: Verso, pp. 58–9.

16 Edmonds, J. E. (1928). *Military Operations, France and Belgium, 1915*, History of the Great War. London: Macmillan, p. 179.

17 Mande, J. (2023). 'Processed Foods Are Making Us Sick. It's Time for the FDA and USDA to Step In'. *Harvard Public Health Magazine*. https://harvardpublichealth.org/nutrition/processed-foods-make-us-sick-its-time-for-government-action/

18 Biakolo, K. (2020). 'A Brief History of the TV Dinner'. *Smithsonian Magazine*. https://www.smithsonianmag.com/arts-culture/brief-history-tv-dinner-180976039/

19 Fu, J. (2022). 'Can $1 Billion Really Fix a Meat Industry Dominated by Just Four Companies?' *The Counter*. https://thecounter.org/big-four-meatpackers-antitrust-consolidation/

20 *Food and Water Watch* (2021). 'The Economic Cost of Food Monopolies: The Grocery Cartels'. Washington, DC: Food & Water Watch.

21 Nuwer, R. (2014). 'The World's Most Endangered Food'. *BBC*. https://www.bbc.com/future/article/20140401-the-worlds-most-endangered-food

22 Mathews, R. (2023). '7 Extinct Fruits'. *AZ Animals*. https://a-z-animals.com/blog/7-extinct-fruits/

23 Newman, L. (2019). *Lost Feast: Culinary Extinction and the Future of Food*. Toronto: ECW Press.

24 Kristeva, J. (1982). *Powers of Horror: An Essay on Abjection*. Translated by Leon S. Roudiez. New York: Columbia University Press.

25 Herman, E. and Chomsky, N. (1988). *Manufacturing Consent: The Political Economy of the Mass Media*. New York: Pantheon Books.

26 Debord, G. (1967/1983). *Society of the Spectacle*. Detroit: Black & Red.

27 Baudrillard, J. (1996). *The Perfect Crime*. Translated by Charles Turner. London: Verso.

28 Ibid, p. 27.

29 Ion, F. (2013). 'From Touch Displays to the Surface: A Brief History of Touchscreen Technology'. *Ars Technica*. https://arstechnica.com/gadgets/2013/04/from-touch-displays-to-the-surface-a-brief-history-of-touchscreen-technology/

30 Nancy, J-L. *Corpus*.

31 Ibid, p. 45.

32 Ibid, p. 91.

33 Ibid, p. 93.

Chapter 8

1. In 2022, the Queenstown-Lakes district council rejected Thiel's planning permit for the 200-hectare complex due to its adverse ecological impact. It is difficult, however, to imagine that Thiel will simply give up there. I predict he will persist and gain consent within the next decade. In the meantime, the billionaire's other 'elite exit' strategy is 'Seasteaders', floating communities on the sea that are inaccessible to land dwellers and exempt from sovereign laws and regulations. Conceived by Thiel and Patri Friedman (Milton Friedman's grandson), these so-called 'startup communities' will enjoy complete political autonomy: 'The world needs a place where those who wish to experiment with building new societies and new technology can go to test out their ideas. Currently, it is very difficult to experiment with alternative social and governance systems on a small scale; countries are so enormous that it is hard for an individual to make much difference.' *The Seasteading Institute* (2023). 'Why Seastead?'. https://www.seasteading.org/faq/
2. Surpran, G., Rahmstorf and Oreskes, N. (2023). Assessing ExxonMobil's Global Warming Projections'. *Science*, 379. https://www.science.org/doi/10.1126/science.abk0063
3. Buis, A. (2022). 'Too Hot to Handle: How Climate Change May Make Some Places Too Hot to Live'. *NASA*. https://climate.nasa.gov/explore/ask-nasa-climate/3151/too-hot-to-handle-how-climate-change-may-make-some-places-too-hot-to-live/
4. Byron, G. (Baron) (1816/1994). 'Darkness'. In *Lord Byron: Selected Poetry*. Oxford: University of Oxford Press, p. 73.
5. Carrington, D. (2023). 'Cop28 Host UAE Planned to Promote Oil Deals during Climate Talks'. *The Guardian*. https://www.theguardian.com/environment/2023/nov/27/cop28-host-uae-planned-promote-oil-deals-climate-talks
6. Bregman, R. (2017). *Utopia for Realists: And How We Can Get there*. London: Bloomsbury; Wright, E. O. (2010). *Envisaging Real Utopias*. London: Verso Books; Levitas, R. (2013). *Utopia as Method: The Imaginary Reconstitution of Society*. Basingstoke: Palgrave; Ghodsee, K. (2023). *Everyday Utopia: What 2,000 Years of Wild Experiments Can Teach Us about the Good Life*. New York: Simon & Schuster.
7. Levitas, *Utopia as Method*, p. xi.
8. Bloch, E. (1923/2000). *The Spirit of Utopia*. Translated by Anthony A. Nasar. Stanford: Stanford University Press.
9. This is close to what Adorno termed *social physiognomics* where eidetic description is fused with genetic interpretation so that ostensibly isolated – *sui generis* – individual traits can reveal the overarching social structures that

produced them. See Adorno, T. W. (1993/2000). *Introduction to Sociology*. Translated by Edmund Jephcott. Stanford: Stanford University Press.
10   Wright, *Envisioning Real Utopias*, p. 1.
11   Benjamin, W. (1923/1978). 'Surrealism: The Last Snapshot of the European Intelligentsia'. *New Left Review*, 1(108): 47–56, p. 55.
12   Also see Traverso, E. (2016). *Left-Wing Melancholia: Marxism, History, and Memory*. New York: Columbia University Press.
13   Bloch, E. (1954/1986). *The Principle of Hope, Vol 1*. Translated by Neville Plaice, Stephen Plaice and Paul Knight. Cambridge, MA: MIT Press.
14   See Hayek, F. A. (1949). 'The Intellectuals and Socialism'. *University of Chicago Law Review*, 16: 417–33.
15   Marcuse, H. (1967/2005). 'The End of Utopia'. In *Marxists Internet Archive*. Translated by Jeremy Shapiro and Shierry M. Weber. https://www.marxists.org/reference/archive/marcuse/works/1967/end-utopia.htm
16   Bastani, Aaron (2019). *Fully Automated Luxury Communism: A Manifesto*. London: Verso. Mason, P. (2015). *Postcapitalism: A Guide to Our Future*. London: Allen Lane.
17   See Bender, F. (1981). 'The Ambiguities of Marx's Concepts of "Proletarian Dictatorship" and "Transition to Communism"'. *History of Political Thought*, 2(3): 525–55.
18   Mason, P. (2019). *Clear Bright Future: A Radical Defence of the Human Being*. London: Penguin.
19   Segal, L. (2017). *Radical Happiness: Moments of Collective Joy*. London: Verso.
20   Ibid, p. xiii.
21   Wilderson, F. B. III, Hartman, S., Martinot, S., Sexton, J. and Spillers, H. J. (2017). *Afro-Pessimism: An Introduction*. Minneapolis, MN: Racked & Dispatched.
22   R. L. (2013). 'Wanderings of the Slave: Black Life and Social Death'. *Mute*. https://www.metamute.org/editorial/articles/wanderings-slave-black-life-and-social-death
23   Wilderson, F. B. III. (2020). *Afropessimism*. New York: W. W. Norton & Sons, p. 225.
24   Anders, G. (1956). *Die Antiquiertheit des Menschen Bd. II: Über die Zerstörung des Lebens im Zeitalter der dritten industriellen Revolution*. C.H Beck: Munich.
25   Brecht, B. (1976). 'To Those Who Come after Us'. In *Bertolt Brecht Poems 1913–1956*. Translated by John Willett and Ralph Manheim. New York: Methuen, pp. 318–20.
26   Ibid, p. 320.

27 Blanchot, M. (1980/1995). *Writing of the Disaster*. Translated by Ann Smock. Lincoln: University of Nebraska Press.

Conclusion

1 Powell, Secretary Colin L. (5 February 2003). 'Remarks to the United Nations Security Council, 5 February 2003'. New York City: US Department of State. https://2001-2009.state.gov/secretary/former/powell/remarks/2003/17300.htm
2 Burnham, G., Lafta, R., Doocy, S. and Roberts, L. (2006). 'Mortality after the 2003 Invasion of Iraq: A Cross-Sectional Cluster Sample Survey'. *The Lancet*, 368(9545): 1421–8.
3 Escalona, A. (2012). '75 Years of Picasso's Guernica: An Inconvenient Masterpiece'. *Huffington Post*. https://www.huffpost.com/entry/75-years-of-picassos-guernica_b_1538776
4 Lukács, G. (1971). *History and Class Consciousness: Studies in Marxist Dialectics*. Translated by Rodney Livingstone. Cambridge, MA: MIT Press, p. 83.
5 Walker, M., Fleming, P. and Berti, M. (2021). 'You Can't Pick Up a Phone and Talk to Someone: How Algorithms Function as Biopower in the Gig Economy'. *Organization*, 28(1): 26–43.
6 Adorno, T. W. (1970/2021). *Negative Dialectics*. Translated by Dennis Redmond. Frankfurt am Main: Suhrkamp Verlag, p. 90.

Selected bibliography

Adorno, Theodor W. *Introduction to the Sociology of Music*. 1962. Translated by E. B. Ashton. New York: The Seabury Press, 1976.

Adorno, Theodor W. 'Perennial Fashion – Jazz'. In *Prisms*. 1967. Translated by Samuel and Shierry Weber, 121–32. Cambridge, MA: MIT Press, 1988.

Adorno, Theodor W. *Introduction to Sociology*. Translated by Edmund Jephcott. 1993. Standford: Stanford University Press, 2000.

Adorno, Theodor W. *Critical Models: Interventions and Catchwords*. 1963 and 1969. Translated by Henry W. Pickford. New York: Columbia University Press, 2005.

Adorno, Theodor W. *Minima Moralia: Reflections on a Damaged Life*. 1951. Translated by E. F. N. Jephcott. London: Verso, 2005.

Adorno, Theodor W. *Negative Dialectics*. 1970. Translated by Dennis Redmond. Frankfurt am Main: Suhrkamp Verlag, 2021.

Anders, Günther. *Die Antiquiertheit des Menschen Bd. II: Über die Zerstörung des Lebens im Zeitalter der dritten industriellen Revolution*. Munich: C.H Beck, 1956.

Arendt, Hannah. *Eichmann in Jerusalem: A Report on the Banality of Evil*. New York: Viking Press, 1963.

Arendt, Hannah. 'Thinking and Moral Considerations: A Lecture'. *Social Research* 38, no. 3 (1971): 417–46.

Autor, David, David Mindell and Elisabeth Reynolds. *The Work of the Future: Building Better Jobs in an Age of Intelligent Machines*. Cambridge, MA: MIT Press, 2022.

Avent, Ryan. *The Wealth of Humans: Work, Power and Status in the Twenty-First Century*. New York: St. Martin's Press, 2016.

Azmanova, Albena. *Capitalism on Edge: How Fighting Precarity Can Achieve Radical Change without Crisis or Utopia*. New York: Columbia University Press, 2020.

Barbrook, Richard and Andy Cameron. 'The Californian Ideology'. *Science as Culture* 6 (1995): 44–72.

Bastani, Aaron. *Fully Automated Luxury Communism: A Manifesto*. London: Verso, 2019.

Baudrillard, Jean. *The Perfect Crime*. Translated by Charles Turner. London: Verso, 1996.

Benanav, Aaron. *Automation and the Future of Work*. London: Verso, 2020.

Bender, Frederic L. 'The Ambiguities of Marx's Concepts of "Proletarian Dictatorship" and "Transition to Communism"'. *History of Political Thought* 2, no. 3 (1981): 525–55.

Benjamin, Walter. 'Surrealism: The Last Snapshot of the European Intelligentsia'. 1923. *New Left Review* 108 (1978): 47–56.

Blanchot, Maurice. *Writing of the Disaster*. 1980. Translated by Ann Smock. Lincoln: University of Nebraska Press, 1995.

Bloch, Ernst. *The Principle of Hope, Vol 1*. 1954. Translated by Neville Plaice, Stephen Plaice and Paul Knight. Cambridge, MA: MIT Press, 1986.

Bloch, Ernst. *The Spirit of Utopia*. 1923. Translated by Anthony A. Nasar. Stanford: Stanford University Press, 2000.

Bolchover, David. *The Living Dead: Switched Off, Zoned Out: The Shocking Truth about Office Life*. Oxford: Capstone, 2005.

Brecht, Bertolt. 'To Those Who Come after Us'. In *Bertolt Brecht Poems 1913–1956*. Translated by John Willett and Ralph Manheim, 318–20. New York: Methuen, 1976.

Bregman, Rutger. *Utopia for Realists: And How We Can Get There*. London: Bloomsbury, 2017.

Brynjolfsson, Erik and Andrew McAfee. *The Second Machine Age: Work, Progress, and Prosperity in a Time of Brilliant Technologies*. New York: Norton, 2014.

Cage, John. *Silence: Lectures and Writings*. London: Marion Boyars Publishers, 2011.

Casilli, Antonio A. *Waiting for the Robots: The Hired Hands of Automation*. Translated by Saskia Brown. Chicago: University of Chicago Press, 2024.

Chomsky, Noam. 'The Relevance of Anarcho-Syndicalism' (1976): https://chomsky.info/19760725/

Crawford, Kate. *Atlas of AI: Power, Politics, and the Planetary Costs of AI*. New Haven, CT: Yale University Press, 2021.

de Jasay, Anthony. *The State*. Indianapolis: The Liberty Fund, 1985.

Debord, Guy. *Society of the Spectacle*. 1967. Detroit: Black & Red, 1983.

Deeming, Richard. *This Exquisite Loneliness: What Loners, Outcasts, and the Misunderstood Can Teach Us about Creativity*. New York: Viking Books, 2023.

Deleuze, Gilles. 'Postscript on the Societies of Control'. *October* 59 (1992): 3–7.

Delfanti, Alessandro. *The Warehouse: Workers and Robots at Amazon*. London: Pluto, 2021.

Epstein, Richard. 'A Common Law for Labor Relations: A Critique of the New Deal Labor Legislation'. *The Yale Law Journal* 92, no. 8 (1983): 1357–408.

Epstein, Richard. 'In Defense of the Contract at Will'. *University of Chicago Law Review* 51, no. 4 (1984): 947–82.

Epstein, Richard. *Takings: Private Property and the Power of Eminent Domain*. Cambridge, MA: Harvard University Press, 1985.

Epstein, Richard. *Forbidden Ground: The Case against Employment Discrimination Laws*. Cambridge, MA: Harvard University Press, 1992.

Epstein, Richard. 'Employment Law: Courts and Contracts'. *California Western International Law Journal* 28, no. 1 (1997): 13–26.

Epstein, Richard. *Simple Rules for a Complex World*. Cambridge, MA: Harvard University Press, 1997.

Epstein, Richard. 'Contractual Solutions for Employment Law Problems'. *Harvard Journal of Law and Public Policy* 38, no. 3 (2015): 789–802.

Eubanks, Virginia. *Automating Inequality: How High-Tech Tools Profile, Police, and Punish the Poor*. New York: St Martin's Press, 2017.

Fink, Larry. 'The Power of Capitalism: Larry Fink's 2022 Letter to CEOs' (2022): https://www.blackrock.com/corporate/investor-relations/larry-fink-ceo-letter

Fisher, Mark. *Ghosts of My Life: Writings on Depression, Hauntology and Lot Futures*. London: Zer0 Books, 2014.

Fisher, Mark. *K-Punk: The Collected and Unpublished Writings of Mark Fisher*. London: Repeater Books, 2018.

Fleming, Peter. 'The Human Capital Hoax: Work, Debt and Insecurity in the Era of Uberization'. *Organization Studies* 38, no. 5 (2017): 691–709.

Ford, Martin. *The Rise of the Robots: Technology and the Threat of Mass Unemployment*. London: Oneworld Publications, 2015.

Frase, Peter. *Four Futures: Life after Capitalism*. London: Verso, 2016.

Freud, Sigmund. *Reflections on War and Death*. 1915. Translated by A. A. Brill and A. B. Kuttner. New York: Mofat, Yard and Company, 1918.

Frey, Carl. *The Technology Trap: Capital, Labour and Power in the Age of Automation*. New Haven, CT: Princeton University Press, 2019.

Frey, Carl and Michael Osborne. 'The Future of Employment: How Susceptible Are Jobs to Computerization?' *Technological Forecasting and Social Change* 114, (2017): 254–80.

Frey, Carl and Michael Osborne. 'Automation and the Future of Work: Understanding the Numbers'. *Oxford Martin School* (2018): https://

www.oxfordmartin.ox.ac.uk/blog/automation-and-the-future-of-work-understanding-the-numbers/

Fritzon, Katarina, Nathan Brooks and Simon Croom. *Corporate Psychopathy: Investigating Destructive Personalities in the Workplace*. Cham: Palgrave Macmillan, 2020.

Gelles, David. *The Man Who Broke Capitalism: How Jack Welch Gutted the Heartland and Crushed the Soul of Corporate America – and How to Undo His Legacy*. New York: Simon and Schuster, 2022.

Ghodsee, Kristen R. *Everyday Utopia: What 2,000 Years of Wild Experiments Can Teach Us about the Good Life*. New York: Simon & Schuster, 2023.

Gillespie, Tarleton. 'Algorithm'. In *Digital keywords: A Vocabulary of Information Society and Culture*, edited by Benjamin Peters, 18–30. Princeton, NJ: Princeton University Press, 2016.

Gioia, Dennis. 'Pinto Fires and Personal Ethics: A Script Analysis of Missed Opportunities'. *Journal of Business Ethics* 11 (1992): 379–89.

Greenhalgh, Leonard and Zehava Rosenblatt. 'Job Insecurity: Toward Conceptual Clarity'. *Academy of Management Review* 9, no. 3 (1984): 438–48.

Handy, Charles. *The Age of Paradox*. Cambridge, MA: Harvard Business School Press, 1994.

Hanlon, Gerard. *The Dark Side of Management: A Secret History of Management Theory*. London: Routledge, 2015.

Hanlon, Gerard. 'The First Neo-liberal Science: Management and Neo-liberalism'. *Sociology* 52, no. 2 (2018): 298–315.

Harvey, David. 'The Body as an Accumulation Strategy'. *Environment and Planning D: Society and Space* 16, no. 4 (1998): 401–21.

Harvey, Eric. *The Leadership Secrets of Santa Claus: How to Get Big Things Done in Your 'Workshop' … All Year Long*. Naperville, IL: Simple Truths, 2015.

Hayek, Friedrich A. 'The Intellectuals and Socialism'. *University of Chicago Law Review* 16 (1949): 417–33.

Hayek, Friedrich A. *The Road to Serfdom*. 1944. London: Routledge and Kegan Paul, 1986.

Hayek, Friedrich A. *The Fatal Conceit*. Chicago: Chicago University Press, 1988.

Hegel, Georg Wilhelm Friedrich. *Elements of the Philosophy of Right*. 1820. Translated by H. B. Nisbet. Cambridge: Cambridge University Press, 1991.

Heidegger, Martin. *Identity and Difference*. New York: Harper, 1969.

Heidegger, Martin. *The Question Concerning Technology and Other Essays*. 1954. Translated by William Lovitt. New York: Harper and Row, 1977.

Herman, Edward and Noam Chomsky. *Manufacturing Consent: The Political Economy of the Mass Media*. New York: Pantheon Books, 1988.

Hilton, Steve. *More Human: Designing a World Where People Come First*. New York: W.W. Norton, 2016.

Horkheimer, Max and Theodor W. Adorno. *Dialectic of Enlightenment*. 1944. Translated by John Cumming. London: Verso, 1997.

Jacoby, Sanford M. *Labor in the Age of Finance: Pensions, Politics, and Corporations from Deindustrialization to Dodd-Frank*. Princeton, NJ: University of Princeton Press, 2021.

Joque, Justin. *Revolutionary Mathematics: Artificial Intelligence, Statistics and the Logic of Capitalism*. London: Verso Books, 2022.

Kets de Vries, Manfried. 'The Psychopath in the C Suite: Redefining the SOB'. *Working Paper 119/EFE* (2021): https://papers.ssrn.com/sol3/papers.cfm?abstract_id=2179794

Kneale, Nigel. 'The Road'. *BBC Television*. London, 1964.

Kristeva, Julia. *Powers of Horror: An Essay on Abjection*. Translated by Leon S. Roudiez. New York: Columbia University Press, 1982.

Kwon, Spencer, Yueran Ma and Kaspar Zimmermann. '100 Years of Rising Corporate Concentration'. *SAFE Working Paper No. 359* (2023): https://ssrn.com/abstract=3936799

Laporte, Dominique. *The History of Shit*. 1976. Translated by Rodolphe el-Khoury. Cambridge, MA: MIT Press, 2000.

Lazzarato, Maurizio. *The Making of the Indebted Man: An Essay on the Neoliberal Condition*. Cambridge, MA: MIT Press, 2012.

Leeson, Nick. *Rogue Trader: How I Brought Down Barings Bank and Shook the Financial World*. Boston, MA: Little, Brown & Co, 1996.

Lemann, Nicholas. *Transaction Man: The Rise of the Deal and the Decline of the American Dream*. New York: Farrar, Straus and Giroux, 2019.

Levitas, Ruth. *Utopia as Method: The Imaginary Reconstitution of Society*. Basingstoke: Palgrave, 2013.

Lübke, Christiane. 'How Self-Perceived Job Insecurity Affects Health: Evidence from an Age-Differentiated Mediation Analysis'. *Economic and Industrial Democracy* 42, no. 4 (2021): 1105–22.

Lukács, Georg. *History and Class Consciousness: Studies in Marxist Dialectics*. 1919–1923. Translated by Rodney Livingstone. Cambridge, MA: MIT Press, 1971.

Malik, Kenan. *Not So Black or White: The History of Race from White Supremacy to Identity Politics*. London: C. Hurst & Co, 2023.

Marcuse, Herbert. 'Some Social Implications of Modern Technology'. 1941. In *The Essential Frankfurt School Reader,* edited by Andrew Arato and Eike Gebhardt, 138–64. New York: Continuum Publishing, 1982.

Marcuse, Herbert. *One-Dimensional Man: Studies in the Ideology of Advanced Industrial Society*. 1964. Boston: Beacon Press, 1991.

Marcuse, Herbert. 'The End of Utopia'. 1967. In *Marxists Internet Archive*. Translated by Jeremy Shapiro and Shierry M. Weber, 1967/2005. https://

www.marxists.org/reference/archive/marcuse/works/1967/end-utopia.htm, 2005.

Marx, Karl. *Grundrisse: Foundations of the Critique of Political Economy (Rough Draft)*. Translated by Martin Nicholaus. London: Penguin, 1973.

Marx, Karl. *Capital: A Critique of Political Economy – Volume One*. 1867. Translated by Ben Folks. New York: Penguin Books, 1976.

Marx, Karl. *Economic and Philosophic Manuscripts of 1844*. Translated by Martin Milligan. New York: Promethean Books, 1988.

Mason, Paul. *Postcapitalism: A Guide to Our Future*. London: Allen Lane, 2015.

Mason, Paul. *Clear Bright Future: A Radical Defence of the Human Being*. London: Allen Lane, 2019.

McTaggart, J. M. E. 'The Unreality of Time'. *Mind* 17 (1908): 457–73.

Mirowski, Philip. *Never Let a Serious Crisis Go to Waste: How Neoliberalism Survived the Financial Meltdown*. London: Verso, 2014.

Nancy, Jean-Luc. *Corpus*. Translated by Richard A. Rand. New York: Fordham University Press, 2008.

Newman, Lenore. *Lost Feast: Culinary Extinction and the Future of Food*. Toronto: ECW Press, 2019.

Noble, David. *The Forces of Production: A Social History of Industrial Automation*. New York: Knopf, 1984.

Noble, Safiya U. *Algorithms of Oppression: How Search Engines Reinforce Racism*. New York: NYU Press, 2018.

O'Neil, Cathy. *Weapons of Math Destruction: How Big Data Increases Inequality and Threatens Democracy*. New York: Broadway Books, 2016.

Pasquinelli, Matteo. 'How a Machine Learns and Fails'. *Spheres: Journal for Digital Cultures* (2019): https://doi.org/10.25969/mediarep/13490

Pitron, Guillaume. *Dark Cloud: How the Digital World Is Costing the Earth*. Melbourne: Scribe, 2023.

Polanyi, Karl. *The Great Transformation: The Political and Economic Origins of Our Time*. 1944. Boston: Beacon Press, 2001.

Postone, Moishe. *Time, Labor, and Social Domination: A Reinterpretation of Marx's Critical Theory*. New York: Cambridge University Press, 1992.

Power, Nina. *One-Dimensional Woman*. Winchester: Zer0 Books, 2009.

R. L. 'Wanderings of the Slave: Black Life and Social Death'. *Mute* (2013): https://www.metamute.org/editorial/articles/wanderings-slave-black-life-and-social-death

Resnikoff, Jason. *Labour's End: How the Promise of Automation Degraded Work*. Champaign: University of Illinois Press, 2021.

Rhodes, Carl and Peter Fleming. 'Forget Political Corporate Social Responsibility'. *Organization* 27, no. 6 (2020): 943–51.

Russell, Stuart. *Human Compatible: Artificial Intelligence and the Problem of Control*. New York: Viking, 2019.
Sandberg, Sheryl. *Leaning In: Women, Work and the Will to Lead*. New York: Alfred A. Knopf, 2013.
Sartre, Jean-Paul. *Critique of Dialectical Reason: Volume One – Theory of Practical Ensembles*. 1960. Translated by Alan Sheridan-Smith. London: Verso, 2004.
Sartre, Jean-Paul. *Being and Nothingness: An Essay on Phenomenological Ontology*. 1943. Translated by Sarah Richmond. New York: Atria Books, 2021.
Segal, Lynne. *Radical Happiness: Moments of Collective Joy*. London: Verso, 2021.
Skelton, Leona J. *Sanitation in Urban Britain, 1560–1700*. Milton Park: Routledge, 2020.
Smith, Brian Cantwell. *The Promise of Artificial Intelligence: Reckoning and Judgement*. Cambridge, MA: MIT Press, 2019.
Solanas, Valerie. *SCUM Manifesto*. 1967. London: Verso, 2004.
Stigler, George J. 'The Cost of Subsistence'. *Journal of Farm Economics* 27, no. 2 (1945): 303–14.
Susskind, Daniel. *A World without Work: Technology, Automation and How We Should Respond*. London: Allen Lane, 2020.
Taylor, Astra. 'The Automation Charade'. *Logic(s)* (2018): https://logicmag.io/failure/the-automation charade/
Taylor, Frederick Winslow. *The Principles of Scientific Management*. 1911. New York: W.W. Norton, 1967.
Theocarakis, Nicholas. 'Metamorphoses: The Concept of Labour in the History of Political Economy'. *The Economic and Labour Relations Review* 20, no. 2 (2010): 7–38.
Thompson, Gabriel. *Working in the Shadows: A Year of Doing Jobs (Most) Americans Won't Do*. New York: Nation Books, 2010.
Tooze, Adam. *Crashed: How a Decade of Financial Crises Changed the World*. New York: Penguin, 2018.
Traverso, Enzo. *Left-Wing Melancholia: Marxism, History, and Memory*. New York: Columbia University Press, 2016.
Van Zee, Art. 'The Promotion and Marketing of OxyContin: Commercial Triumph, Public Health Tragedy'. *American Journal of Public Health* 99, no. 2 (2009): 221–7.
von Mises, Ludwig. *Bureaucracy*. New Haven, CT: Yale University Press, 1944.
Wailes, Nick. 'Professor Richard Epstein and the New Employment Contracts Act: A Critique'. *California Western International Law Journal* 28, no. 1 (1997): 27–43.

Walker, Michael, Peter Fleming and Marco Berti. 'You Can't Pick up a Phone and Talk to Someone: How Algorithms Function as Biopower in the Gig Economy'. *Organization* 28, no. 1 (2021): 26–43.

Weber, Max. *From Max Weber: Essays in Sociology*. Translated by H. H. Gerth and C. Wright Mills. New York: Oxford University Press, 1946.

Weber, Max. *The Rational and Social Foundations of Music*. Translated by Don Martindale, Johannes Riedel and Gertrude Neuwirth. Carbondale: Southern Illinois University Press, 1958.

Welch, Jack. *Jack: Straight from the Gut*. New York: Headline Publishing Group, 2001.

Wilderson, Frank B. III. *Afropessimism*. New York: W.W Norton, 2020.

Wilderson, Frank B. III., Saidiya Hartman, Steve Martinot, Jared Sexton and Hortense Spillers. *Afro-pessimism: An Introduction*. Minneapolis: Racked & Dispatched, 2017.

Wolin, Richard. 'Benjamin's Materialist Theory of Experience'. *Theory and Society* 11, no. 1 (1982): 17–42.

Wright, Erik Olin. *Envisaging Real Utopias*. London: Verso Books, 2010.

Yunkaporta, Tyson. *Sand Talk: How Indigenous Thinking Can Save the World*. Melbourne: The Text Publishing, 2019.

Acknowledgements

Numerous good friends and colleagues helped me to write this book. As per usual, these ideas evolved out of long discussions with Gerry Hanlon, Stefano Harney and Matteo Mandarini. I'm indebted to their intellectual generosity, but most of all their friendship. Both Gerry Hanlon and Albena Azmanova gave excellent feedback on the initial proposal, which was so helpful. Katrina Calsado, Ben Piggott and Liza Thompson at Bloomsbury have been super supportive. When travelling together in Italy (Summer 2024), Carl Cederström graciously tolerated my preoccupation with editing the manuscript and gave invaluable advice on style, cadence and argumentation (including one paragraph that we spent literally hours on). Many of the arguments were road-tested at the annual Lake Como Summer School of Advanced Studies. I thank students and participants, and especially my co-organizers Mauro Magatti, Hans-Peter Müller, Monica Martinelli and Cesare Silla, for engendering such fruitful conversations over the last few years. My colleagues at the University of Technology Sydney have also been much inspiration, particularly Carl Rhodes, Bronwen Dalton, Simon Darcy, and the late Dean Jarrett. Jana Costas kindly double-checked my German, which I'm grateful for. Many thanks to Amelia Seddon for her wonderful cover image. And finally, any mistakes or inaccuracies remain my responsibility alone.

Index

absent leaders 46, 48
Adorno, T. W. 37, 56–7, 70, 138, 140–2, 175, 178 n.9
   Dialectic of the Enlightenment 178 n.9
   mass commodification of music 191 n.11
   Minima Moralia 142
   'Perennial Fashion – Jazz' 191 n.11
   social physiognomics 193 n.9
   work/non-work dichotomy 56
advanced capitalism 39, 42, 89, 102, 135, 160
Advent International (company) 72
afropessimism 163
aggregative capitalism 183 n.22
AIDS epidemic (1980) 133–4
algocracy 114, 121–2
Amazon, warehouse worker life in 92–4, 105–6
American capitalism 61
   militarization of 35
American sociality 37
amoral man 17–18, 27
analytical rite 75
Anarchism xii
anarcho-capitalists 57, 65, 77, 157
Anders, G. 123
   naked apocalypse 164
anorexia 132, 147

Anthropocene 29, 40
anti-Black violence 163
anti-moral man 22, 27
antitrust laws 87
anti-work movement 96
Arendt, H. 11, 24
   non-thought 14
   trial of Adolf Eichmann (1961) 11–14
Aristotle 123–4
artificial intelligence (AI) 101, 118–19
   AI-architecture 122
   AI-driven mechanization 96
   AI-power chatbot 119
   algorithms 89, 95
   faking AI 100
Australia, overpayment cases 109–13
automated feudalism 96
automation/automation technology 76, 93, 94, 95
   ideology of 97–8
   and job substitution 90
   new-wave 95
   semi-automation 98–9, 103
Azmanova, A., precarious capitalism 183 n.22

Babbage, C. 116
Babylonia 116

Bankman-Fried, S. 29
bannus malum 11
Barings Bank 21
Bastani, A., *Fully Automated Luxury Communism* 162
Baudrillard, J., *The Perfect Crime* 149
Bayesian mathematical modelling 118
Beam (robot) 1–4
Becker, G. 88
Bell Laboratories (company) 140
Benjamin, W. 134–5, 140
   'always-the-same' (*das Immergleiche*) 135
   deeper solitude 36
   organized pessimism 158
   Trauerspiel study and 'Elective Affinities' 190 n.3
Bezos, J. 97
Biden, J. 87
Big Data 120
biodiversity crisis 146
BlackRock (company) 25–6
Blanchot, M., *The Writing of the Disaster* 166–7
Bloch, E.
   The Principle of Hope 159
   secular spiritualism 156
Bloodworth, J. 92
Bolchover, D., *The Living Dead* 45
Boudica, Queen 5
Brecht, B. 178 n.9
   'To Those Who Are Born Afterwards' 166
Bregman, R., *Utopia for Realists* 157, 159
brutality (brutal) xii
   of dematerialization xi
   e-brutalism 114, 122
   separation and individuation ix–xi
   statistical brutalism 121
   and violence xi
Buchanan, J. M. 88
burdened individuality xii
bureaucracy 60–1, 64–5, 67, 110, 125, 160
   anti-capitalist critique of 69
   bureaucratic rationality 63
   paperless 47
   pro-capitalist critique of 69
business-as-usual approach 4, 153

Cage, J. 141, 191 n.12
Californian Ideology 57
Cameron, D. 65
capital accumulation process 48, 74, 90
capitalism viii, 14, 21, 41, 75, 158, 172. *See also* racial capitalism
   aggregative 183 n.22
   and bourgeois individualism xi
   debureaucratize 65
   disorganized 183 n.22
   identity of ix
   socially correct 25
   spirit of 3, 16, 44
capitalist labour process 105
capital-labour compact 61
carbon emissions, effects 153–4
carbon reduction schemes 154
Carillion (company) 28
catastrophic equilibrium 43–4
Cathode-Ray-Tube 147
Cato Institute 84
causality, types of 123
   causa effiens 123–5, 128–9
   causa finalis 123–4
   causa formalis 123
   causa materalis 123
Centrelink, overpayment cases 109–13

Chaplin, C. 99
charismatic leadership 21, 44
Chicago Schools of Economics and Law 73, 83
China
   bureaucracies 60–1
   IT-despotism in 114
Chomsky, N. 148, 181 n.25
Cobb, G.
   impossible machines 5–6
   slavery 5
coercive abstraction 174–5
cognitive capitalism 40
collective aphantasia xi, 28
Coltrain, J. 191 n.11
Common Crawl 117
computational systems 113
computerization 95, 116, 118
Constellis/Blackwater (company) 25
contemporary capitalism 2, 5, 28, 34, 69
COP28 climate summit 155
corporate cultures 19, 21, 33, 53, 62–3, 103
corporate feminism 51–2
corporate governance 48
corporate psychopathy 22, 24
Corporate Social Responsibility (CSR) 25
corporate unthinking 14
cost-saving reforms 63
Cotard, J., delirium of negation/walking corpse syndrome 180 n.4
Covid-19 pandemic 4, 39, 72, 83, 99, 133
   Communications Itinerary Card app 114
   creative-writing possibilities of loneliness 135
   food 146
   social ramifications 134
   tocuh 150
Crawford, K. 99
critical theory 2, 44, 69, 95, 104, 121, 158
cultural materialism 137
cybernetics and authoritarianism 114

dark realism 155–6, 167
Debord, G., *Society of the Spectacle* 148–9
deep machine learning 100, 121–2
deindustrialization of Western economies 15, 20, 141
de Jasay, A., *The State* 65
Deleuze, G. 43, 62
democratization of sovereignty x
Department of Human Services (DHS) 110–12, 127–8
dialectical materialism 182 n.6
Diamond, B. 24
Diana, Princess 134
diaper-wearing workers 187 n.35
Dick, P. K. 53
Diggin a Hole in Our Heart (painting) 29
digital capitalism 115, 121, 189 n.20
digitalization 4, 19, 99, 104, 116, 121
digital machinery 114
digital media platforms 151
digitization 115–16
disorganized capitalism 183 n.22
double-bind functions 157–8
driverless trains systems 95
Dunlap, 'Chainsaw Al' 44
Dutch East India Company 26
dystopian moment 159–60

e-brutalism 114, 122
economy (economic) 35, 41, 45, 49–50, 69, 74

automaticity 28
equality 32, 51, 73
gig 71–2, 74, 80, 85, 105, 172
independence and self-determination 73, 133
inequality 32, 51, 73, 96
insecurity 81–2, 183 n.22
liberalism 77
problem 96
rationality 172
scarcity 4, 82
time 57
universalism 58
eco-socialism 157
Edison, T. 23
Eichmann, A., trial of 11–14
elite exit strategy 153, 193 n.1
Ellis, B. E., *American Psycho* 22
Employee Free Choice Act 84
employer and employee 60, 62–3, 65, 67, 81, 83–6, 104, 184 n.38
employment law 72, 83–4, 87
employment relationship 63, 75, 80
English Factory Acts 56
enlightenment 36
Enron (company) 20, 23
Environment, Social and Governance (ESG) programmes 155
Epstein, R. 83–8, 183 n.38
exit option 85
Hoover Institution 83
equal temperament of twelve 140
ethical degenerations (economic sphere) 27
ethico-sadism 24
ethno-nationalism 40
'Evil Boss' 68–9
exclusive inclusion 74
Exxon (company) 154
'Eye in the Sky' analytics 89

faking AI 100
false interiority 59
false truth telling 48
fast-food workers 91, 93, 99
Fastow, A. 24
fatalism and resignation 5, 155–6, 167
faux-moral man 26–7
Federal Arbitration Act 85
Ferreira Da Silva, D. ix
financial capitalism 21, 26, 49–50
Fink, L. 25–6
First World War 143
fiscal policies 160
Fisher, M. 4–5
Food and Drug Administration 145
food production 144, 146
Fordism, crisis of 15, 17–20, 56
Fordist period, dominant industrial relations paradigm 60
Ford, M. 96
formal deformalization 66
formal freedom 56, 85
Frase, P. 96
free time 56–7
Freud, S. 55, 133, 163
Friedman, M. 57
Friedman, P. 193 n.1
Frito-Lay (company) 146
Fuchs, E. 190 n.3
Fuld, R. 24, 44
Fulfilment Centre 94
future of work 3

gas warfare 143–4
Gay, R. 112, 128
GE Capital (company) 23
gender inequality 51
General Electric (company) 18, 62
gig economy 71–2, 74, 80, 85, 105, 172

Index

Gillespie, T. 121
global capitalism 23, 46, 167
global economic system 164–5
global financial crisis 23–7, 44
good stewardship 46
Goodwin, F. 'The Shred' 24
gothika economica 76, 89–90
GPT-3 117
GPT-4 99–100, 118
Gramsci, A., optimism of spirit 157–8
'Grand Refusal' 39
Great Disengagement 45
Great Stink of London 142
green capitalism 153
Green, J. 29
Grothendieck, A. 179 n.14
Guattari, F. 43

Habermas, J. 186 n.19
hallucinations 118
Handy, C. 64
haphephobia (touch phobia) 133
Harlow, H., mating farm 131–2
Hartman, S. xii
Harvey, E., *The Leadership Secrets of Santa Claus* 46–7
Hassall, T. 5
hauntology xiii, 4
Hawks Nest Tunnel incident 61
Hayek, F. A. 57, 74, 77–81, 84, 88, 133, 159, 183 n.16
  'The Intellectuals and Socialism' 77
  organized socialism 82
  political universe 82
  pragmatism 77
  The Road to Serfdom 80
heat maps model 89
Hegel, G. W. F. 2
Heidegger, M. 59, 125–6, 129
  enframing 124
  'On the Question of Technology'

  (*Die Frage nach der Technik*) 122–4
  standing reserve 124
Herman, E. 148
Hermes UK (company) 72–3
Hilton, S. 65–6
  More Human 65
  'Red Tape Challenge' 181 n.21
Horizon 114
Horkheimer, M. 142, 178 n.9
Howson, R. 28
humachines 94–5
human capital theory 76
human labour 90, 98, 115, 186 n.19
  and capitalist machine 97
human remainder 93–4, 98
human robotic mimesis 95, 99–100, 102
human touch 131–4
  blendticity 137
  and cancellation 136
  deracination 135
  phenomenology 136
Hussain, S. 169–70
Hyowon Healing Centre 53, 55–6, 58
  death workshop 66
  wellness workshop 53

ideology ix, 3, 16, 21, 57, 61, 63, 79, 88, 101, 142, 152, 175
  of automation 97–8
  ideological distortion 171
  ideological mystification 170–1
  Ideologiekritik 170
  management 63
  of mass sanitation 143
  of objectivity 121
inclusive exclusion 74
individual employment contracts 84–5
  at-will contracts 86–7

individuality/individuation x, 10, 63
  bourgeois xi
  burdened xii
  cataclysmic fantasy of x
  collective individualism 36
  principium individuationis 59
  psudo-individualism 142
  self-determination 56
industrial development 61
industrial food production techniques 146
inequality 15, 24, 32, 113, 160
  economic 51
  gender 51
  socio-economic 80, 96
  and workers' rights 73
institutional man 16
isolation principle 132–4

Al Jaber, Sultan 155
Jameson, F. xiii
Jevons, W. S. 75
Jones, R. 22
Joque, J. 118
Joy Division, 'She's Lost Control' 141
Juukan Gorge 10, 29

Kamper, D. 116
Kant, I. 12–13
Kenyan workers, GPT-4 100
King, M. L. 37
K-means clustering 117
Kneale, N., *The Road* 5–6
Kodak (company) 18, 62

labour 18, 23, 72, 74, 77, 82, 84, 90, 95, 173. *See also* paid employment
  cypherization of 173
  dematerialization 76
  de-representation of 75
  digital transposition of 173
  as disutility 79
  generalizability 75
  ideational effacement of 78
  law 84
  and liberty 57
  life and 14, 57–8
  modern capitalism 60
  normative evacuation of 76
  privatization of work 175
  reconceptualization 74
  semi-invisibilization 75
  and shopping 35
  unit-price of 80
labour-power 180 n.6
labour time 54, 97, 186 n.19
  social 104
  temporal bifurcation of 56
laissez-faire capitalism 73
Lancet study 169
Late Glacial Period 9
Leeson, N. 20
Lemann, N., *Transaction Man* 16
Leskov, N. 190 n.3
Leverkühn, A. 138
Levin, I., *The Stepford Wives* 37
Levitas, R. 156
LG Prada 150
liberal capitalism 16, 24, 35
Lovelace, A. 116

machine learning 118
  deep 100, 122
  and digital statistical modelling 120
  and neural nets 115
machine music 138, 140–1
machines 5, 99, 101–2, 107, 120, 125–7
  digital 113–14
  humachine 94–5

and human 103, 150
impossible 6, 90
and organism 103
smart 98, 100, 187
Mad Men 103
magnetic tape 140
managerial ethics 14, 20
    corporate psychopathy 22, 24
managerialism 15–18, 20, 26, 74
    banalization of 175
    formal deformalization 66
    reformulation 61
Mann, T., *Doktor Faustus* 138
Marcuse, H. 35–40, 42–3, 50, 178 n.9
    economic domination 35
    'The End of Utopia' 161
    One-Dimensional Man 35,
        38–9, 43, 50 (*see also* one-
        dimensional man/one-
        dimensionality)
    'On Some Social Implications of
        Technology' 101–2, 105–7
market individualism 63
Marxism xii
Marx, K. 56, 60, 64, 85, 98, 104–5,
    161–3, 180 n.6
    alienation (*Entäusserung*) 187
        n.35
    Grundrisse 186 n.19
    relative surplus value 97
    value and material wealth 186
        n.19
Mason, P., *Postcapitalism* 162
mass communications 147
mass incarceration movement 134
mass media 38, 147
mass sanitation 143
mass visuality 149
maternal/infant bond 131
Mazie 71–2
McTaggart, J. M. E. 43

Mengers, C. 75
mergers/acquisitions 20
Metal Machine Music 141
methodological anachronism 3
Metropoulos, A. x
Mises, L. von 133
    Bureaucracy 65
modern capitalism 60, 134, 151
modernity 125, 133, 135, 139, 174
modern technology 101, 124–5
Modern Times 99
monopoly capitalism 87
Moten, F. xi
mother-surrogate (experiments) 132
Mozart Muzak 129

naïve systems 2
Nancy, J.-L. 136
    Corpus 151
National Industrial Labour Relations
    Board 84
National Security Agency 171
neo-blindness 28, 48
neoclassical economics 64, 73–4, 88,
    93, 172
neoclassical economists 57, 63, 74,
    88, 133, 159
neoliberal capitalism 16, 24, 160
neoliberalism 20–1, 40, 73, 134
neoliberalization of society 75
neoliberal revolution 133
neo-Luddism 101
New Deal 84, 86
new economy 69, 85
new utopian movement 155–9
new-wave automation technology 95
The New Yorker magazine 83
New Zealand
    apocalypse bunkers 153
    industrial relations system 87–8
nihilolithic dimensionality 44, 50

meta-structural level 48
non-feminism 52
nihilolithic hauntology xiii
no-dimensional man/no-dimensionality 33–5, 39, 42–4, 50, 52, 175
non-routine-mental work 95
non-work, concept of 79
nothingness philosophy 7, 40, 42, 58, 75, 103, 141, 167, 171, 174–5
now-time 2–3, 135–6

ocean acidification 154
The Office 66
one-dimensional man/one-dimensionality 35–6, 39, 43, 50
   absolute technique, hypostatization 37–8
   administrative superego 42
   consciousness, collapse of 40
   elemental indivisibility 37
   labour and shopping 35
   monolithic world of conformity 43
Onionhead (Christian movement) 66–7
Online Compliance Intervention (OCI) 110–11, 127–8
ontological totality xii
OpenAI 99, 117
optimization 127
organized ignorance xi, 47–8
organized non-thinking, theory of 11
Otto Group (company) 72
overpayment cases 109–13
Oxfam America 91–2
OxyContin 31–4, 41–2

paid employment 4, 58, 60, 66, 70, 76, 96–7, 160
   ideological landscape 56, 76
   radical individualization 60
Panama Papers 49
paperless bureaucracy 47
Paris Agreement 153
part-time employment 64, 111, 171
Pasquinelli, M. 120
Paycheck Fairness Act 84
performative principle 44
pessimism 126, 158, 163
   dejection and 161
   organized 158
   revolutionary 158
Pfleumer, F. 140
Picasso, P., *Guernica* 169–71
Playboy magazine 50
poiēsis 124, 126, 128
Point Blank Capitalism 28
Polanyi, K. 77
population policy 70
post-industrialization (post-industrial) 17, 56, 58, 104, 148
   capitalism 172, 175
   economy 70, 93–4, 162
post-millennial commerce 41
Postone, M. 186 n.19
post-Second World War 61, 144
post-war America 35
poultry workers 91, 95
Powell, C. 169–70
Power, N., *One-Dimensional Woman* 50
precarious capitalism 183 n.22
predictive policing/algorithms 114, 120–1
principium individuationis 59
Proximal Policy Optimization 118
psudo-individualism 142

psychoanalysis 42, 55, 147, 192 n.15
Purdue Pharma (company) 32
   business model 33
   marketing approach 33
Puutu Kunti Kurrama and Pinikura (PKKP) people 10

quantitative psychosis 18–19, 27

racial capitalism viii–ix, xii
   brutal separation and individuation ix–xi
   geocidal and genocidal separation xi
   material and intellectual, separation x
Reagan, R. 61
Reed, L. 141
religion of technology 4
reorganized capitalism 183 n.22
Replika 119
Rio Tinto (company) 7, 10–11, 14, 29
   Cultural Heritage Management System 27
Robinson, C. viii–ix, xii–xiii
Robodebt 110, 113–15, 117, 120, 122, 126–8
robotic marine submersibles 95
Rousseau, J-. J. 20
routine-mental work 95
Royal Commission 128
Rumsfeld, D. 48
Russell, S. 95
Ryanair or Frontier Airlines 41

Sackler, R. 33–4, 41, 44
Sandberg, S., *Leaning In* 51
Sartre, J.-P. 42, 99
Schillinger, J. 139–40

The Schillinger Theory of Musical Composition 139–40
Sebald, W. G. 166
Second Machine Age 95
secular spiritualism 156
security, types 81–2
Seductive Operational Bully (S.O.B.) 24
Segal, L., *Radical Happiness* 162
self-mockery 26
semi-automation 98–9, 103
sensations
   decline of vision 147–50
   smells 141–4
   taste 144–7
   touch 150–2
sensibility 135, 137
   accumulation strategy 136
   corporeality 137
   sensory sociology 136, 147
separability (separation) ix, xii–xiii, 41
   geocidal and genocidal xi
   and individuation ix–xi
   material and intellectual x
Seyfarth Shaw LLP 86
shadow banking system 49–50, 171
shareholder value and financialization 20–3
Shultz, H. 26
Silverstein, T. 'Terrible Tom' 134
Simpson, O. J., trial 149
Skilling, J. 24
Slacker, R., pathological privacy 47
smellscape 142
Smith, A. 145
Smith, B. C. 100–1
social body 48–50, 76
social control 43
social equity 111

socialism 79, 124, 157, 160
   eco-socialism 157
   organized 82
   rudimentary components of 160
sociality 37, 132, 134, 161
social pain 32
socio-economic conditions 3, 70, 155
Solanas, V., *SCUM* ('Society for Cutting up Men') *Manifesto* 51–2
soulful corporations 67
South Korea, capitalism 53–4
   death workshops 54–5, 58
   team-building evenings 54
spirit of corporation 145
Stalinism 80
stark utopian streak 77
statistical science fiction 120
stewardship and budgetary conservatism 21, 46
Stigler Diet 78
Stigler, G. 78
supervised algorithms 117
surplus cybernation 126
surveillance capitalism 114, 121
Swanston & Sons 145
system crashes 49

Taylor, A., fauxtomation 97
Taylor, F. W. 15, 17–18
   The Principles of Scientific Management 18
technical rationalization 42, 124
technicity 5, 106, 125, 152
techno-capitalism 104
technological fatalism 5
technology 90, 96, 122–3, 153, 187 n.23
   automatic system of machinery 97
   causality 123–5, 128–9
   religion of 4

retroactive universality 125
technological rationality 102, 106–7
touchscreen 152
techno-optimism 162
Thatcherism 133
Thatcher, M. 61
Theocarakis, N. 78–9
theory of the stranger (Simmel) 174
Thiel, P. 153, 193 n.1
Throbbing Gristle 141
touchscreens 150
   tactility, stages 150–1
   technology 152
transaction man 16
The Truman Show 149
Trump, D. 25, 83
two-dimensional man/two-dimensionality 35–6, 38–9
Tyson Foods (company) 91, 93

Uber
   Geosurge and batch matching algorithm 115
   pay rate 173
Uber-badness 164
Übermensch 23
UK Post Office 114
unemployment 59, 86, 98
   mass technological 96
unionism 63
Unite 92
United Arab Emirates 155
United Health Programs of America 66–7, 181 n.23
United Kingdom
   generic French varieties 146
   predictive policing 114
The United States 170
   fentanyl crisis 59
   food industry 145–6

industrial relations system 84
labour relations consultants 89
liberal capitalism 35
New Deal 86
poultry industry, working conditions 91, 95
predictive policing 114
US healthcare system 32
Unmanned Combat Aerial Vehicles 117
unsupervised algorithms 117
utopia/utopianism 77–8, 156–8, 161

vacuity syndrome 45, 173
vibrant economy 82
violence xii, 21, 28, 61, 73, 84, 163
 brutality and xi
 imperial 171
 security, types 81
 symbolic 94, 114

wage labourer 163–4, 172
Wagner Act 86
Wag the Dog 149
Walmart 89
war on loyalty 23
Weber, M. 16, 60, 65, 102, 124, 138, 140, 174
 musical instruments 139
 neo-Kantian critique 65
 scientific specialization and formalization 174
 sound discriminations 138
 Zur Musiksoziologie (*The Rational and Social Foundations of Music*) 138

Weil, S. 147
Welch, J. 22–3
 Jack: Straight From the Gut 23
Western philosophy x, 147, 166
Western politics x, xii
white supremacy 163
Wicksteed, P. 79
Wilderson III, F. B. 163
win-win doctrine/financial outcome 18, 26, 153
women's liberation movement 50
workers' rights 73, 93
workforce 2, 23, 36, 61–4, 100, 104, 115
 invisibilization 88
 neo-boredom 104–5
 secretization 173
workplaces viii, 2–3, 36, 60, 64, 67, 70, 106
 beneath-the-radar interactivity, valorization 68
 informalism 68
 modern 65, 93
 neo-boredom 104
 new age 57
 superficial gloss of formalism 67–8
work-related suicides 54
Wright, E. O., *Envisioning Real Utopias* 157–8

xylazine 32

Zink, E. 31. *See also* OxyContin
Zuckerberg, M. 121, 189 n.20